W H A T   A

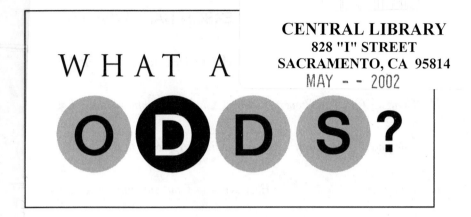

OTHER BOOKS BY JEFFERSON HANE WEAVER

The Compact Guide to Contract Law: A Civilized Approach to the Law

The Compact Guide to Property Law: A Civilized Approach to the Law

The Compact Guide to Tort Law: A Civilized Approach to the Law

The Conquering Calculus: The Easy Road to Understanding Mathematics

The Conquering Statistics: Numbers without the Crunch

The World of Physics, 3 volumes (editor)

With Henry A. Boorse and Lloyd Motz:

The Atomic Scientists: A Biographical History

With Lloyd Motz:

The Concepts of Science from Newton to Einstein

Conquering Mathematics: From Arithmetic to Calculus

The Story of Astronomy

The Story of Mathematics

The Story of Physics

The Unfolding Universe: A Stellar Journey

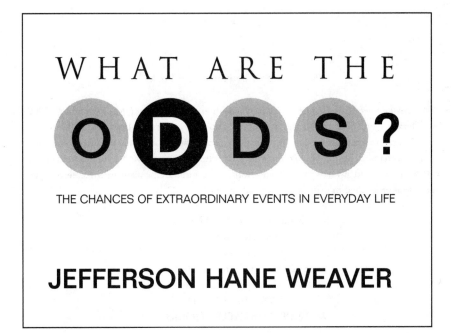

WHAT ARE THE O D D S ?

THE CHANCES OF EXTRAORDINARY EVENTS IN EVERYDAY LIFE

JEFFERSON HANE WEAVER

Prometheus Books

59 John Glenn Drive
Amherst, New York 14228-2197

Published 2001 by Prometheus Books

Inquiries should be addressed to
Prometheus Books
59 John Glenn Drive
Amherst, New York 14228–2197
VOICE: 716–691–0133, ext. 207
FAX: 716–564–2711
WWW.PROMETHEUSBOOKS.COM

06 05 04 03 02   5 4 3 2 1

Library of Congress Cataloging-in-Publication Data

Weaver, Jefferson Hane.
  What are the odds? : the chances of extraordinary events in everyday life / Jefferson Hane Weaver.
    p. cm.
  Includes index.
  ISBN 1–57392–933–6 (pbk. : alk. paper)
  1. Probabilities—Popular works. 2. Mathematical statistics—Popular works. I. Title.

QA273.15 . W43 2001
519.2—dc21

2001034961

Printed in the United States of America on acid-free paper

This book is dedicated to my mother, Helen Wood Weaver

CONTENTS

PREFACE

Statistics and probability theory are not topics that cause most people to jump for joy or even admit to a passing interest. This indifference—if not outright hostility—to these topics is undoubtedly due in large part to the prevailing attitudes toward mathematics in general and statistics in particular. When asked if they would be interested in learning more about statistics, most people will cringe as though they were in the presence of an insurance salesman. Yet the subject is fascinating and, when properly explored, can provide hours of amusement and entertainment.

This is not a book about statistics except to the extent that the examples we are using do involve basic probability calculations and how they apply to our lives. It was written primarily to entertain and inform readers about the odds that certain events will occur, such as a meteorite landing on your house or you becoming a rock star or even you getting audited by the Internal Revenue Service. But the book was motivated by the desire to provide a lighthearted treatment of the subject matter because mathematics in general and statistics in particular have very poor public images even though these fields are absolutely crucial to the continued functioning of our modern technological society.

So we have tried to create a breezy narrative that wanders from subject to subject while offering certain calculations as to the possibilities that particular events will occur while also informing the reader of the basic limitations of both the collection of data and the interpretations that can be drawn from such data. Moreover, the limitations of probability theory and statistics—to the extent it is relevant for this book—are also discussed where appropriate. But this is not a book on statistical concepts and will not delve into the fundamental ideas of statistics; we are instead interested purely in the likelihood that certain events will manifest. It is my hope, however, that the reader will approach the subject with an open mind and, after reading this book, will at least have a better understanding of how we determine the probability that particular events and outcomes—both good and bad—will occur. In this way, the reader should develop a greater appreciation for and enjoyment of the predictive powers of statistics and probability theory.

Jefferson Hane Weaver

1

IN SEARCH OF
ROMANCE

PERFECT MATES

Have you ever sat alone in the dark after your most recent romantic relationship crashed and burned like the *Hindenburg* dirigible? Have you wondered whether you would ever find that certain person who would be the perfect match for you? Do you often wake up in the morning after a drunken night of carousing on the town and gaze into the peaceful face of a person whom you have no recollection of having met and no desire to ever see again? These are the dilemmas that confront those wanting to find true love.

Love, even though it may be offered over the phone for $3.95 a minute, is among the most difficult and fleeting of things to find. And finding that certain perfect person in a cacophonic world strewn with dysfunctional personalities and neurotic behavior is a Herculean task. Fortunately, we can pick ourselves up off of our barstools, cast aside our feelings of self-pity, and grab the arm of the nearest statistician to reduce this quest for true love to a more definable (and, hopefully, solvable) mathematical problem. After all, we are living on the threshold of a new millennium in which our sciences have tamed a chaotic world and enabled us to bring rational analysis to bear on even matters of the heart.

13

So what would this statistician tell us about our likelihood of finding our perfect mate? He would first demand payment for services to be rendered and then he would proceed to ask us some questions about the population in which we wish to carry out our search. Do we want to confine our search for true love to our town? Our state? Our country? Or do we want to go for broke and open our search for that perfect person throughout the entire world, whether it takes us to the huts of the Serengeti or the bathhouses of Bangkok or the lumber camps of Siberia? If we opted to take on the entire world, our statistician would notify us that there are about 6 billion people whom we would need to consider in our search. This type of quest poses enormous logistical problems because it is very difficult to meet 6 billion people, even if one devotes all of his or her waking hours to this task. Moreover, there are expenses—plane fares, hotels, room service, bribes to customs officials—which cannot be ignored. Fortunately, we can reduce this search by defining the type of person we would like to meet. First, we can limit our search to a single sex (say, men), thereby cutting the potential pool down to 3 billion people. Second, we can focus on a particular age group such as those men between 30 to 40 years of age because we may not be very interested in dating men who ride around in baby carriages or those who take their teeth out at night before they go to bed. As a result, we would be considering no more than 600 million men. Now we might want to further qualify our search, perhaps by eliminating those who do not speak our language, those who have disfiguring diseases, and those who belong to terrorist cells. We might thus find ourselves considering no more than 50 million men. This is certainly a much more promising approach than simply buying a book of plane tickets and rushing around to the world's capitals in a furious attempt to find Mr. Perfect. But it still presents a challenge to us because finding true love requires such things as meeting potential perfect mates, dating potential perfect mates, and actually taking the time to get to know these potential perfect mates.

When you are trying to court 50 million men, time is at a premium. Given the fact that the average woman lives to be 75 years of age, and is an adult for fifty-seven of those years, then the average woman has, at most, fifty-seven years of possible dating time or approximately 20,800 dating days. This of course ignores those times in which that woman is ill, recovering from jet lag, or simply sick of men. Broken down further, we see that if a woman devotes her entire adult life to dating, beginning her dating from the time she gets up in the morning to the time she goes to bed, then we might be able to count on a total dating time of 332,800 hours (assuming sixteen-hour dating days). For such an endeavor to be successful, it is very helpful to be independently wealthy because such a rigorous dating schedule will preclude gainful employment in all but the highest levels of the federal government.

Assuming that we are still enthusiastic about the task at hand, we may want to focus on the efficiency of our dating arrangements. If we are trying to root through some 50 million men, we cannot afford to spend hours and hours getting to know them and learning about their hopes, dreams, and fears because the whole dating process will break down. Moreover, we want to be able to determine early on whether our potential soul mate is the perfect match. This may be accomplished by mailing each man a detailed questionnaire before the start of the first date which he can fill out while you are driving to the restaurant. You can then mark his test while waiting for the appetizers to arrive and, if he fails to make the grade, you can then make a hasty exit before having to order the entree (perhaps offering the excuse that you must attend a wake for your recently deceased grandmother—who can serve as a convenient excuse for short-circuiting many dates in the future). For those who find computerized tests to be too cold and impersonal, you could devise a series of questions which you could mix with the small talk over drinks in a very subtle manner:

He: This is a lovely restaurant.

She: Yes, it is. Is there a history of heart disease, cancer, or diabetes in your family?

He: No, I don't think so. Oh, look at the beautiful moon outside the window.

She: It's very nice. Have you been sexually active in the past three months?

He: That is a rather personal question—

She: By the way, have you ever had been tested for a sexually transmitted disease?

He: I don't know what to say—

She: By the way, did you remember to bring your prior three years of personal and corporate tax returns?

He: But we are on a date!

She: I'll take that as a yes. And what about your mental health? Have you ever been committed to a mental institution for psychiatric evaluation?

He: I have never been so insulted in my life!

She: Now, now, I'm just trying to find out a little bit about you! Why waste a lot of time on meaningless chitchat when you can go straight to the heart of the matter and find out whether you are impotent—

He: (indignantly) Impotent! I should say—

She: —and if so, if you have found E.D. pills to be a successful treatment—

He: I can't believe this conversation! I'm leaving! (He exits.)

Although this type of probing dialogue is not for the faint of heart, it enables our protagonist to determine very quickly if her date is emotionally unstable, quick to anger, and therefore unlikely to be that perfect life partner. The need to carry out dating activities in an efficient manner requires that one avoid the "happy talk" that causes so many dates to bog down and drag late into the night. To further increase dating efficiency, one could schedule fifteen-minute dating slots at the same restaurant and arrange for prospective dates to come in for preliminary screenings. Your turn-out rate will likely be much higher if you do not inform any of your dates that they will be "interviewed" along with twenty or more other men over the course of the evening.

So if you are able to perfect the fifteen-minute date, spending all of your adult waking hours dating men, you could conceivably develop deep, meaningful relationships with about 1.2 million men before you were due to leave this world. But that would still exclude some 48.8 million possible matches from your dating process. This is completely unacceptable because it could render the results of your exhaustive search meaningless. One possibility would be to get the pictures of all 50 million men beforehand and flip through the photographs to see who might strike your fancy. If it takes two seconds to look at a photograph and decide after deep contemplation that the subject may or may not be the perfect mate for you, then it would only take about 100 million seconds to go through the entire collection of photographs of all the world's eligible men. As there are 31,536,000 seconds in a year (of which you would be devoting all of your waking hours or sixteen hours a day or approximately 21,024,000 seconds to reviewing photographs), then you would be able to look at about 10,512,000 photographs each year. At that rate, you would make short work of the entire pile in about five years. Assuming that you are very selective and pick 50,000 photographs for further consideration, then you will be way ahead of the game. Of course this process ignores the fact that some of these men will be aging out of your 30- to 40-year group and new ones will be joining it at the same time but these are the messy details which we must finesse when we are involved in important scientific matters.

Having narrowed your choices down to a select few tens of thousands, you could then utilize a variety of more selective techniques, ranging from impromptu telephone calls to showing up on a whim at the front doors of your more reluctant prospects. Whether they open the door gladly or urge their bull mastiff to bite your leg is an unknowable risk that you will not be able to ascertain beforehand but it is a hazard that one must consider when seeking the perfect mate.

So what are the odds that you will meet the man of your dreams, the one charming and handsome fellow who causes your heart to pound and your blood to race, the divine masculine hunk who dumbfounds your very senses? Our brief excursion has revealed that if you assume that there is only a single person in the world who is your perfect match, then you have quite a tough road ahead of you. After all, you are betting that you will succeed when you have only about a 1-in-50-million chance, assuming that you decide to focus on your desired age group. If you are unsure of your preferences, wondering aloud whether you might indeed be happier with a 95-year-old leper who lives alone on a Tibetan mountain or perhaps a 22-year-old "roadie" who feeds lions in the Barcelona circus, then there is scant hope that you will find that perfect someone because you will not yet have made up your mind about the type of man with whom you wish to spend your life and you will have little more than a 1-in-3 billion chance of success. And pity the poor bisexuals who must grapple with the entire human population, feeling enamored with muscular men one day and shapely women the next, completely overwhelmed at the prospect that the perfect match is lost somewhere in the 6 billion souls of humanity. Of course the bright side of the poor bisexual's dilemma is that he or she may have double the chance of finding that perfect someone.

But is it truly realistic to propose that there is only one perfect person for any single individual wandering around somewhere else in the world? It is hard to imagine why the human race would not have died out many centuries ago if everyone spent all of their time looking for that one person who was the perfect match. But the fact that we are here today is a testament to our having abandoned the notion that we must find the perfect person. Most of us have decided that we can love more than one person, sometimes at the same time. But modern convention, hot-tempered spouses who carry sidearms, and ravenous divorce attorneys have joined together to deter all but the most suicidal of us from actually acting out those fantasies of multiple bed partners. Most of us have managed to compromise instead of insisting on blindly pursuing an image of flawless beauty. Instead, we have set our sights on finding someone with whom we can be compatible and comfortable. This does not guarantee a perfect match but it does help to ensure that the human race will survive for yet another generation. Because it is difficult to be indescribably happy about anything for any great period of time—whether it be the local baseball team winning the World Series or a despised boss who sexually harassed you falling off a cruise ship—perhaps it is folly to think of a perfect mate. After all, you can be married to the most handsome man in the world but the novelty of his beauty will eventually wear off. He will become somewhat less extraordinary in your eyes while the youthful, heavily biceped gardener who pours herbicides on your next-door neighbor's rosebushes may seem increasingly exciting. So while the idea that there is a single perfect person somewhere in the world is an appealingly romantic notion, it is probably without any kind of evidentiary support. People's tastes change over time and even those few who are fortunate enough to stumble across that perfect mate may not realize it at the right moment or fail to remain enamored with that once perfect person for all time.

THREE IS NOT A CROWD

Most people involved in romantic relationships eventually move beyond the kissing and hand-holding stage, where they feel obligated to pretend to be interested in each other's deepest thoughts and desires, to a more physical stage in which they engage in a variety of activities with puzzling Latin names. For most of the population, however, their venture into the world of sexual intimacy is made with but a single partner at one time. Two people with active imaginations can offer literally thousands of creative activities and positions which will provide them with the stimulation, satisfaction, and exercise that they so desperately crave.

However, there are some people who find a single partner to be too pedestrian and, frankly, too dull for their tastes. This is not to say that most people have not fantasied at one time or another about having two, three, or even four members of the opposite sex cavort with them in a vat of whipped cream. But the reality is that most of us do not have such "open-minded" groups of friends or vats filled with whipped cream. Moreover, those of us who are married do not usually find that our spouses are terribly keen on the idea of sharing us with another person or two and will in fact express their displeasure by threatening to cut off our legs or some other handy appendage with a machete if we dare suggest the idea again. This sort of hostile response will deter most people from bringing up the topic again but there are a few hardy souls who do not believe that they should have to suffer the isolation and loneliness of having to engage in sexual relations with a single person at any given time. For these people, the mattress is a canvas on which bodies of all shapes, sizes, and colors can become entwined in a quivering mass of sweaty flesh.

Because society is so inundated with sexually oriented advertising, magazines, movies, books, and television programs, we would not be surprised that there are many people who engage in threesomes, foursomes, and even moresomes. But to try to determine the odds that you will become involved in a threesome is precarious at best. First, we do not have enough voyeurs on the payroll to sweep through the country's neighborhoods late at night and peer through open windows to get a head count as to how many persons are jumping into flesh piles. Sadly, there are no blank spaces on the U.S. Census forms whereby one may state the frequency and the number of multiple partners he or she may enjoy.

If we cannot use official surveys of the population to determine the percentage of the entire population engaged in sexual activities with multiple sex partners, then we must rely on our own surveys. This is unfortunate because it means we must not only mail out our own surveys but that we must try to make sure that the survey is sent to a representative sample of the population. If we want a true idea as to the odds that you or I will become involved in a ménage à trois at some point in our adult lives, then we want to make sure that our survey is received by an accurate cross section of the population. We would not want to send all of our surveys to the subscribers of *American Swingers* magazine because these readers are more likely than the general population to share a box of cornflakes with two or three naked adults, never mind the sexual activities. Their responses would presumably be much higher than those of the general population regarding their sexual activities with multiple partners. Similarly, we would not want to send all of our surveys to the local convent or monastery which we assume, due to the vows of celibacy taken by the members, would reflect a much lower rate of participation in sexual activities with multiple partners than the population as a whole. So the trick is to send a few to the swingers, a few to the nuns and monks, and distribute the rest in a representative manner among the other groups which make up the entire population.

Even if our mailing goes well and we receive enough responses from each group (something which only happens in the wet dreams of statisticians), we are still going to have to consider whether or not the results are worth the paper they are printed on. Many people like to brag when asked about their sexual history, adding a few additional partners to the résumé or a few additional minutes to tales of their endurance. If we are asking someone whether they have ever engaged in a threesome, we need to keep in mind that this is a very common fantasy, particularly among males, and that they may say they have participated in a ménage à trois when in fact they may not know the difference between a ménage à trois and a coup de grâce. So the social scientist who must go through these surveys and draw some type of meaningful conclusions from his results may not feel very comfortable with the results due to this tendency by most persons (particularly men) to exaggerate all things sexual. Indeed, the statistician may be surprised at the percentage of people who respond positively to such a question, reasoning that neither he nor any of the other statisticians with whom he plays poker and factors prime numbers for fun has ever said anything about being involved in a threesome. But, like it or not, there may be no alternative but to accept the results of the survey, assuming that the sample adequately represents the population, and report the findings.

What have national surveys said about the chances that even very ugly people will become involved in a threesome? Although the political pollsters do not typically ask households about their sexual activities, there are a few published surveys that have tried to uncover the frequency with which people like you and me have sex with multiple partners at the same time. These surveys typically utilize small samples and may therefore not be representative of the entire population. Yet the Kinsey Institute has collected the results of several of these surveys together in June M. Reinisch and Ruth Beasley's *The Kinsey Institute's New Report on Sex* (1990) to try to bring some clarity to the subject.

After being informed by the authors that the phrase *ménage à trois* translates to mean "household of three," the authors then proceed to discuss some of the findings that have been derived from surveys purporting to examine the frequency in which people engage in group sex. Of particular interest is that the traditional form of the ménage à trois is something of a family activity—with the three people in question consisting of a married couple and the lover of one of the spouses. Whether this lover comes along on cross-country trips with the rest of the family is not discussed but it appears as though the lover is accepted almost matter-of-factly in such situations. Moreover, such situations do not necessarily involve all three persons engaging in sex together—the spouse without the lover often watches his or her spouse be seduced by the third person. But this does raise the question as to how frequently married people become involved in ménage à trois affairs. According to the Kinsey Institute, only 3 percent of married men and 1 percent of married women admit to having sex with another person while their spouse is present and most of these respondents would admit to having only done it once. Of course one has to wonder about the truthfulness of the responses in general because this is not the type of activity for which Congressional Medals of Honor are awarded. Indeed, we might wonder not only whether a greater percentage of the respondents had dabbled in group sex but also whether they had actually discontinued the practice after only one attempt. Because this is an activity for which some people might harbor feelings of shame, we can be skeptical about the accuracy of such responses. But the nature of the subject matter and the reluctance of most people to discuss such matters in any detail with pollsters and social scientists would probably preclude more forthright admissions of such unconventional behavior.

What about those lonely single people whom married people read so much about? As far as group sex is concerned, single persons as a whole seem to relish jumping into flesh piles with far greater frequency than those fuddy-duddy married swingers we just discussed. Indeed, the Kinsey Institute reports that a survey of unmarried persons revealed that 24 percent of all men and 7 percent of all women had engaged in group sex. As with our hardy ménage à troisers, however, most of the respondents said that they had only engaged in group sex once—perhaps because of curiosity or the solicitations of a friend or perhaps even boredom.

What about the proclivities of the entire adult population to engage in such unconventional sexual activities? According to the Kinsey Institute, a study concluded that 2 percent of the entire adult population—without qualifying for age, race, gender, or marital status—had tried group sex. Even though many may have tried to take on a half-dozen sexual partners at the same time for medicinal purposes, the fact remains that most of these persons found a onetime experience to be enough. Indeed, this study showed that only about one-half of 1 percent of the entire adult population of the United States engage in group sex on a regular basis. If the entire adult population of the United States (above the age of 19) numbers about 210 million persons, then an extrapolation of this percentage would cause us to conclude that about one million adults are swingers of some sort or, alternatively, that one out of every 210 adults is a swinger. Of course some age groups (e.g., 18–24, 25–34) are more likely to have group sex than others (85 and older) because it is difficult to imagine many of the approximately 4.3 million persons above the age of 85 having much affinity for the group-sex scene. So we would expect the 26,258,000 persons in the 18-to-24-year-old age group who make up 12.5 percent of the adult population and the 37,233,000 persons in the 35-to-44-year-old age group who make up 17.7 percent of the adult population to contribute more than their combined 30.2 percent of the adult population to the ranks of America's swingers. Yet we cannot speak with any great certainty as to the degree to which these two age groups are overrepresented in the nation's swing clubs. Moreover, we still have to be skeptical about the results that we obtain from these surveys even though we do not have available to us the means to conduct truly reliable tests of the frequency in which Americans engage in group sex with each other—short of sending an army of researchers outfitted with video cameras out to document the activities of these persons in vivid color.

In the interest of advancing the frontiers of human knowledge, we should also point out that the group-sex scene does not always involve massive collections of strangers rolling all over each other in a massive room filled with oil and whipped cream. In fact, the Kinsey Institute tells us that groups engaging in sexual behavior may have very specific, sometimes even very discriminatory rules, that must be followed by their participants (e.g., the women may have sex with each other but no men can have sex with each other; all the members of the group are single; all the members of the group are married to other persons participating in the group).

Whether the day will actually come in which we stroll into the bedroom and find two naked bed partners waiting for us is unclear because the probabilities of participating in such activities are probably much greater in certain age groups and less frequent in others. Moreover, such things as where you live and your income level and even your educational background may affect your likelihood of success in the group-sex world. Because of the limitations inherent in surveys about intimate personal activities, we can never be too certain that we truly know the odds that we will become involved in such activities but for now it may be the best that we can do.

LIVING TOGETHER

Marriage is not for everyone. Indeed, there are many married people who would agree with that statement, considering themselves to be experts on the subject, particularly with their vision having been honed by hindsight. There are also many people who have opted not to bother with marriage at all. The reasons cited by these persons who would tread lightly around church altars and wedding chapels range from disliking the idea of being legally bound to another person to an inability to spell the word "commitment." But the sociologists from the U.S.

Census Bureau have documented the increasing popularity of couples living together without the benefit (or burden) of marriage; an increase of nearly 1,000 percent in a little more than thirty years as discussed below. So it does present an interesting question to inquire as to the odds that any single person will actually cohabitate with another individual outside of a marital relationship during their lifetime. Of course there is a certain amount of "self-selection" in this type of analysis in that whether a person lives in a nonmarital relationship is completely voluntary—except in those rare instances where an unwitting person is kidnapped and dragged off to live with a love-starved stalker.

Now one could plow through dozens of densely footnoted studies purporting to analyze the changing structure of the American family or one can simply resort to a deep philosophical masterpiece such as this book to get a succinct yet sweeping overview of the decreasing primacy of legally structured family relationships. According to the U.S. Census Bureau, the number of unmarried couples cohabitating has risen from some 439,000 in 1960 to approximately 4.2 million in 1998. This represents an almost tenfold increase in absolute numbers during a time in which the population has, according to the U.S. Census, increased by about a third from about 180,000,000 in 1960 to 268,000,000 in 1998.

There are a number of theories that have been offered to explain the growing phenomenon of cohabitating unmarried couples, ranging from the "sex without shackles" theory which suggests that some persons are drawn to committing themselves to relationships in which they are free to leave at any time to the "free love" perspective which highlights the advantages of being able to leave a partner without having to hire a platoon of attorneys to help divvy the spoils. There is also the navigationally challenged theory, which suggests that some people are simply very bad at directions and unable to locate either a justice of the peace or a minister to "tie the knot," and the "marriage as masochism" view which argues that marriage is inherently painful and causes many

Unmarried Couples Living Together 1960–1998

Year	Total
1960	439,000
1970	523,000
1980	1,589,000
1985	1,983,000
1990	1,996,000
1995	3,668,000
1998	4,236,000

Sources of Statistics: U.S. Census Bureau; Marital Status and Living Arrangements (March 1998)

persons to turn away in fear, particularly those who grew up watching their own parents rant and rave at each other and, in many cases, divorce. Whatever the reason, it is clear that couples no longer view a marital relationship as the inevitable outcome of the dating process. The adage about not needing to buy the cow when the milk is free— while understandably insulting to some—does seem to have some truth in it as it is no longer necessary for most people to enter into a marital relationship in order to enjoy a sexual relationship. Indeed, some persons have found that it was necessary for them to get out of their marriages in order to enjoy a sexual relationship whereas still others have found that it was their repeated involvements in trysts and flings that brought an end to their marriages. But it is intrinsically easier for people to find partners who will engage in sexual activity without the benefit of even a wedding ring or pledged stock portfolio.

Living together does have a certain appeal for persons who are intimidated about the prospect of planning a formal wedding or unsure as to whether they will still like each other by the time their first anniversary rolls around. According to the most recent statistics offered by the government statisticians, more than one-half of all the male-female couples who tie the knot will have, at some point in their relationship, lived together. This represents an increase of nearly 500 percent in a generation. What is surprising is that the greeting card marketers and jewelers have not hopped on the bandwagon and begun hawking cards and nose rings for "housemates" and "cohabitants." In a calendar which sets aside a day each for mothers and fathers, it seems unfair that there is no special day for "cohabitants" or "significant others."

Researchers who study unmarried couples living together fear that such couples are more individually oriented because they are lacking a connection to each other that manifests in ceremony, is celebrated by religion, and is sanctioned by law. The fact that either person can go out the door without a second thought seems to trivialize whatever relationship does exist between the couples. Of course this is not to say that the couples themselves agree with this view even though many must wonder at least some of the time as to whether they should actually formalize their relationship with each other. Although some persons may genuinely dislike the idea of marriage and see the marriage certificate as merely a piece of paper, others may settle for cohabitation for lack of a more attractive alternative. In other words, Jane may decide to live with Harry, a lifelong hobo, because she simply has not met a man who has traveled across the country as extensively as Harry, albeit in a railroad boxcar. Or Bob, an accountant, may be tantalized by the prospect of living with Ellen, a renowned table dancer, because he finds very few women can keep up with him on the dance floor.

People may also be drawn toward cohabitation out of desperation, particularly as they get older and begin to fear that they will never meet "Mr. Right" or "Ms. Sort of Okay." But they may not perceive that they become more used to getting their own way as they age and, as a result, less inclined to be overly concerned about adjusting their lifestyles to adapt to the concerns of others. Certainly it is easier to deal with living with another person, who may actually have thoughts and opinions distinct from your own, if you are forced to begin compromising at an earlier age. For those persons who manage to avoid becoming ensnared with another "significant other" until they have reached middle age and begun in earnest that long, long decline toward what some refer to as the "golden" (as opposed to olden) years, the prospect of facing the second half of their lives by themselves can be somewhat daunting. Their fears may be more pronounced due to the negative images that are commonly associated with living alone. The outdated term "spinster" (a word used to refer to an unmarried woman, for example) does not typically evoke images of glamour and beauty. This is not to say that this image was ever accurate. Yet, for some reason, the word "bachelor" does not seem to have as much of a negative connotation. However, lifelong bachelors may find themselves the subject of gossip whereby their acquaintances openly wonder about their sexual orientations. In either case, the images may become more negatively pronounced as the person ages. One can almost see the greeting card for a bachelor's 65th birthday party: "Hope you have another miserable birthday alone!" Obviously, the author of such a card would have to be a person who was trapped in an unhappy relationship and not wishing to see anyone else enjoy a footloose and fancy-free existence.

But one needs to put misty-eyed sentiment aside and look at this growing phenomenon of unmarried cohabitators because it appears to be a trend that is here to stay. But the odds that any person will become involved in such a relationship is certainly dependent upon that person's attitude toward such a lifestyle. If you are unalterably opposed to the idea of living with another person (presumably of the opposite sex) outside of marriage, then you probably have very little chance of becoming a cohabitator or marrying again because this is often a necessary prerequisite in today's society.

Leaving aside the notion of voluntariness, however, we can draw upon the works of various statisticians and demographers and construct a portrait of the cohabitant household, in which children are an increasingly common part. According to *USA Today* (April 18, 2000), nearly half of all previously married cohabitators and more than a third of cohabitators who have not been married have children in the household. But the presence of children apparently does not ensure that cohabitator households are as stable as married households. Of course, whether the cohabitator household is a stable and loving one or one fraught with tension and anger is more dependent on the personalities of the individuals involved and less dependent on the legal relationship or lack thereof of the parties. But it seems that the fact that either party can easily end the cohabitation arrangement would be a source of problems because of the inherent instability of the relationship.

One interesting finding about today's cohabitating singles reported by that same article is that these people are about 8 percent less likely to end up marrying each other than they were in the early 1980s. Even more striking is the conclusion that the probability cohabitating couples will break up has risen nearly 20 percent in that same period of time. Perhaps the lessening invariability of taking a stroll down the wedding aisle is due to the fact that cohabitating singles are less likely to be publicly reprimanded or ostracized than they were even twenty years ago. Cohabitation is not so widely accepted that it will receive heavenly praises from the local clergymen, but society's attitude toward such living arrangements has become much more tolerant, if not enthusiastic. Perhaps society's tolerance is nothing more than another way of referring to society's apathy in a more positive manner. Although there are many segments of our society that are opposed to people living together without the benefit of marriage (including bridal gown manufacturers, wedding cake bakers, and divorce attorneys), mainstream society basically shrugs its shoulders at the prospect of persons living under the same roof who are not legally joined at the hip. But the question arises as to whether this is more a question of style over substance because most couples reportedly either break up or marry within two years. As the duration of the average marriage is only a few years, there may not be much difference between living together and being married because the end result is the same: embittered partners and, in the case of a failed marriage, at least some redistribution of wealth to a member or two of the state bar association.

At this point you might want to consider the probability that you will become a cohabitator. With over 4 million "cohabitating" couples out of nearly 78 million families in the United States, the U.S. Census Bureau would give the average adult a 1-in-20 chance of living with an unmarried partner. Not every adult family member can freely choose to take advantage of this lifestyle, particularly if they are already married. Most spouses are not usually very excited about the prospect of their husband or wife moving to another home with their lover. But for those persons who are single, there are ample opportunities available, particularly given the tendency of many existing unmarried (and married) relationships to fracture.

2

SEX IN AMERICA

Sex is a topic that is of particular interest to statisticians because they like to have have wild and crazy times when they are not busy calculating standard deviations and the averages and means of groups of values. Although nothing will send statisticians into a passionate frenzy quicker than a rousing debate over the role of statistics in the social sciences, statisticians also enjoy engaging in all kinds of physical activities—some of which involve acts containing too many Latin phrases to be easily translated. But some statisticians have combined their personal and professional interests to actually study aspects of sex in America—particularly such topics as the frequency with which Americans have sex with each other. Other topics that have been studied in exhaustive detail include the rate at which persons engage in extramarital sex, the percentage of Americans preferring sex with members of the same gender, the number of sex partners enjoyed by the average American in a given period of time, and the percentage of the population which engages in sex for money.

As these are topics which are of critical importance to the future of sociology, it is important for us to maintain a scholarly dialogue and to resist the temptation to engage in titillating, shallow speculations designed more to attract a wider audience than to actually advance the frontiers of human knowledge. So let us now begin our statistical analysis of that unique area of human behavior—sexuality—that has inspired artists and poets through the ages and has undone some of the greatest politicians and thinkers of all time. Because sex involves a wide range of emotions and sensations it provides an area of study that is uniquely of interest to both professional statisticians as well as the lay audience—particularly when pictures are involved. But social scientists like to know about the basic patterns of human behavior and statistical studies of sexual conduct certainly provide a unique perspective as to the conduct of human beings—married, single, or otherwise.

When one conducts statistical analyses of any subject, it is necessary for the researcher to observe the population they are studying. For studies dealing with sex, the job of the researcher becomes somewhat more problematic because he cannot directly observe the behavior of the persons being studied unless he spends much of his time peering through bedroom windows with a night-vision camera to "document" his investigations in cinematic color. Moreover, there is the simple logistical impossibility of trying to draw generalizations about the behavior of large groups of people. Although there may be no shortage of willing volunteers ready to go stand outside the bedroom windows of the nation's swingers, it is simply not practical to equip literally tens of millions of research assistants and tell them to go out and invade the privacy of their neighbors. As a result, statisticians must devise ways in which they can obtain "snapshots" of the nation by resorting to a representative sample of the population. In the case of sexual conduct, which they cannot easily monitor unless they wish to risk committing one or more felonies, the primary means by which statisticians gather information about the sexual behavior of couples is to ask them directly. The obvious danger to such an approach is that it requires the statistician to accept the answers of the respondents and provides no real way in which the statistician can verify these answers through direct observation. But such are the limitations of the social sciences that they can provide only approximations of behavioral pattern and cannot claim the accuracy of the physical sciences. The trick is to design a survey that will ensure a certain level of accuracy and find a representative sample to answer the survey truthfully. Many of the nation's most reputable polling organizations will select random samples that they believe are representative of the population that they wish to study and these samples will typically number no more than, say, 1,500 persons. And so it is with surveys of human behavior as shown by the National Opinion Research Center (NORC) at the University of Chicago, which polls a nationwide representative sample of 1,500 adults each year to try to find out what sorts of things are happening in the nation's boudoirs.

MORE! MORE! MORE!

One of the things that seems to concern most Americans is whether they have sex more or less frequently than their friends and neighbors. After all, very few people want to believe themselves to be underachievers in the sexual Olympics—even though sex can often get in the way of watching television and talking on the phone and eating two or three pieces of pie. But because people tend to brag about their sexual conquests and their proficiency in the bedroom, it is difficult for most of us to know what are the average numbers of times that people engage in sexual activities. After all, most people like to portray themselves as being sexual animals—primitive beasts who ooze sensuality and passion. Because such posturing typically occurs when people are talking to each other about sex or snapping each other's rear ends with towels in locker rooms, surveys may be more likely to elicit more truthful responses because the respondents are usually anonymous and respond to the questions in writing. There is no face-to-face contact with the questioner and so there is hopefully a better likelihood of obtaining answers that are not tainted by concerns of embarrassment.

Now that the mechanism by which the desired information is obtained has been settled, we can look at the results obtained by the NORC and educate ourselves as to the frequency of sexual intercourse by Americans and have a better idea as to when people are "blowing smoke" in discussing their most intimate activities at weddings, funerals, and church socials. But the most surprising thing revealed by the NORC survey is that the respondents had sex 59.1 times a year. The survey was unclear as to what one-tenth of a sexual experience would be (e.g., kissing, hugging, fondling) but it showed that Americans were not exactly posting Olympian numbers in the bedroom—with their rates of sexual intercourse averaging a little more than once a week. Now this was admittedly a "mean" value which averaged all sorts of reported frequencies—some of which were less than once a week and some of which were greater than once a week—into a single aggregate average for the population as a whole. But in a blow to the image of the swinging single life, the survey revealed that married persons have sex an average of 66.1 times a year, about 10 percent greater than the national average. Not clear was whether these married persons were having sex with their spouses or with some of the more enterprising single persons included in the survey. But it is logical to conclude that married persons would, on average, engage in sexual relations more frequently than single persons because the marital relationship is a far more efficient framework for carrying out sexual activities. The husband does not have to do a great deal of wining and dining because he already went through that process prior to convincing his wife to spend her life with him in the bondage of holy matrimony. This means that husbands and wives do not have to go to bars and restaurants and talk to dozens of persons whom they have little interest in meeting to try and find someone who is reasonably acceptable as a sexual partner. One bypasses the entire "meat market" process and thereby saves days, weeks, or even months and greatly cuts down on the "down time" involved in trying to get a prospective partner to disrobe and come to bed.

The frequency of sexual intercourse does not vary appreciably by race with the reported differences in frequencies among blacks and whites, for example, varying by about 2.5 incidents of sexual intercourse per year—a measure that is virtually insignificant from a statistical standpoint. Of course it raises the question of how many people actually keep a tally of the number of times they have sexual intercourse in a year. Many of us have difficulty remembering what we ate for breakfast this morning and we would probably be hard-pressed to count the number of times we had done anything in a single year—even something as enjoyable as sexual intercourse. So one has to wonder about the accuracy of the responses in a general sense because most people simply do not have such accurate memories that they can recall with unquestioning accuracy the frequency with which they participate in any given activity in a single year. You can test this theory out for yourself by trying to remember the number of times you had pancakes for breakfast or the number of times you washed your car or the number of times you cut the grass with a lawnmower or even the number of times you read a literary masterpiece such as this volume. And even if you think you have a fairly accurate answer, you may still find yourself doubting whether your answer is completely accurate—unless of course you keep a diary and steadfastly record each and every aspect of your life in sickening detail. So one must wonder about the accuracy of the response and—because the questions deal with sex—as to whether there is any type of systematic bias in the answers given by the respondents.

Do most married couples have sexual intercourse about 1.2 times a week or are the survey respondents engaging in sexual intercourse on a less frequent basis and padding their averages for fear of appearing to be too repressed or even, dare we say, British? Or might the survey respondents be so embarrassed about the line of questioning that they would systematically understate the frequency in which they engage in sexual intercourse because they might believe that such activities somehow reflect poorly on them? Of course such an attitude would be puzzling in a "happening" society such as ours but any analysis of the results of any survey must take into account the varied ways in which the respondents might alter their answers based upon their attitudes toward the subject matter contained in the questions.

But let us assume that the respondents have infallible memories and that married couples engage in sexual intercourse about sixty-one times a year. Whether they do it well or properly or actually with each other is not really of great concern to the questioner. He merely wants to obtain some quantitative information about the rate at which married couples have sexual intercourse and he is not interested in passing judgment or evaluating their techniques or even serving as a tag-team member in any unique marital games. Whether he provides an actual definition of "sexual intercourse" to the people he questions or simply assumes that they know what he is talking about when he asks them about their bedroom behavior is his decision. He wants to make sure that the respondents understand the questions being posed and that they answer them accurately.

Of course accurate responses may or may not be forthcoming and the social-science researcher must anticipate that some persons will modify their answers to make themselves appear better in some way or even to please the questioner. But these are the psychological issues that every sociologist must contend with in dealing with human subjects. They lack the predictability of the inanimate atomic particles that are the province of the physicist. But imperfect information is better than no information at all because no information means that the survey cannot be completed and its results evaluated. So even though the researcher may suspect that the respondents are either understating or overstating their answers regarding the frequency in which they engage in sexual intercourse, the researcher really cannot grill the respondents too much in order to determine if they are telling the truth. After all, the respondents are volunteers and it is difficult to find people to fill out lengthy surveys—particularly if you are not paying them. So

Age and Average Frequency of Sexual Intercourse by Age and Marital Status—1998

| | Number of Times Per Year | |
Age	Married	Unmarried
18–29	111.6	69.1
30–39	85.7	65.6
40–49	69.2	49.8
50–59	53.8	31.2
60–69	32.5	15.7
70+	16.2	2.6

Source of Statistics: National Opinion Research Center (NORC), General Social Survey, 1998

researchers are generally reluctant to scream at respondents or slap them across the face even though they may suspect that the answers they are being given are not completely truthful.

How does the age of the respondents affect the frequency with which they have sexual intercourse? One obvious conclusion is that younger people will typically engage in sexual relations more frequently than older people because, quite frankly, older people are tired and have spent so much of their energies trying to survive their children. The NORC survey found that married adults between the ages of 18 to 29 engaged in sexual intercourse 111.6 times a year whereas single adults of the same age group lived a comparatively monastic life—having sex only about 69.1 times a year. Those between 30 to 39 years of age reported having sexual intercourse 85.7 times (married) or 65.6 times (single) per year whereas those between 40 to 49 years of age claimed to have sexual intercourse 69.2 times (married) and 49.8 times (single) per year. At the other end of the spectrum, those respondents older than 70 years of age stated that they had sexual intercourse 16.2 times (married) and 2.6 times (single) per year. Of course the study did not specify whether sexual intercourse had to be with another human being or even a nonlatex object but the general trend seems to indicate that there is an inverse relationship between age and frequency of sexual activity: the younger you are, the more times you have sexual intercourse. As with everything else, this does not mean that the younger are better at it but only that they have more opportunities to improve their techniques. It also means that you are less likely to drop dead during sexual intercourse when you are younger. Two somewhat sad findings of the NORC survey was that about 17 percent of all respondents reported not having sex in the past year and 11 percent claimed to have not had sex in the past five years. Of course this is not the type of competition that most persons wish to participate in—let alone win.

So the moral of the story is that your odds of having sexual intercourse will decline over time as you age. Of course no single individual has to be shackled to these admittedly depressing statistics. You can be as much of a lothario as you like at age 40 or 50 or 60 or 70 so long as your body and your partner are willing to cooperate. Are you not as young as you feel? Maybe or maybe not. But the point of this roundabout discussion is that snapshots of the nation's behavior or conduct does not mean that every individual must invariably follow those very same patterns. As a result, you can have young people who are very lethargic—if not downright comatose when it comes to the frequency of their sexual activity—and you can have very energetic senior citizens who could compete for a medal in the sexual Olympics. But these are the exceptions, and surveys—like all statistical studies—deal with groups of events (e.g., responses, numbers, events) and are not so concerned with individual aberrations except when they alter the expected outcome of the studies themselves.

FLESH PILE

Because most people like to view themselves as being sexually desirable beings (even though these views may not be shared by any other mammals), they have a certain curiosity about the number of sexual partners that their lovers, friends, and neighbors have had in the past (e.g., years, months, weeks, days). Fortunately for our purposes, the NORC has also seen fit to try to determine the numbers of sexual partners which Americans have had over one- and five-year periods of time. In this way, the NORC has tried to provide important insights into the human condition while also enhancing the appeal of its survey should they ever decide to offer it for sale in a brown paper wrapper to the general public. In any event, the researchers carrying out the NORC survey plunged ahead and asked the same 1,500 adults with whom they had already spoken about the frequency of their acts of sexual intercourse additional questions about the numbers of sexual partners they had enjoyed (or tolerated) in the past. As with much of the NORC survey, some of the results were surprising and others were to be expected.

America is a land that prides itself on its monogamous lifestyle and the Founding Fathers would be very pleased to find that this tradition appears to be borne out in the frequency with which Americans swap sexual partners. The NORC survey reported that nearly 70.7 percent of all respondents had sexual intercourse with only one partner in the previous twelve-month period of time (1998). When this time period was extended to five years, there was still 59 percent of the respondents who had clung to but a single sexual partner like a life vest. Given all the talk about the "sexual revolution" and "sexual freedom," this strong streak of monogamy is a little surprising. As pointed out above, however, the second largest group (17.4 percent of respondents) reported having no sexual partners at all in the previous twelve-month period. When this time period was expanded to five years, the "no-sex" group declined to 11.2 percent of the respondents. So those persons who were determined not to have sexual intercourse with another person (we do not know if any shepherds were included in the survey sample group) continued to remain surprisingly high. But as we have pointed out before, these surveys cannot possibly provide us with every possible facet of information that we might desire so we do not know if the members of this group had merely shifted their interests to intimate relations with other types of things such as blow-up dolls. On the other hand, we do not know if some of the respondents who said that they had one or more partners in the previous year were actually deflating their partner(s) after each use and folding them up to put away in a drawer. So one has to be careful in drawing any definitive conclusions about these results because it is not always clear what conclusions can be drawn. But we are probably fairly safe in concluding that the great majority of Americans (17.4 percent [no partners] and 70.7 percent [one partner]) in the previous twelve months were more likely to be spending their time with the same loved one (or no loved one) than to be hotfooting it through the neighborhood bars and clubs in search of new intimate friends.

But if 88.1 percent of the population were content to be with no person or one person in the previous year, that means that there are still 11.9 percent who are fun-loving types put on this earth to help dispel the general perception that Americans are a bunch of prudes. It is this tiny but sexually hyperactive group that is not content to be a single partner but wishes to go from bed to bed much like the bumblebee that meanders from flower to flower. Now this is not to say that all of the members of this group are frivolous, carefree individuals because 6 percent of them had just two partners in the previous twelve months in the survey and 2.2 percent had three partners in the past year. When added to the 88.1 percent having one or no partners in the previous year, we are left with a total of 96.3 percent of the respondents having three or fewer partners in the previous year. This of course means that the true party animals—those who have had four or more partners in the previous year—make up about 3.7 percent of our survey. These are the heavy hitters in the boudoir, the major league champions of the bedroom; the reigning kings and queens of the swing clubs. These are the people whom the rest of us secretly aspire to emulate even as we decry their egotism as well as their lack of morals and self-restraint.

The NORC survey reveals that the percentage of persons having multiple partners in the past year thins out very quickly. Whether this is due to the fact that some of these ladies and gentlemen get caught by their spouses and are forced to lay low for a while or is simply due to fatigue or boredom is unclear. But it is probably the case that fewer and fewer people simply have the time, energy, and inclination to try to meet and bed more and more people in a given period of time. There is arguably a certain point unique to each individual where the thrill and excitement of putting one additional notch on the bedpost is offset by the costs—both emotional and financial—of racking up yet another conquest. Now while this quest for ever greater numbers of sexual partners is arguably the ultimate romantic quest for some, there are others who would describe such an attitude as being shallow and meaningless. But everyone is entitled to their opinion and we should all respect each person's right to disagree with others.

Because only a few percent of all individuals have had four or more sexual partners in the past year, that small percentage engages in a lifestyle that is obviously foreign to the bulk of the population. (And many of us have conveniently forgotten our numbers some twenty years or so back in time.) But we do see that 1.5 percent claimed four partners in the previous year and 1.4 percent claimed five to nine partners in the past year, leaving a grand total of 0.4 percent claiming to have had sexual relations with ten or more persons in a twelve-month period of time. In a nation of 280 million people, this would represent a group numbering about 1,120,000. This may strike us as somewhat surprising because it means that about one out of every 250 persons is living life to the fullest, indulging in his or her carnal passions, and throwing every caution to the winds. As most of us can claim to have known at least 250 people in our lives, it means that, on average, each of us knows at least one person who is living this freewheeling lifestyle. But there are no common characteristics revealed by the survey to give us clues as to who these people might be in real life. In other words, they could be doctors, lawyers, teachers, carpenters, ministers, ice cream truck drivers, government officials, bankers, bus drivers, camp counselors, or any other occupation. So sexual proclivities and appetites cannot be easily characterized as being the province of a particular group or sect. Nor can one draw any conclusions along ethnic, gender, or age lines—except to say that the rate at which one engages in multiple sexual relationships will probably decline with age for most individuals.

In returning to the figures which broke down the number of sexual partners over the prior five years, the NORC survey revealed that 11.2 percent had no partners in the past five years, 59 percent had one partner in that time, 9.2 percent had two partners, and 6.0 percent had three partners. As a result, 85.4 percent had limited themselves to three or fewer sexual partners in the preceding five-year period—a level of experimentation that might not greatly impress the Marquis de Sade. But we might find that the reason most people did not have greater numbers of sexual partners was that most people were basically happy with their partners or—at the very least—too tired or lethargic to bother trying to find more exciting bedmates. But the decision not to seek additional partners is essentially the decision to remain with the same partners, so one must assume that most people have a certain bare minimum level of satisfaction with their existing situation. In any event, only 14.6 percent of the population had four or more sexual partners in the preceding five years, which is actually quite a low figure given the rootlessness and social mobility that characterize American society.

And should we pass judgment on those few persons who can claim double-digit conquests in a reclining position? Those persons who administer surveys are not interested in passing moral judgments; they merely want to collect the data needed to complete their surveys. Many are content to leave it to the newspaper columnists and television commentators to make sweeping generalizations and characterizations. Besides, it is not that difficult to have sex with ten different people in a given year so we should not really be so impressed with such a feat. After all, you could accomplish that task by having sex with a different person every thirty-six days. Now this is not a rate of sexual activity that will impress anyone, let alone anyone participating in a locker-room discussion of sexual conduct. Indeed, we find that this is a very anemic rate of sexual activity, which, if our lotharios are having only one tryst with each of their ten partners, is easily outdone by even those married adults older than 70 years of age. So perhaps we should not be so quick to covet the lifestyle of the monastic swinger because he or she would have sex only on average every five weeks or so. Of course this conclusion presumes that the person in question is having only a single encounter with each partner. Whether this assumption is meaningful is unclear. It may be that swinging persons have single encounters with some partners in a given year and multiple encounters with other partners. And it further stands to reason that those engaging in multiple contacts with other persons have the same outlook toward sex and would not be adverse to being involved with each other on a more frequent basis. The net result is that the survey results noted above do not provide us with enough information to draw any conclusions about whether these ten-plus performers see a different person each time or whether they oscillate back and forth among a number of persons.

MONEY FOR SEX

The NORC survey also attempted to determine the extent to which the respondents had paid for sex. As this is not an activity which most people discuss over polite dinner conversation (e.g., "So, dear, how was your day?" "Great! I had sex with two prostitutes"), one has to be concerned about the accuracy of the responses. Moreover, the offering of money for sex is illegal in most states and many respondents could be expected to be very reluctant to reveal that they might have knowingly engaged in a criminal activity. So it is not surprising that only a minority of those questioned (17 percent) ever admitted to the NORC to having paid for sex. The survey was quick to point out, however, that only 0.7 percent admitted to having paid for sex in the past year. As this is the type of question that will not necessarily elicit the most accurate response due to the fact that paying for sex does not say much for an individual's own sexual prowess, one has to be suspicious of the given responses. Of course there is the argument that sex for money merely speeds the dating process to a particular end result without all of the turgid dating and uncomfortable meals with the prospective in-laws. It may also be less expensive than having to spring for all of those pricey restaurant meals and theater tickets, but there is the slight drawback that the escort then leaves, moves on to the next job, and may carry a problematic ailment. So if one does not mind the somewhat temporary nature of relationships with paid escorts and the fact that one always needs to bring several hundred dollars in cash and risk contracting sexually transmitted diseases, then escorts may be a viable alternative for those who simply do not have the interest or the energy to develop meaningful monogamous relationships. Of course there is also the slight risk of fines, imprisonment, and public humiliation should you be swept up in the local vice squad dragnet while you are having a romantic dinner with your escort. But for some people, any publicity is good publicity and even a public humiliation is a ringing affirmation of their joie de vivre. Some may even find the prospect of being the lead story on the evening news with their shirt pulled over their head while being shoved into the backseat of a police cruiser to be invigorating.

EXTRAMARITAL SEX

Sometimes persons who have become bored with their spouses begin to look elsewhere for sexual fulfillment. Sex with a nonspouse is called an affair and often results in divorce when the innocent spouse learns of the tryst. Family lawyers consider affairs to be unfortunate but their disappointment that so many marriages are destroyed by affairs and then terminated by divorce is tempered somewhat by the knowledge that they can help right the wrongs suffered by the innocent spouse (particularly in community property states). These attorneys can also help to engineer a redistribution of the family wealth to the injured spouse. But it is also true that many marriages do manage to weather an affair . . . or two . . . or three . . . and the partners do manage to try to put their lives back together. But we are really more interested in the pure statistical numbers regarding admissions of extramarital activity than we are in the consequences arising from those infidelities because we are really not very compassionate statisticians.

In the NORC survey, the respondents' answers indicated that infidelity is a rare phenomenon in America. In fact, 16.5 percent of those questioned admitted that they had engaged in extramarital sex at one time or another during their married lives. But there was some discrepancy between the percentage of men who admitted to going astray as compared to the percentage of women respondents who admitted to engaging in extramarital relations. For the male respondents, 4.9 percent of those surveyed admitted to having engaged in extramarital sex in the past year and 20.8 percent admitted having engaged in extramarital sex at some point during their adult married lives. The female respondents were more guarded in their responses, with 2.5 percent of those surveyed admitting to having engaged in extramarital sex during the previous year and 13.4 percent having walked on the wild side at one time or another during the course of their marriage. Whether these figures are reliable is open to debate because we are once again dealing with an issue that does not reflect positively on the respondents admitting to the infidelity in any way. Whether it is better to engage in extramarital sex with a friend or to pay a professional is open to debate because both strike at the very heart of the marital partnership. But such acts do have one positive aspect in that they help to employ large numbers of attorneys and their staffs who remain ready and willing to help assist in marital property divisions of any size and type.

But there is something puzzling about the discrepancy between the percentages of males and females responding that they had engaged in extramarital sex and that is the fact that any such discrepancies do exist. We would think, at first blush, that the rates of infidelity among men and women would be essentially the same because we are dealing with equal numbers of men and women in the survey sample. But there are several problems with this line of reasoning. First, the men and women who were in this survey probably did not have extramarital sex with each other because the survey itself consisted of a nationwide sample of 1,500 individuals. Second, we may be making the tacit assumption that these men and women engaged in heterosexual extramarital sex and forgetting that some might have indulged in homosexual or lesbian extramarital sex. Third, we are also assuming that the male and female partners must have had extramarital sex with the same partners the same number of times—which is admittedly a very remote possibility. Fourth, we are assuming that there may be some underreporting of extramarital activity—particularly among women—due to the shame and embarrassment commonly felt by straying spouses who would probably not be overly anxious to reveal their darkest secrets to a clip-board-clutching research assistant. Moreover, problems might arise if the husbands of these women noticed that their offspring did not really seem to bear any resemblance to them. These discrepancies may simply exist because a greater percentage of the male population engaged in sexual relations with a slightly smaller percentage of the female population. Or it may be that members of the two genders matched up very nicely with most of the extra men finding solace in the company of their fellow men. As you can see, such surveys can offer information but they can raise more questions than answers because any statistics that reveal significant differences in the behavior of men and women will necessarily challenge prevailing assumptions regarding the common behavioral traits of men and women. But the important thing is that we have managed to cover all of the important matters that could possibly arise in any discussion concerning sex in America in these few very abbreviated pages.

3

DEATH, DISASTER, AND MAYHEM

THE SKY IS FALLING! THE SKY IS FALLING!

When we look into the nighttime sky and watch the starry carousel turn overhead, we will sometimes be treated to the spectacle of a shower of meteors streaking through the black sky toward Earth. We may remember that old adage from our childhood and make a wish but will usually be saddened to find that our boss is still at the office the next day. Notwithstanding the improbability of falling rocks as wish granters, astronomers inform us that Earth is repeatedly bombarded by millions of such objects from outer space, some smaller than a grain of sand and others the size of a baseball. Most of these objects do not reach the surface of the planet because they burn out in the atmosphere. But there are a few larger objects which are simply too massive to be incinerated before they hit the ground. Moreover, meteors do not dilly-dally on their way down to terra firma but instead hurtle toward Earth at rates of up to 40 miles per second or 144,000 miles per hour. Because meteors are not made of sponge cake or foam rubber, they can wreak widespread devastation when they hit the ground. Should you be out for a walk in the country admiring the wild flowers and a meteor no larger than a compact car falls out of the sky and lands on your head, then you will probably be killed. Although one can never rule out the strength of the human will to survive, very few people who have been squashed to no taller than the thickness of a human hair are able to live very vibrant lives. Fortunately, we do not have any records which would suggest that a meteorite has ever killed anyone in the modern era.

It is indeed surprising that even relatively small meteors can create large amounts of damage due to the tremendous amount of force they build up when being accelerated toward Earth. The famous English physicist Isaac Newton would be pleased to point out that the force of a meteor is equal to its mass times its acceleration or, expressed mathematically, $F = ma$. This equation shows that even a very small meteor, when it is traveling at very high speeds, can have an explosive impact upon landing. If you happen to look up in the sky while you are enjoying your walk through the meadow and see a flaming rock plummeting toward you, then you should make your best guess as to where you believe the meteor will land, turn in the opposite direction, and run as fast as you can. This strategy may not appeal to those persons who like to stand near dikes to see if the earthworks are strong enough to contain raging flood-

Explosive Impact of Meteors Striking the Earth

Diameter (feet)	Force (megatons)	Area Destroyed (square miles)	Frequency (intervals in years)
150	10	—	1
300	100	1	1,000
500	1,000	20	5,000
800	10,000	1,000	15,000
2,000	100,000	50,000	60,000
5,000	1,000,000	160,000	1,000,000

Source of Statistics: Morrison, Chapman, and Slovic,
Hazards Due to Comets and Meteors (ed. T. Gehrels)

waters or look directly at solar eclipses to see whether their retinas will in fact be burned. But it is a useful approach to consider when your survival is at stake even though you may not be able to run far and fast enough to do any good before the rock hits Earth.

How do we go about determining the odds that a meteor will hit you on the head? This is a difficult statistic to calculate because we can only roughly estimate the number of objects which plummet toward Earth in any given time. Astronomers believe that several hundred tons of cosmic debris enter Earth's atmosphere each day but the vast majority of these objects are not much larger than specks of dust. Moreover, these very small meteors will be slowed down dramatically by the friction created by Earth's atmosphere. This is why the vast majority of meteors burn up long before they reach the ground. Unfortunately, the atmosphere is not quite so effective an incinerator when larger objects are involved. A space boulder of 500 tons, for example, will suffer little more than a bad sunburn as it passes through Earth's atmosphere. But there is a direct relationship between the size of the plummeting meteor and the impact with which it hits the ground. And it is very surprising to learn that even small boulders from space can have massive impacts when they hit Earth. A meteor that is big enough to be rolled up against a building and reach the fourth-floor window would strike Earth with the force of several Hiroshima-type atomic bombs.

What about even bigger objects? The Barringer Crater near Winslow, Arizona, which is nearly 4,000 feet across and more than 600 feet deep, is an ominous testament to the ferocious power of falling objects. This massive crater was believed to have been created some 50,000 years ago when an object no more than 150 feet in diameter struck the surface of the planet with a force of some 600 Hiroshima-type fission bombs. Astronomers estimate that meteors of this size probably do not strike Earth more than once every thousand years. A recent event—possibly similar in nature—may have been the 1908 Tunguska incident in which a meteor or comet is believed to have landed in remote Siberia, flattening all the trees within a 30-mile radius like matchsticks. But the largest single meteor hit which scientists have been able to document with some certainty may have occurred about 65 million years ago when an object measuring about 100 miles across landed near Chicxulub in the Yucatan Peninsula. This is the event which many believe may have brought about the extinction of the dinosaurs as such an object would have scattered so much dust as to plunge the entire planet into virtual darkness (a so-called nuclear winter) for many months, thus killing much of the planet's vegetation. We are told by people who care to calculate such things that such a meteor would hit Earth only about once every 100 million years. Mind you, we have no proof were there a Creator of the universe that he or she would agree with these statistics and might not in fact be preparing to send some meteors the size of the state of Pennsylvania hurtling our way. But our best estimates are only estimates based upon what we have observed in the past, so we have to be careful not to put too much weight on these statistics.

Let us suppose that there are 1,000 asteroids careening around the solar system which are larger than one-half mile in diameter. Astronomers suggest that one of these objects will strike Earth every 250,000 years. But these estimates presume that these objects are evenly spaced and will hit Earth at regular intervals. The reality is that many of these meteors could be tightly bunched together and pelt Earth, one after another, in a comparatively short time. This would be akin to a host of nuclear bombs inexorably heading our way. Even if we had a functioning missile defense system, the system would have a difficult time knocking out each and every asteroid hurtling toward Earth.

Because we do not know the true number of asteroids that might ultimately collide with Earth or the periods of time in which the collisions can be expected to occur in the future, we can only make approximations based upon the evidence of past meteorite landings. The physical universe sometimes has a way of ignoring the predictions offered by probability theory. It might be that Earth will not be hit by a meteorite of any substantial size for another billion years. Or, on a sadder note, it may be that a meteorite the size of the Moon is about to obliterate Earth. Nevertheless, we are curious beings who still would like to quantify in some way the risks associated with debris falling from the sky. As a result, we need to determine the odds of a meteor reaching Earth and beaning us. This tendency of small meteors to create comparatively large pockmarks on Earth's surface should make us feel somewhat less sanguine about the extent to which the meteor's damage could be contained, particularly if you happen to break its fall. Three learned individuals named Morrison, Chapman, and Slovic have contributed a handy reference guide, *Hazards Due to Comets and Asteroids* (edited by Tom Gehrels, University of Arizona Press, 1994), for those of us who wish to know what will happen when a certain-sized meteor hits our planet and the frequency at which such an event will occur. No doubt these authors would offer the caveat that these estimates are only estimates and that they represent a best-effort guess based upon both the number of observed craters on Earth and the identified asteroids tumbling through space.

According to Morrison, a meteor 150 feet across, for example, would strike Earth with a force equal to a 10-megaton bomb, and could be expected to hit the planet once a year. Most of these meteors burn up in the atmosphere before reaching Earth, so we would not see too many of them. A meteor 250 to 350 feet across in diameter would strike Earth with the impact of 100 megatons and create a crater the size of the Barringer Crater or a leveling blast like that which destroyed Tunguska. Such a meteor would certainly be powerful enough to carry out the ultimate form of urban renewal of any city but would strike only about once every 1,000 years. If we are willing to wait 5,000 years, then Morrison and friends inform us we can expect a meteor at least 500 feet across which will hit the ground with the force of 1,000 megatons and lay waste to an entire metropolitan area such as New York or London. Every 15,000 years or so will bring us a meteor that is 800 feet or so across, which will strike with the force of up to 10,000 megatons and destroy a small state. So if you live in Rhode Island or Delaware, you might want to move to a big state and improve your odds of survival! Well, not exactly. But the arrival of a meteor some 2,000 feet across every 60,000 years or so will bring a blast of up to 100,000 megatons, which can destroy a medium-sized state such as any of those square states in the middle part of the country that are featured in trivia games. Finally, a meteor spanning a mile in diameter would come along every quarter of a million years and hit Earth with the force of up to 1,000,000 megatons and flatten an area the size of California or France. Now francophobes and owners of landlocked properties in Nevada might be delighted with such a prospect but the event would throw so much dust in the air that it could bring about the end of the food supply and life itself on the planet.

For our purposes, we might want to focus on the smaller class of meteors referenced above which do not exceed 150 feet in diameter and ignore the larger meteors due to the infrequency in which they occur. Because most of these meteors will burn up in the atmosphere, we will adopt a very conservative estimate and assume that one out of every 100 will reach Earth; a rate of one every 100 years. So once every 100 years we may expect a big rock to land somewhere in the world and strike the ground with the force of up to 10 megatons. Now 10 megatons is a substantial explosion, one that will rattle the windows, shake the walls, and possibly kill a few million people in the right area. Here we do not have to worry about radioactive fallout but we still need to be concerned about being in the wrong place at the wrong time. Using our brilliant mathematical powers, we can thus determine that we have a 1/100 or .01 probability that a meteor of this size will hit Earth in any given year. Now all we need to determine the probability that this meteor will land on our house is the amount of surface area of the planet and the estimated area that will be destroyed by the meteor itself. Earth's land surface is about 57,000,000 square miles, which is in turn about 30 percent of the total land mass of 196,000,000 square miles. If our 150 foot meteor strikes Earth once every 100 years and creates a dead zone of, say, 10 square miles, then the likelihood that your home will get squashed by a meteor can be determined by dividing the surface area of Earth by the area of damage caused by the meteor and then multiplying that quotient by .01. If Earth's surface is 196,000,000 square miles and the meteor will destroy 10 square miles, then we have a 1-in-19,600,000 chance of being struck by a meteor in a given century or a 1-in-1,960,000,000 chance of being struck by a meteor in a given year. (The reader will undoubtedly applaud the author's apparent effort here to utilize the tried and true "miles" as a standard of measurement when most of the world is rushing to embrace the trendy metric system.) But remember that we are talking about 10 square miles of devastation. If we want to be more specific and figure out the chance that the meteor will actually land on our house in a given year, then we would determine the ratio of the area of our house (e.g., 3,000 square feet) to the square footage of the 10 square miles (278,784,000) which is 92,928 and then multiply that number by 1,960,000,000, thus giving us a probability of 1 in 182,138,880,000,000.

These numbers sound so technical and antiseptic that it is easy to forget that we are dealing with a disastrous event. If our meteor veers at the last moment and hits the house at the end of the street, we will not be able to draw a deep sigh of relief and go back to watching the television because we will still be within the potential damage zone. It is unlikely that the rest of the people in the neighborhood will be able to resume their normal business either because our meteor will do more than merely squash the unfortunate home which is at Point Zero (and now greatly reduced in resale value). Instead it will hit the ground with the force of 200 Hiroshima bombs and obliterate all the houses within a range of 3 to 5 miles. This catastrophe will certainly put a huge damper on the upcoming neighborhood block party. But its impact will be felt even beyond the immediate devastation because it may cause tremendous amounts of dust and dirt to be scattered across the sky, perhaps causing day to appear as night throughout surrounding areas for several days and sending massive steams of rock and debris to rain down on nearby towns and farms. But we will be able to tell our grandchildren that we were the chosen few who were able to experience firsthand the spectacle of a falling meteor: "In our day . . ."

UP, UP, AND AWAY!

Although the spectacle of global annihilation from the impact of a massive meteor strike is very exciting, humanity is perfectly capable of creating its own kinds of disasters. Sometimes these disasters result from warfare such as the bombings of cities and the destruction of the countryside. But many disasters result from the failure of man-made devices—due to either their inherent design and manufacturing flaws or certain external factors such as "acts of God." Airplane crashes are perhaps one of the most dramatic and poignant kinds of disasters because they typically result from either a failure of the plane itself, pilot error, or the conditions of the exterior environment.

Seldom does a week go by where we do not hear the sad story of a plane slamming into the ocean or the side of a mountain or a remote village or a quiet neighborhood. Air disasters make for great news coverage because the horror is quite visible and immediate, generating big television ratings. The specters of these crashes also rekindle concerns about air safety in the minds of prospective passengers because nearly everyone flies on airplanes today—regardless of whether they are wealthy or poor. But those fears are usually assuaged by the calming reassurances of airlines spokespersons who have been trained in the voice of composure and who know where to find the parachutes if the plane starts to dive.

Perhaps the most common line offered by the airline industy is that air travel is far safer than automobile travel. On the surface of it, the fact that about 42,000 people died on the nation's roads in 1997 but only two persons died aboard large commercial carriers in 1997 would seem to ring the bell in favor of the airplane for those who wish to improve their odds of avoiding a hideous death on their vacation. Yet this comparison would not be entirely fair because the auto fatality figure includes all automobile-related accidents of any kind whereas the large commercial carriers are but one part of the general aviation industry (albeit the most reliable, safest, and popular part). A further point should be made that the number of fatalities in the large commercial carrier market was unusually low in 1997; the previous three years (1994–1996) had seen 239, 166, and 342 persons, respectively, die aboard large commercial carriers. The statistics provided by the National Transportation Safety Board do not necessarily suggest that there was a dramatic improvement in the level of aviation safety when the holiday revelers rang in the new year of 1997. Indeed, there were the same number (3) of fatal aviation accidents in both 1996 and 1997. The main difference is that the 1996 accidents were much bloodier than 1997. But the level of complexity involved in operating large commercial airliners coupled with the staggering numbers of passengers who climbed aboard U.S. airliners in 1997 (598 million) to fly some 605 billion passenger miles would seem, at first glance, to suggest that the extremely low number of fatalities was an aberration. But a review of the fatality figures provided by the Air Transport Association of America for 1998 and 1999 reveal that extremely low numbers of fatalities in the aviation industry may be more the norm than the exception because 1998 saw only one fatality arise from an on-ground accident and 1999 saw twelve lives claimed in two accidents.

But before we get too carried away with the wonderful safety record of the major airlines, we need to consider the safety records of the general aviation industry as a whole. When we add commuter carriers, air taxis, and private planes to the mix, we find that the number of fatal accidents recorded by the aviation industry as a whole in 1997 rises to 350 with a total of 640 fatalities. The fact that each accident averaged fewer than two fatalities suggests that the vast majority of these crashes involved small planes having only a few passengers. As many private planes may be less stable and have far less sophisticated instruments, it is not difficult to imagine why small planes would tend to have disproportionately higher rates of accidents than the commercial jetliners.

So what are the odds of dying in a plane crash? Well, some might argue that it depends on the skill you exercise (or the luck you have) in selecting the plane you wish to board. If, for example, you select a flight which ends up falling 5 miles out of the sky into the ocean, then the chances are fairly good you will not live to see the ball drop again next New Year's Eve in Times Square. But if you pick a plane that successfully completes its journey, then you will not have as much to worry about the status of your life insurance policy. The trick here, of course, is knowing ahead of time which flight will actually make it to its destination. For those of us who are not able to predict the future, however, we can rely only on our statistical analyses to help us predict the probability that our plane will be the one which actually blows up in the air or slams into a bucolic neighborhood.

How might we determine the safety of a given airline's flight? We could begin by asking how many people flew on planes in a given year, treating each separate ticketed journey as a different person. We know that some people fly more than once a year whereas others never climb onto a plane. But if we take the total number of tickets sold and then divide that number by the total number of tickets sold to passengers who died in a plane crash, then we could obtain a good idea of the odds that we will perish in a plane crash when boarding a given flight.

We need to use a little common sense in approaching this issue. We would not want to climb aboard a plane in which the fuel tanks are leaking and a flame is burning near the rear of the engines because we would know that something was amiss. Similarly, we would not be very eager to board a plane in which a wing had fallen off onto the tarmac. These subtle clues are things that the experienced traveler learns to look for in trying to determine which airline he should use for his flights. Instead we may want to check the prevailing safety statistics to see which airlines have better safety records and then allocate our business accordingly. Our review of the plane crash statistics might reveal that certain airlines are extremely accident-prone ("Fly Darwin Airlines: For those few who are strong enough to walk away from a crash") whereas others would boast of an unparalleled safety record ("Angel Airlines: Bringing Your Loved Ones to You in Safety"). You might quickly determine that the vast majority of fatal crashes occurred with a fairly small group of airlines such as Darwin and that most, if not all of the major American carriers, had very good safety records. Or you could just decide that this whole effort was not worth the trouble and buy a rail pass for your summer vacation.

But the simplest approach is to retrieve the appropriate government statistics and look at both the most current statistics regarding aviation accidents as well as the figures from past years to see if there is a trend toward lesser or greater mayhem on the nation's tarmacs. The NTSB calculated that the rate of fatal accidents per 100,000 aircraft hours is 0.02 for the large commercial carriers but rises to 1.42 for all aircraft—nearly a seventyfold increase. If we go back to 1985, however, we find that the rate of fatal accidents per 100,000 aircraft hours was 0.048 for large commercial carriers and a comparatively lofty 1.75 for all aircraft. So it would appear that the rate at which deadly crashes are occurring and passengers are disembarking to that giant fuselage in the sky are heading downward over time. This is good news for those of us who would prefer the speed of the airplane to the ambience of the bus station.

BORN TO BE WILD

Although few things in life can compare to the thrill of riding a plane downward to a fiery crash, you would probably get some arguments from motorcyclists who spend their every waking moment trying to think of ways to sneak out of school or work so that they can go ride their bikes and feel the cool wind blowing in their face and the flies smashing against their teeth. Motorcycles provide their riders with a feeling of freedom that many of them find difficult to equal in even the flashiest sportscars. Motorcyclists have virtually no protection from the dangers of the road; it is this vulnerability that makes motorcycles appear both attractive and dangerous at the same time to their riders.

Many of us who have ever watched a motorcycle roar past us on the highway have thought that it would be fun to be dressed in a leather jacket and boots, our hands wrapped around the handlebars of a gleaming silver and black cruiser, the sun shining brightly on the polished chrome as we raced up the highway, hoping that no highway patrol cars are within range with radar guns in hand. It might also inspire thoughts about the possibility of dying a horrible death on a motorcycle.

Now we have seen that estimating the probabilities of any event depends on the information we have about the total number of events in a given population and the frequency at which these events occur within that population. In this case, we would be interested in the total number of motorcyclists and, within that population, the number of deaths among motorcyclists each year. But we need to be careful how we define the term "motorcyclist" as there are persons who would consider themselves to be motorcyclists even though the extent of their riding involves little more than dropping a coin in the vibrating plastic motorcycle located at the front of the local toy store. These would clearly not be persons whom we would want to include in our population of motorcyclists. The same would hold true for those enthusiasts who attend motorcycle racing events and cheer on their favorite riders but do not actually ride a motorcycle itself.

Of course we might try to focus on those persons who have motorcycle licenses, but we will have no guarantee that we are including all the motorcyclists in the country. Some states do not require that riders obtain licenses in order to operate motorcycles or even dirt bikes. So there could be thousands upon thousands of unlicensed motorcyclists driving around, not caring one whit that they are frustrating our statistical analyses. Alternatively, we could focus on the national sales figures for all the motorcycle dealers combined but that, of course, would not include sales by private individuals through such things as newspaper classifieds and garage sales. So it becomes clearer that the task handed to the statistician is not one which can be performed by any namby-pamby but instead is one which only a few heroic persons possessing unflinching courage and rare tenacity can tackle with any hope of success. Certainly the task of identifying the population of motorcycle riders is one which is laden with semantic quicksand. But it is also clear that we must have some idea as to the nature of the population we are trying to examine. We want to look at motorcyclists as a whole and then determine the probability that these individuals will suffer deaths fit for viewing only by television audiences who love crashes.

Moving further along, the Centers for Disease Control reports that motorcyclists do their best to keep the funeral homes profitable, suffering some 2,100 deaths and an additional 50,000 serious injuries each year. Now this seems like a lot of death, particularly when one is riding a motorcycle decked out in chrome and leather trinkets, but the fact remains that motorcyclists are at a distinct disadvantage when they run into automobiles and trucks on the highways or automobiles and trucks hit them. Except for disoriented hotdog-cart vendors, motorcycles are the least massive vehicles on the highway and their drivers are virtually unprotected except for the windshields on their bikes' handlebars and the helmets on their heads. This means that motorcyclists do not usually fare very well in the games of "chicken" which routinely take place on the nation's roads. The CDC underscores this seemingly common-sense observation by pointing out that motorcyclists are fourteen times more likely to die than automobile drivers and three times more likely to suffer serious injury in a crash. Emergency rooms refer to motorcycles as "donorcycles" since many of the riders who die in accidents ultimately become donors for organ transplants.

Perhaps one should applaud the bravado shown by these daring knights and ladies of the highway, but it is unfortunate that the roads are a virtual killing field, despite the fact that most accidents are not caused by the motorcyclists themselves. Instead, motorcyclists are more often the casualties of motorists who do not see the two-wheeled chariots trying to pass them or changing lanes in front of them or behind them.

A person has about a 1-in-200,000 chance of dying on a motorcycle if he or she is a member of the general population. But if that person is the operator of a motorcycle in the United States—where there are some 7 million such vehicles—then the odds increase about sevenfold to about 1 in 30,000. We all know that there is a certain element of risk involved in everything we do but few activities offer as much potential for a gloriously fiery end as does a speeding motorcycle. Whether this situation will improve in the future—particularly when the roads are becoming more and more choked with bigger, heavier vehicles—remains to be seen.

WHY DID THE CHICKEN CROSS THE ROAD?

The advantage of living in an urban society bustling with people and overrun with all types of motorized vehicles which hurtle down narrow city streets is that you can occasionally see a minor fender bender or perhaps a spectacular crash. Of course you can be more aloof when confronted with the cacophonic spectacle of a cement truck slamming into the side of a city bus when you are standing on the sidewalk—as opposed to the crosswalk where the two behemoths merged.

But it is this distance that enables us to wonder about the probability that we might end our days crushed underneath the wheels of an eighteen-wheeler or the metal tracks of a bulldozer.

It is an unfortunate fact of modern society that very few people take the time to ponder weighty philosophical issues or even to consider the statistical likelihood that they might be squished by a taxicab or a runaway hotdog cart while trying to cross a busy city street. Yet there are a few unfortunate souls who are destined to serve as road cushions for public-transit vehicles and there is nothing that even the most marginally accurate television psychic can do to prevent these tragic stories from unfolding.

How you determine the probability that you will be staring at a truck axle when you draw your last breath should be quite simple. You would look at the total number of fatalities resulting from auto accidents and then isolate those deaths involving pedestrians. Once you determined the number of pedestrian deaths, then you would be free to divide that number by the population as a whole. If you were an accident hobbyist who wished to determine the probability that a given death arising from an auto accident would involve a pedestrian, however, your population would consist only of auto accident victims instead of the entire national population.

We are fortunate that the Insurance Institute for Highway Safety (IIHS) has gone to the trouble to count the number of pedestrians who are run over, battered, smacked, bulldozed, flattened, crushed, and clobbered on the nation's roads. Needless to say, there are many gory pictures of the unfortunate pedestrians who happened to be in the wrong place at the wrong time. The IIHS tells us that some 6,000 pedestrians each year die in or near the nation's roads; they make up nearly one out of every six traffic-related deaths. As all of the citizens of this country can be considered pedestrians at one time or another (even those persons confined to wheelchairs who occasionally venture across the street), we are once again dealing with the entire national population.

If we assume that the nation has 300,000,000 inhabitants (excluding household pets and wildlife), we each have a 1-in-50,000 chance of being killed while trying to cross the street. But this estimate must be qualified because some people live in areas that are crisscrossed by very dangerous streets whereas other people make their homes in regions with very little traffic on their roadways. Of course one can be killed on a lightly traveled road just as easily as a heavily traveled one but it would seem that the likelihood that one would become a highway statistic would be greater in areas with heavier traffic. But one could also argue that people who live in high-traffic areas are much more aware of the dangers of the road and correspondingly more vigilant when they cross the road. However, these are merely arguments and are not necessarily easily proven by statistical analyses.

But theory and reality are not always perfectly melded. Suppose that a cement mixer rammed a city bus as an elderly man crossed the street half a block away and suddenly dropped dead from a heart attack. Assuming that the authorities eventually noticed the body lying in the road, they would have to determine whether the man's death resulted from the colliding vehicles. If they performed an autopsy and found that his heart had stopped, then they would likely conclude that the elderly man had died from natural causes even though it was arguably caused by the shock of seeing the accident itself. So statisticians must always deal with the question of how to classify a given event in estimating probabilities.

How might you improve your chances of crossing the street safely? Many traffic engineers believe that a pedestrian should look both ways before proceeding into the thoroughfare. This advice is simplistic but it does seem to have some intrinsic merit. It makes sense to see if there is an oncoming truck before plunging ahead. We can test the merit of this idea by blindfolding the low-ranking member of the research team, placing him next to a high-powered, grossly overpaid executive member of that very same research team, and then telling them both to cross a busy boulevard. Even though the blindfolded staff member may be more tentative in stepping out into the street, hands outstretched as though feeling for an oncoming vehicle, he is much more likely than the sighted executive to get catapulted to the next block by a speeding taxicab. So there does appear to be some value in the "look both ways" approach.

Another less risky approach involves crossing only those streets in desolate areas where the cars and trucks appear with the frequency of ballet performances in maximum-security prisons. The advantage of such a road-crossing policy lies in its very low likelihood of roadway death. Unfortunately, it necessitates that all crossings take place in areas devoid of human inhabitants. As a result, it is not terribly practical to use in most areas in which people actually live.

STAIRWAY TO HEAVEN

Nearly every person who has a home with a flight of stairs has taken a nasty fall at one time or another and spent days or even weeks recovering from their bruises and, in many cases, broken bones. But some persons go beyond the pale and, quite unintentionally, end their existence at the foot of the stairs. The sad fact is that stairs can prove to be deadly to the unfortunate person who catches his foot on a loose board or trips over the dead body of a previous fall victim who has not yet been removed by the medical examiner.

How deadly are the stairs of America? We can certainly say, based on no evidence of any kind at all, that you are more likely to die on a flight of stairs than you are to command a rocket to the planet Pluto or walk across the surface of the Caspian Sea. Of course this sort of statistic merely states the obvious—that the likelihood of becoming a victim of the stairs is greater than nil. But to get a more accurate picture of the true peril we face when we stand on the landing, we have to look at the household accident figures kept by insurance companies to derive some idea as to the probability of taking a deadly fall.

Although the figures vary, it appears as though some 300 people on average die each year from falling down the stairs. In a country of almost 300,000,000 persons, this would give any individual the likelihood of a 1:1,000,000 chance of taking a fatal fall. But we need to remind ourselves that statistics do not provide any sort of guarantee that a particular event will or will not occur unless the defined event is one which has either no probability of occurring (the sun rising in the west and setting in the east) or certain to occur (the eventual death of every human being). If we go back to our stair example and we find, for example, that any person has a 1-in-1,000,000 chance of dying on the stairs (perhaps prompted by the gentle push of an insurance policy beneficiary), we have no assurances that we will not be a statistical casualty. If we find, in other words, that 300 people died last year on the nation's stairways (which would jibe with that 1:1,000,000 probability in a country of almost 300 million people), the fact that it is December 28 and the 300 people have already bitten the dust on the stairs does not mean that you can do a swan dive off the landing or strap on a pair of roller skates on the way to the cellar and expect to emerge unscathed. You can still die on the stairs even if the statistical quota for stairway carnage for the year has already been satisfied. There is nothing akin to a statistical prophylactic to keep you from harm when you insist upon throwing yourself in harm's way. So statistics are not very useful to those of us who are truly bent on self-destruction.

THE THRILL OF THE HUNT

Falling down a flight of stairs does not provide enough excitement for certain adrenaline junkies who are constantly in search of bigger thrills. For many persons, the obvious remedy to a tedious workweek is to get out of the suit and tie and get the ammunition out of the kitchen drawer and go hunting. Indeed, it is hard to believe that some people do not enjoy slinging a high-powered rifle (with infrared night vision scope) over their shoulders, donning brightly colored flak jackets ringed with several belts of ammunition, and heading off into the woods to obliterate some of nature's most dangerous creatures such as the sinister squirrel and the terrifying rabbit. The pursuit of deadly game is an exciting business for many weekend warriors but it is also one in which occasional accidental deaths occur.

Now the object of hunting is to kill unarmed animals and not other gun-toting humans. But carrying a big gun and lots of armor-piercing shells does not ensure good judgment in deciding whether another hunter's jacket resembles an article of clothing or the flank of a moose. The simple truth of the matter is that hunters sometimes get shot by other hunters. Most of these tragedies are not intentional but result from the victims being mistaken for two-legged deer or six-foot-tall grouses. Compounding the problem is the tension that invariably surrounds the life-and-death struggle for survival between man and pheasant or man and beaver. When a hunter fears for his life, he is prone to make mistakes in judgment and, sometimes, pulls the trigger before he can clearly see his target. So the invariable deaths occur even though the unintended victims may be clad in colorful jackets and hats.

How can you determine the chance that you will fall victim to a hunter's bullet? You must first define the population which you are studying. Here you would tally the total number of persons who can be considered hunters (those who use guns to shoot at targets or animals as opposed to those who use their guns to relieve liquor store owners of their spare cash). As far as the sample is concerned, you could focus on all the people who die in a given year, regardless of whether or not they are hunters, or you could limit the sample to only those persons who are actual hunters with actual loaded weapons, extra bottles of vodka, and enormous chips on their shoulders. But we should go further and try to distinguish between those hunters who live off the land and only occasionally "go into town" for a few provisions and those gun-toters who toss their munitions in their sports cars and head out into the wilderness to experience the great outdoors.

To avoid a definitional morass, we are probably better off if we include all persons who hunt in a given year—whether they are habitual warriors or merely lollygaggers. From this pool of worthy individuals we can then take the number of deaths resulting from hunting accidents and then try to determine the statistical probability of becoming another "victim" lying facedown on the forest floor and being nibbled on by the gentle woodland creatures.

But we may have to confront another definitional problem in tallying our sample because there may be cases where it is inappropriate to classify a hunting accident as such. The fact that someone who likes to wear hunting garb as a matter of course decides to end his or her life while standing out in the woods is not an event which we would normally consider to be a "hunting" accident. But as hunters do not commit huge numbers of suicides, this potential problem should not be significant. Similarly, the hunter taking aim at a moose who is suddenly hit on the head by a falling meteorite or even a motorcycle dropping from the wheel well of a passing cargo plane would not be considered a hunting accident statistic. Even though the reader may marvel at the adeptness with which the preceding example brought together the various parts of this chapter, the point is that one must be somewhat arbitrary in deciding what will be or not be considered a "hunting accident." Indeed, we all owe a debt of gratitude to hardheaded statisticians who, throughout recent history, have unilaterally decided how to define the parameters of their studies while thumbing their noses at the masses who demanded a more democratic process for setting up statistical analyses.

In view of all of the potential ambiguities surrounding our effort to figure out the number of hunters venturing after big game each year as well as those who return from their hunts in bodybags, we are probably best served by relying on that government entity—the U.S. Fish and Wildlife Service (USFWS)—which knows more about hunters and wild animals than any other governmental agency—except, perhaps, the U.S. State Department. In any event, the USFWS informs us that there are about 14 million hunters in the United States, each of whom averages about 17 days of hunting per year. How many people die as a result of these 14 million warriors venturing out to do battle with Bambi? The answer is something on the order of about 130 each year. Mind you, this is a figure that is subject to criticism for many of the reasons already noted above but it is perhaps as comprehensive a tally as we will get without sending an army of staffers out to do a hunting "census." But if America's hunters go out about 238 million hunting days each year (we get this figure by multiplying 14,000,000 by 17 days), we find that the rate of death from hunting accidents is 0.0000005 (we get this figure by dividing the number of deaths— 130—by 238 million hunting days per annum). Well, this rate is admittedly very low and certainly puts the entire risk issue in perspective because there is only about one hunting fatality for every 2 million hunting days each year. This should make us feel very good—unless, of course, we are one of the unfortunate few who happen to get gunned down by our fellow hunters. But it does underscore the fact that our likelihood of suffering the fate of Bambi's mother is very, very small.

CONCLUSION

As with everything else in America, there are many ways to die and this chapter has touched upon only a few of the ways in which Americans perish. While the death of any person is a tragedy, it is also true that many people put themselves at risk unnecessarily with little thought for the consequences of their actions. But this chapter has touched upon a few of the ways in which people can die through no fault of their own such as a plane crash or getting hit by a car. These deaths are, in many ways, the saddest of all because they are so senseless and undeserved.

But it is an inescapable part of the human condition that everyone will die at some point; some people simply manage to do it with a little more notoriety and flair.

4

GOING TO WAR

Few things excite the bloodlust of some people more than mortal combat—regardless of whether it occurs in a boxing ring or on a battlefield or even in a department store during the holiday season. But when a nation goes to war the mettle of its people is tested and its soldier-warriors must step to the forefront to defend the vital interests of their country or, if the nation is an imperial power, squash a pesky insurgency of grubby guerrillas who have deluded notions about their entitlement to self-determination.

Death is not a topic that military recruiters like to dwell on when they explain the many advantages of a military career to potential recruits. After all, one's personal demise is admittedly something of a depressing topic to consider after one has watched thrilling videotapes of fighter planes shooting down enemy aircraft in aerial dogfights or navy ships dropping depth charges on enemy submarines or formations of massive tanks pounding through enemy lines. But it does bear mentioning somewhere in the small print of the multimedia presentation given by the representatives of the army, navy, air force, and marines that soldiers (as well as civilians unfortunate enough to be caught in the line of fire) do get killed. So for the would-be soldier who is considering whether to sign up

Combat Fatality Rates from the Revolutionary War to Vietnam

War	Number of Troops	Number of Deaths	Fatalities (percentage)
Revolutionary War	250,000	4,435	0.017
War of 1812	286,000	2,260	0.007
Mexican War	78,700	1,733	0.002
Civil War			
Union	2,210,000	140,000	0.063
Confederacy	1,050,000	74,500	0.070
Spanish-American	306,760	385	0.012
World War I	4,735,000	53,400	0.011
World War II	16,120,000	291,800	0.018
Korean War	5,689,000	33,750	0.005
Vietnam War	8,730,000	47,355	0.005

Source of Statistics: U.S. Department of Defense

for a stint in the military, it may be a good idea to try to get some idea as to the likelihood that a recruit might take a fatal bullet.

We can then compare that cold hard statistic with the many benefits of a military career, including the fine gourmet meals available at the mess, the enormous starting salaries (including stock options), and the custom-tailored uniforms. But this weighing of the costs (death) and benefits (too numerous to mention) of the military life is a tricky endeavor because one cannot really know in advance the odds that one will die in combat—no more than one can know the odds that your lover's spouse will show up at home unexpectedly during the middle of the day and empty both barrels of his or her shotgun into you. One can try, however, to estimate the odds of a premature demise by looking at some of the earlier wars in which the United States has been involved and then trying to to calculate the mortality rates for soldiers who fought in these campaigns.

Because we Americans are by nature an optimistic people, we might suspect that our increasingly technologically sophisticated military arsenal has, over the years, made military duty a substantially less dangerous undertaking. Yet we would have to examine the casualty rates for various wars throughout the history of the United States to see if increased technology has led to increased insulation from the ultimate costs of warfare. Moreover, we would probably like to find out whether particular branches of the military service are more dangerous than others so that we can at least pick a career path in the military in which the odds of survival are more in our favor.

The statistics for many of the earlier wars such as the Revolutionary War (1775–1783), the War of 1812 (1812–1815), the Mexican War (1846–1848), and even the Civil War (1861–1865) were fought when statistics on battlefield casualties were sketchy at best and often nonexistent at worst. The value of being able to track quantities of resources (men and matériel) was not a widely shared view among military officers even though those in charge were responsible for equipping military forces with basic necessities.

Because the vast majority of soldiers served in the army in these earlier wars, it is probably not very helpful to try to discern whether it was safer to be in the army than the navy or the marines. There simply were not enough persons outside the army to draw any meaningful conclusions about the dangers of serving in one branch or another. But we can draw upon statistics provided by the U.S. Defense Department to try to get a handle on the perils faced by those persons serving their country in these earlier conflicts. The most straightforward approach would be to examine the number of persons serving in any given war and then divide that number by the number of combat deaths (giving due credit to the number of noncombat deaths) to arrive at the all-important combat death ratio: the rate at which military personnel perished in conflict compared to the total number in uniform (e.g., one out of every 500, one out of every 50, etc.). Alternatively, we might reverse the numerator and the denominator, thus dividing the number of battle deaths by the number of military personnel serving in a given war, to arrive at a percentage figure as to the probability that a particular member of a specific branch would indeed not survive to the end of the conflict. Although many soldiers suffer nonfatal wounds which can be slight to extremely serious, we will disregard any nonfatal wounds in this chapter so as to focus solely on the mortality rates endured by American soldiers in their military campaigns.

Although estimates vary as to the number of soldiers under arms during the Revolutionary War, the U.S. Defense Department has estimated that no more than 250,000 soldiers served under the colonial military command and that a total of about 4,435 combat-related deaths occurred in that conflict. Because the role of the navy and marines was negligible aside from several well-publicized sea battles, we can assume that the casualties were almost exclusively derived from that of the army. We therefore divide 250,000 by 4,435 to get a ratio of 56.36 which tells us that one out of nearly every fifty-six persons serving in the Continental army died during the war. If we reverse the numbers and divide 4,435 by 250,000, we find that there was a casualty rate of about 0.017—a little less than 2 percent. Doubtless this seemingly low death rate probably owed a great deal to the limited range and uneven quality of most of the firearms of that era. Indeed, it was not uncommon for soldiers to be injured due to their firearms blowing up in their faces. But it was also an era in which skirmishes were the norm and field commanders were not particularly keen on fighting to the death of the last man.

How does the War of 1812 compare to the American Revolution? It has always been a poor stepchild in relation to its more famous 18th-century namesake because the War of 1812 did not give rise to a day of fireworks or a constitution or even a tricolored flag. It did bring us an early example of urban renewal when the British burned Washington, D.C., and it did prompt Francis Scott Key to write a national anthem that only three people on the planet can sing without stripping their vocal cords. But the War of 1812 is known for the years in which it occurred and therefore lacks the grand title of many other conflicts in American history such as the MEXICAN War, the CIVIL War, and the really impressive-sounding global conflicts—WORLD WAR I and (for those who did not get enough carnage the first time around) WORLD WAR II. But one advantage of fighting in a dull, nondescript war such as the War of 1812 was that the survival of the nation was not at stake. The passions that had erupted in the Revolutionary War were largely absent in the War of 1812 and, indeed, neither the American nor the British side really had any clear and compelling idea as to why they had gone to war in the first place. Most people seemed to lack strong convictions as to the point of the war and this may be one reason that the rates and percentages of deaths among soldiers declined markedly from the time of the Revolutionary War.

The U.S. Defense Department states that 286,000 soldiers served during the War of 1812 but only 2,260 died in combat. As with the Revolutionary War, there are no reliable figures for noncombat-related deaths so we will ignore them here. But we see that dividing 286,000 by 2,260 gives us a combat death ratio of 126.54, which tells us that one out of about every 126 soldiers died in the War of 1812. Reversing the numerator and denominator and dividing 2,260 by 286,000 gives us the miniscule mortality rate of 0.007 percent—less than 1 percent. These low numbers do not make for very good television documentaries but they do illustrate the fact that the War of 1812 was a good war to be in if you were interested in being a soldier and assuring your own survival.

The Mexican War (1846–1848), which saw the United States seize the northern two-thirds of Mexico, did not involve extraordinarily large armies as only about 78,700 soldiers participated in the military operations in Mexico. Battle-related deaths totaled 1,733 whereas other deaths, such as those arising from illness and disease, totaled 11,550—almost six times the number of deaths from combat. These numbers do not speak well for the sanitation and hygiene practiced in the war zones nor does it say much about the level of medical care received by the troops. As far as the combat death ratio is concerned, however, we see that about one in forty-five soldiers died in battle; this means that a little more than 2 percent of all the soldiers who served in that war perished on the battlefield. Of course this figure represented a tripling of the battlefield casualty rate over that which occurred during the War of 1812. But one has to expect that a few additional deaths will result when trying to take a million square miles of territory from another country. If we add the battlefield and noncombat deaths together, we get a much more grisly picture—a death ratio of 5.92 and a probability of death equal to 0.168. Imagine trying to recruit new soldiers when your most recent war saw one out of about every six soldiers die from either combat or other war-related causes, thereby creating a wartime mortality rate of almost 17 percent! This would not be very impressive to report, particularly in view of the comparatively miniscule numbers posted in the American Revolution and the War of 1812.

The United States had not yet experienced the widespread devastation that would come with the Civil War. The death and suffering would be unprecedented and, of course, nearly every casualty would be an American. The U.S. Defense Department has estimated that about 2,210,000 soldiers served in the Union military, all of whom except for about 84,000 soldiers were in the Union army (the rest being in the other branches of the military). These troops suffered about 140,000 battle-related deaths and about 224,000 other deaths, most of which resulted from poor medical treatment, disease, and periodic outbreaks of illness. Unfortunately for these soldiers, the level of medical care had not evolved greatly from the time of the Mexican War or, for that matter, from the time of the Revolutionary War. Infectious diseases killed many tens of thousands of soldiers on both sides because antiseptics had not yet begun to be utilized. Compounding the problem was the large numbers of prisoners taken by both sides and the inability of either side to care adequately for these soldiers. The Confederacy was particularly hard-pressed to care for Union soldiers due to its lack of adequate food and clothing for its own population. As a result, the lives of Union prisoners of war were particularly dreary. Andersonville, Georgia, was perhaps the most notorious prison camp in which some 30,000 Union prisoners were crowded into a log stockade consisting of about 16 acres—which necessitated stuffing about 1,875 prisoners on each acre of land. When you realize that there is about 43,560 square feet in an acre of land, the dire nature of the conditions endured by these men becomes clearer: Each soldier had an average of about 23 square feet to himself. The severity of the Andersonville camp conditions becomes more obvious when we realize that 23 square feet is an area of land less than 5 feet by 5 feet. This extreme overcrowding combined with contaminated water, poor food, and primitive sanitation contributed to the severity of epidemics that periodically swept through the camp and kept the gravediggers in the area very busy. One can only imagine how many fights broke out when somebody dared to step across a line drawn in the dirt into a neighboring prisoner's 5-foot by 5-foot square.

Notwithstanding our discussion of prison life in a Confederate stockade, our figures showed that the Union armies continued to suffer far greater numbers of deaths (224,000) from poor medical conditions than from actual battlefield conditions (140,000). The combat death ratio (excluding noncombat deaths) is 15.7, which tells us that nearly one out of every sixteen soldiers in the Union army died in glorious carnage on the battlefield. If we add the other 224,000 deaths, then our combat death ratio shrinks to 6.07, which tells us that one out of every six Union soldiers died from military service—whether that death occurred on the battlefield, in a Union hospital, or in a Confederate prison camp. In reversing the numerator and denominator, we obtain a casualty rate that is equal to 6.3 percent for combat-related deaths and 16.4 percent for both combat- and noncombat-related deaths.

These types of heady numbers might make a prospective recruit want to reconsider his options. And it was indeed the growing reluctance of young men in the North to volunteer to become cannon fodder that prompted all-knowing government officials to institute that most popular of recreational activities—the military draft. But it was laden with a number of features to appeal to those having an entrepreneurial spirit and some extra cash in that the draftee could pay a fee to the government and be released from military service altogether or hire a substitute to serve in his place.

But what about the casualties suffered by the Confederate troops? The available figures are even sketchier as to the number of men who served in the Confederate forces with the estimates by the Provost Marshal General as reported by the U.S. Defense Department ranging from a little more than 600,000 to nearly 1,500,000. To make an educated guess and not simply wring our hands over the widely varying estimates of the total number of Confederate troops, we shall proceed by using the very scientific method of splitting the difference and assuming that a total of about 1,050,000 men served in the Confederacy. We are told by the Provost Marshal General that about 74,500 soldiers died in battle and about 59,200 soldiers died of other causes. As a result, we can use these numbers to determine that the combat death ratio was 14.09 for battlefield deaths and 7.85 for all deaths, meaning that one out of every fourteen Confederate soldiers died in combat and one out of nearly every eight Confederate soldiers died from serving in the Civil War itself. As far as the casualty rate was concerned, we would obtain a rate of about 7 percent for battlefield deaths and a rate of about 13 percent for all deaths. We should also point out that we had to make an educated guess at the outset regarding the number of Confederate soldiers under arms because the numbers offered by various sources differ considerably.

If we compare the rates for battlefield deaths for both the Union and Confederate soldiers, we find that they are about the same (6.3 percent in the Union army versus 7 percent in the Confederate army). There is a slightly greater divergence in the aggregate number of deaths of military personnel (battle-related and other) with about a 16.4 percent rate for the Union army and a 13 percent rate for the Confederate army. Given the fact that the Union army was better fed, equipped, and supplied than its Confederate adversary, it seems probable that the higher rate of nonbattlefield deaths suffered by Union troops was caused in large part by the extremely poor conditions of the Confederate prisons. This casualty rate did not reflect any real improvement since the time of the Mexican War so it seems reasonable to conclude that very little had occurred in the interim in the improvement of the level of medical care and the quality and provisions given to Union troops.

At this point in history, the odds a soldier faced in trying to survive a war were not terribly good as nearly one out of every six could be expected to die either on the battlefield or in the field hospitals or the enemy's prison camps. For those soldiers who did survive the war, they were still given the dubious opportunity to enjoy the day-to-day routine of the foot soldier which included monthly pay of about $15 per month and an unsteady diet of pork, biscuits, beans, and corn. When the soldiers went marching into battle, their diets were even more spartan. Their uniforms were typically a scratchy, uncomfortable wool that were less than pleasurable in the dead of summer and typically omitted from consideration for any "Best New Fashion Design" award. Moreover, many soldiers, particularly those in the Confederate army, had to do without shoes, even in the dead of winter.

Certainly there was some hope that the passage of time would improve the lot of the common soldier and breakthroughs in medicine and health care would reduce the noncombat casualties suffered by military troops. Of course the inexorable march of progress would also lead to improvements in firearms and ammunition and, hence, greater vulnerability on the part of the ground troops. But such is the price of progress in the sciences and it is often a nation's army that is the greatest beneficiary of these advances and, simultaneously, the greatest victim of these technological improvements.

By the beginning of the 20th century, warfare was about to undergo revolutionary changes with the advent of the airplane and the tank. But the military tactics and the actual mechanics of warfare were still very much anchored in the 19th century as shown by the Spanish-American War which lasted for less than a year (1898) and involved headline-grabbing charges by Teddy Roosevelt's "Rough Riders" in Cuba. Of the 306,760 persons who served in the Spanish-American War, 280,500 were in the army, 22,800 were in the navy, and 3,300 were in the marines. The corresponding battlefield casualties numbered 369, 10, and 6, respectively, and the noncombat deaths numbered 2,061 (army only). The obvious conclusion is that combat-related deaths continued to be a small fraction of all wartime casualties due to the age-old problems of inadequate medical treatment, poor sanitation and hygiene, and spoiled food and contaminated water. But we see that the combat death ratio broken up by service branch was as follows: army (280,500/369 = 760), navy (22,800/10 = 2,280), and marines (3,300/6 = 550). If we add the noncombat deaths to the army combat death (the only branch with available figures), we obtain 280,000/2,430 = 115.5. So we find that the likelihood of dying in combat or dying from combat-related wounds declined markedly between the time of the Civil War and the Spanish-American War. If you were in the army during the Spanish-American War, for example, you would have a 1-in-760 probability of dying in combat and a 1-in-115 chance of not surviving the war due to either battlefield wounds or noncombat-related issues. Even though the noncombat mortality rate continued to constitute the vast majority of all wartime deaths, it is striking how the probabilities of surviving the participation in the conflict increased so much in this war. Not surprisingly, the rates of casualties were far lower as shown by rates of battlefield deaths among the three branches of the military: an 0.13 percent combat death rate in the army, an 0.04 percent combat death rate in the navy, and an 0.18 percent combat death rate in the marines. These rates were absolutely dwarfed by those suffered in earlier wars, particularly the Civil War.

But numbers are only numbers and we can only surmise as to some of the reasons for the vast differences in mortality rates in the Civil War and the Spanish-American War. First, the stakes were infinitely higher in the Civil War because the survival of the United States was gravely threatened by the secession of the Confederate States. The Spanish-American War was sparked by public furor over Spain's treatment of its colonies in the Caribbean and the Pacific, a noteworthy concern but one that did not have the gravity of a conflict that threatened the existence of the nation itself. Accordingly, the armies in the Civil War continued to pummel each other for four long, bloody years. The military campaigns in the Spanish-American War, by contrast, were brief and decisive, with the United States enjoying decisive advantages in men, matériel, and logistical support. Second, a greater portion of the standing armies of both the Union and Confederacy engaged in battle with each other due to the fact that there were simply not enough able-bodied men to support the armies and also maintain bloated military bureaucracies. In the Spanish-American War, by contrast, a comparatively small part of the military saw action on the battlefields because there was no compelling need to draw upon all of the resources of the United States. The quality of the Spanish military forces was not great and they lacked the desire to engage in battle with a nation that was so eager to fight. In summary, the Spanish-American War was fought against a decisively inferior adversary who was at an enormous disadvantage in terms of its ability to carry on sustained warfare in an area that, for the most part, was in the backyard of the United States.

But the "fun" of the Spanish-American War and the almost nonexistent casualties suffered by the military were not destined to be the model for warfare in the future. World War I was just around the corner and the unbridled joy of "trench warfare" and the aromatic delights of "mustard gas" would soon become known to the entire world. As with the Civil War, World War I would bring massive armies into conflict with each other who would use every lethal means at their disposal to liquidate each other and thereby defend their respective national governments and cherished ways of life. Certainly the Allied nations believed that Kaiser Wilhelm's Germany was a mortal threat to the democratic traditions of western Europe, particularly after it had sent its armies through neutral Belgium in an effort to crush the French armies and ensure its hegemony over the Continent. Not even the most adept public relations firm could have managed to put a positive spin on the ominous actions of the German military.

The United States was fortunate enough to avoid becoming entangled in World War I for nearly three years, during which time Great Britain and France fought Germany to a standstill on the western front but Russia was forced to surrender and cede large amounts of territory in the east. The ability to sit on the sideline was a good thing because the United States was able to continue life as usual while the major European powers gradually exhausted each other in a bitter stalemate in which huge numbers of troops were lost on both sides in often futile attempts to take even a few yards of enemy territory. Moreover, the United States was able to profit from the misery on both sides by selling goods and matériel to all of the warring parties. But public opinion in the United States gradually swung in favor of the Allied cause, particularly after the Germans began unrestricted U-boat activity and sank the ships of neutral nations.

In any event, the United States jumped into the war in 1917 and found that it was one thing to train for warfare and quite another thing to face battle-hardened German troops who knew how to fight. The United States managed to mobilize 4,735,000 soldiers during World War I and suffered a total of 53,400 battle-related deaths and 63,100 noncombat deaths. The army itself had a total of about 4,057,000 men and suffered 50,500 battlefield deaths and 55,800 other deaths. The navy boasted about 600,000 men and lost 430 men in combat and 6,850 sailors in other noncombat circumstances. The marines themselves had 79,000 men and suffered 2,460 combat deaths and 390 other deaths. One striking fact about these casualties is that the battlefield deaths and other deaths for the army were almost equivalent to each other. The navy, by contrast, saw nearly a sixteenfold increase in the number of nonbattlefield deaths over combat-related deaths whereas the marines saw nonbattlefield deaths consist of only about 15 percent of all mortal casualties. The fact that medical services and procurement had vastly improved since the Civil War no doubt contributed greatly to the flattening of the discrepancy between battlefield and noncombat deaths for the army. But the problems with U.S. Defense Department statistics, as with all statistics, is that they provide quantitative snapshots but do not necessarily provide explanations; this task is left to the historians, politicians, and other comedians. As a result, we can understand the relative equivalence of combat and noncombat deaths suffered by the army but we are also perplexed by the huge discrepancy in naval casualties. But more to the point, we can look at these figures and determine whether in fact the soldier (and sailor's) life in wartime had become more or less safe since the time of the Civil War.

As far as the U.S. Army was concerned, a soldier had about a 1-in-38 probability of not returning from World War I alive. Accordingly, the casualty rate (deaths only) for U.S. soldiers was a little more than 2 percent. Sailors in the U.S. Navy had a 1-in-82 likelihood of dying during World War I and, as a result, a mortality rate of about 1.2 percent. Finally, the marines, who played a somewhat more peripheral role in the war, had a 1-in-32 chance of dying during the war and, as a result, a mortality rate of about 3.6 percent. World War I thus taught the very important lesson that it made far more sense to sit on the sidelines as long as possible, watch all the other major countries bloody each other, and then sweep in at the end and take the lion's share of the credit for the victory. It also showed the wisdom of fighting against other countries as opposed to engaging in civil wars in which all of the casualties were by definition incurred by American soldiers and sailors. No doubt the American citizens who watched Confederate and Union armies grind up the landscape would have also agreed with the desirability of engaging in warfare in foreign countries.

So the deaths rates among military personnel dropped significantly from the time of the Civil War but had increased following the Spanish-American War—which was less of a war and more of a military maneuver involving Spanish troops. But the truer test of the danger of the war zone would be more severely tested with the advent of World War II because the United States would not have the luxury of waiting until the final year of the conflict to enter the squared circle.

So how did our military troops do during World War II? Due to a strong isolationist bent, the nation was able to sit on its hands for more than two years following the outbreak of the war in September 1939, but it was finally forced to jump into the fray when the Japanese attacked Pearl Harbor and sent much of the Pacific Fleet to the bottom of the ocean floor. The sneaky nature of the attack doubtless contributed to the rapid mobilization that saw nearly 11,250,000 soldiers serve in the army, 4,200,000 serve in the navy, and 670,000 serve in the marines. But even though the American citizenry knew they were fighting against regimes in Tojo's Japan and Hitler's Germany that made Kaiser Wilhelm's imperial Germany seem like a troop of Girl Scouts, it would still require nearly four years to defeat the Axis powers and make the world safe for new murderous tyrants such as Joseph Stalin and Mao Zedong. But such is the unfortunate nature of global conflict that the solution of one problem almost invariably leads to the creation of another. Yet that should not detract from the sheer heroic effort that was needed by the United States as well as its European allies to defeat the Axis war machines and ensure the safety of the world for Coca-Cola and McDonald's.

When such stark choices between freedom and totalitarianism are involved, there is little likelihood for peaceful resolution and we would expect that the death rate for the branches would have been significantly higher than World War I. But was that the case or did the statistics confound our expectations once again? The army suffered 235,000 battle deaths and 83,400 nonbattle deaths or a total of 318,400 deaths. This meant that the army suffered from a death rate of about 2.8 percent. The navy suffered about 37,000 combat deaths and 25,700 other deaths or a total of 62,700 deaths. The navy thus incurred a casualty rate of about 1.5 percent. Finally, the marines had 19,800 battlefield deaths and 4,800 noncombat deaths or a total of 24,600 deaths and thereby incurred a comparatively higher death rate of 3.6 percent. But these figures showed little real change in the percentages of deaths among members of all three branches of the military service between World War I and World War II. The greatest increase was recorded in the rate of death for army troops but that amounted to less than a full 1 percent increase whereas the navy casualty rate increased by only a few tenths of a percent and the rate among marines was virtually unchanged.

But World War II ended more than a half century ago and seems as distant as the Stone Age to today's enterprising young persons. So they certainly require some information that is more up-to-date to help guide them in their decision as to the best branch of the military to join if they hope to live a long and happy life. So we need to consider the remaining two wars of the 20th century fought by American troops— the Korean War and the Vietnam War.★ These were not "world wars" in the true sense of the world but proxy wars whereby the United States and the Soviet Union and certain of their allies battled against each other. But both involved American troops in distant lands and were waged, ostensibly, to stop the spread of Communism in Asia. In Korea, the army's troops numbered about 2,800,000 and incurred a total of 27,700 combat-related deaths and 2,500 other deaths or a total of 30,200 casualties for a death rate of a little more than 1 percent. The

---

★For purposes of this discussion, we are excluding more limited military interventions such as Grenada and, due to its comparative brevity, the Persian Gulf War.

navy boasted 1,180,000 sailors with about 650 total deaths or a death rate of 0.05 percent. The marines had 424,000 troops and a total of about 4,600 deaths or a mortality rate of about 1 percent. The Korean War also saw the newly created air force in which a total of about 1,285,000 persons served and which saw about 1,500 persons die in combat and noncombat-related activities for a death rate of about 0.1 percent. These mortality rates were clearly only a fraction of those endured during the two world wars and underscored the wisdom of picking fights with poorly trained developing countries—at least until the Vietnam War.

Those who enjoyed three years of bloody warfare on the Korean peninsula must have been absolutely ecstatic about the nine-year quagmire that ensnarled America's military in the 1960s and early 1970s. As with Korea, this conflict was fought as a holding action and the allocation of resources to the war reflected the somewhat split personality of the American political leadership of the time which desired to fight the war but also manage the domestic economy as though there was no war at all. The army had more than 4,350,000 persons in uniform and lost 38,100 soldiers, thereby incurring a casualty rate of 0.8 percent. For those persons who watched the Vietnam War drag on for nearly a decade, this figure may seem surprisingly low. But the fact of the matter is that the American troops in Vietnam inflicted enormous casualties on the enemy troops but could not achieve a quick and decisive military resolution. And if there is one thing that the American public cannot tolerate, it is anything that takes more than a few weeks to resolve because Americans do not have any patience.

But what about the other branches of the American military in Vietnam? The navy boasted nearly 1,840,000 persons and suffered about 2,500 deaths for a mortality rate of about 0.1 percent. The marines claimed nearly 800,000 persons in uniform and buried nearly 14,900 of its own for a mortality rate of about 1.8 percent. Finally, the air force, which enjoyed virtually unchallenged air superiority and the pleasures of dropping bombs from very high altitudes on very tiny targets, claimed about 1,740,000 persons in uniform and lost about 2,580 persons on and off the battlefields for a death rate of about 0.14 percent.

These numbers paint a very interesting picture and underscore what many of us would consider to be an obvious truth: It is more dangerous to be a foot soldier in the army or a marine dashing onto a beach than it is to sail on a ship or fly in a plane. Another advantage of not being in the ground forces is that one can count on steady meals, a warm bed, and dry clothes. A naval career can ensure that a sailor will be able to visit exotic locales and meet fascinating people and violate local laws and customs. Even though every branch of the service will see some of its own perish during time of war, America's involvement in warfare from the time of the Revolutionary War demonstrates that the navy has consistently offered the most favorable odds of survival. But our review of the statistics of American warfare casualties also shows that the casualty rates are dependent on whether the United State is involved in a global all-out war such as World War II or a more limited engagement such as Korea or Vietnam. The difference may lie not so much in whether the United States is devoting all or merely a part of its resources to an armed conflict but instead the quality and strength of the adversary. Unfortunately, our statistics can provide us only with clues and not concrete conclusions as to why the odds of dying in combat fluctuate from conflict to conflict; it remains for us to determine the true underlying reasons for these discrepancies. However, these figures also suggest that the death rates in the modern era have declined significantly from the higher levels seen during World War I and World War II. Moreover, the number of battlefield deaths has consistently been greater than those deaths occurring outside of battle, which suggests that improved health care and living conditions have had a favorable impact upon casualty rates.

5

STRIKING IT RICH

In any book which deals with statistics and probabilities, one must always devote at least one chapter to the chances of winning a lottery or walking away with a big casino jackpot or even being the first to shout "Bingo!" at the church. After all, far more people care about the lottery than about their odds of falling in love or dying a horrible death. Lotteries are the stuff that dreams are made of, and people can become extremely volatile when you attempt to explain to them in a calm, dispassionate voice that they have a snowball's chance in hell of actually walking away with a few million dollars. But it is not for us to question the wisdom of those who choose to stop at their neighborhood convenience store, bypassing the aisles laden with $6 sponges for the stand holding a two-inch pencil and a computerized card. This is where they can record their favorite numbers and dream their greatest dreams.

Even though the proponents of lotteries (which include many of the states in the Union) are quick to assert that the lotteries are purely entertainment, there are few people playing Lotto who would indicate they are pleased to spend $5, $10, $50, or even more purely for entertainment's sake. Those persons who play the lottery want to win and they want to win big! The fact that their particular state may send a part of the proceeds to the public schools may give them a warm fuzzy feeling but many serious players would rather see a few schools not get built if it would mean their pocketing several tens of millions of dollars.

So if we are to concern ourselves with lotteries, we probably need to study the techniques of winning lottery players. Indeed, there is a very special secret known only to lottery players which is the key to their success: They picked the winning numbers! The fundamental problem with the lottery is one of timing. The winning numbers become known only after they are drawn. Think how easy it would be to win the lottery if only you could see the future and pick the winning numbers before they were even drawn by the lottery officials. In such a happy world, winning would become as mundane as driving a car or eating a sandwich. Every Saturday morning you would pick up a lottery ticket (you would need to purchase only one, after all) and wander back to your house, quivering with excitement about the coming windfall. Fast forward a few hours and you would settle on your favorite couch in front of the television set and watch the inevitable as the attractive young lady selected five or six or seven numbered balls from the bin whose numbers corresponded with your own ticket. But your excitement would become tempered by the knowledge that the result was already a foregone conclusion and that you were going to win a few more million dollars. Even though you knew your bank account would inexorably increase by several million dollars with each lottery and that some weeks you would be the only winner of the lottery, your glee would become muted because the mystery and the surprise of winning a lottery prize would no longer exist. Instead you would tap your fingers and glance around the room as though you had better things to do as the announcer read off the selected numbers and you learned for the umpteenth time that you were the grand-prize winner. As time went on, you might decide to skip the weekly drawings, wondering why you should bother watching an outcome that was never in doubt. Of course your curiosity would get the better of you every now and then and you would stay at home for an evening to see if your unexplainable streak of good luck would stop. But as with every earlier trip to the lottery ticket vendor, you would find that you had once again triumphed in the face of all odds.

Of course the prospect of making a few million dollars a week for doing little more than marking up a single lottery form might be very appealing to those shiftless persons who do not wish to spend their lives engaged in the mind-numbing monotony of a 9-to-5 job. But there are a few hardy souls who would not want a lifetime guarantee of unending riches but instead want to earn that money due them by the sweat of their brow and the dint of their own effort. They would not want to step into the local convenience store knowing that they would invariably and inevitably select the winning ticket. No, they would want to step up to the lottery-form table, take the chewed-off pencil in hand, and slowly, but carefully, consider all of the possible numbers before choosing those very special numbers that might just enable them to quit their jobs and begin their new lives as members of the class of nouveau riche. They could then devote their time to charitable causes and tax write-offs. But because they came up with the numbers on their own, they might feel that they had earned their way into polite society where they could spread malicious rumors about their fellow society-page headline-hogging tycoons knowing that they did not simply obtain their wealth through the time-honored old-fashioned way (inheritance) but instead through their own labors. The fact that they were clever enough to become wealthy through the stroke of a pencil as opposed to a lifetime of honest toil would bring them even more respect among their peers.

Of course this digression could be wrong. After all, what is wrong with having a guarantee that you will win every time you play the lottery? For one thing, you might soon find your life to be in danger as news of your repeated successes got around and people began to notice you were appearing on the lottery program each week to collect a check. Even though there would be nothing to preclude them from selecting the very same winning numbers picked by you, they would somehow convince themselves that you were to blame for their repeated inability to win the big prize. A few of them might try to have you "bumped off" so as to free up the lottery money for the rest of the population. Of course the resourceful lottery winner could resort to a variety of disguises but they would eventually begin to wear thin. In either case, those members of the news media who have nothing better to do than to find out whether it was merely a coincidence that each of the previous thirty-six winners of the state lottery had the same surname would begin to make nuisances of themselves and try to discover the truth behind this amazing situation. Sadly, it would only be a matter of time before it was revealed that all of the recent winners were one and the same person. It is doubtful that there would be very many people sympathetic to the pain you had felt, knowing ahead of time that you were destined to win the lottery no matter how hard you tried to select the incorrect numbers.

PROBABILITIES FOR THE GAMBLER

To engage in any kind of gambling with any degree of success, one must become familiar with the laws of probability. We are not talking about physical laws here but instead mathematical laws that tell us the likelihood that a certain event will occur. As would-be professional gamblers, we would like to know the likelihood that we will roll a five with the toss of a die or pull up an ace when being dealt a hand in blackjack. The benefit of such an approach is obvious in that it enables the gambler to evaluate the likelihood that he or she will get the card needed to win the hand. But this approach may also necessitate that the player "count" cards and thus keep a mental record in mind as to which cards have been drawn. Casinos do not like players who count cards

The Probability that a Six-Sided Die Will Show the Same Number Following Repeated Tosses

Number of Tosses	Probability
1	1/6
2	1/36
3	1/216
4	1/1,296
5	1/7,776
6	1/46,656
7	1/279,936
8	1/1,679,616

because they have a better chance of actually winning substantial amounts of money from the casino. Instead they prefer players who have lots of money, poor card skills, and reckless betting habits. The casinos also try to encourage high rollers to impair their skills by plying them with an unending supply of free drinks.

But if one is to be an informed, competent gambler, one must have some grasp on the laws of probability. Perhaps the simplest example is provided by the six-sided die. Each face has a unique number ranging from one to six. The die itself is constructed in a manner so that all of the faces are as similar as possible. This means that each side should, on a given roll of the die, have the same likelihood of turning up on the table. We would certainly be suspicious if we always obtained a two or a five every time we rolled the die because that would seem to violate a fundamental tenet of probability theory—that every face of the die is equally likely to show on a given toss.

One can become intimately acquainted with probability theory by picking up a die and tossing it over and over again. To determine the probability that a given number—say four—would turn up, we could toss the die 6 million times. This would obviously take some time to complete—perhaps nine or ten months if we devoted at least eight hours each day to our task. But we would push ahead with our task, anxious to find out how many fours would turn up on 6 million tosses of the die. This experiment might necessitate quitting our job or becoming mayor of a major city so that we would have the time to follow our scientific dream. In any event, we would follow a regimen of getting up, brushing our teeth, and sitting down at the table with die in hand, day after day. We would practice various die-tossing techniques—including the two-fingered snap, the overhead twirl, and the split finger toss—trying to bring some degree of professionalism to our task. We would then dutifully record the outcome of each toss of the die in our notebook and then carry on. After ten or so months of this excitement, we would count up all of the times the ones, twos, threes, fours, fives, and sixes each turned up. Although the theory of probability would suggest that each of the six sides of the die would turn up exactly 1 million times each, we would likely find that there were some differences in the number of times which side one as well as each of the other five sides turned up. For example, we might find that we rolled 1,000,036 ones, 999,984 twos, 1,000,017 threes, 998,400 fours, 1,000,089 fives, and 1,001,563 sixes. Would this outcome refute the laws of probability? After all, we would not have exactly 1,000,000 rolls of the die for each of the six faces of the die.

The presumption underlying probability theory is that there are a specified number of events that may occur in a given situation for which distinct probabilities may be calculated. In the case of a tossed die, any one of six events—the six faces of the die—has an equal chance of turning up. When dealing with a pack of cards, the number of events is equal to the number of cards in the deck. Each card should have an equal chance of being pulled from the deck. When we roll the die, the laws of probability tell us that the side with the one or the two or any one of the other four sides is equally likely to be revealed. A game in which the cards are gradually withdrawn from the deck such as black-jack or fish (which the high rollers in the casinos are prone to play) will see a continually increasing probability that any remaining card will be withdrawn because the number of choices (of remaining cards) natu-rally shrink in number with each draw. After an ace of clubs, for example, is taken from the deck, there is no possibility that another ace of clubs will be dealt by the dealer from that deck (unless, of course, you are playing in a second-rate casino in which the house is not particularly concerned about its reputation for integrity). Unlike the toss of a die which can result in repeated rolls having the same value, the shrinking deck of cards lends itself to exact calculations of more favorable proba-bilities for drawing any one of the remaining cards because no single card can be drawn more than once. We could try to mimic this effect with a die by sanding off one face each time it turned up so that we would not be able to roll a clean face. But we would in all likelihood still see the sanded faces showing up from time to time, so it would not be as perfect a model as the deck of cards. We need to bear in mind that we can only test probability theory when every event in a given situa-tion has an equal likelihood of turning up. By contrast, a die in which some sides are smooth and others are chopped up is not going to be one in which we can expect all of the faces will show up, on average, because the uneven faces of the die will cause some sides to turn up more fre-quently than others. Of course this sort of die would be very helpful to a gambler if he were somehow able to sneak it onto a casino table without the knowledge of the dealer. However, even the most dim-witted dealer would eventually notice that the die would always show a two, five, or six. At this point, the jig would be up and the would-be gambler would need to make a hasty exit from the casino or find him-self shuffling across the bottom of a nearby river in concrete galoshes.

But to return to our discussion of probabilities, we know that a deck of cards has fifty-two cards, each of which has a unique face and suit. We would be very surprised to find two queens of hearts in a single deck (unless, of course, we were playing with a street hustler) so we are probably safe in assuming that each of the fifty-two cards has a 1-in-52 chance of being drawn at random. The validity of this assertion is dependent on the fact that the two players are indeed playing with a true set of playing cards. Each card, all things being equal, has an equal chance of being drawn. Every card is therefore equal under the laws of probability: the two of clubs has the same probability of being drawn as the ace of diamonds—1/52. If we are playing a poker game whose outcome is critical to the future of human civilization, we will have to deal with probabilities that change as cards are removed from the playing deck following the play of successive hands. If, for example, we play one hand and use twelve cards, then the probability that any player will draw one of the remaining forty cards is 1/40 instead of 1/52. But because every card is different, every card should still have the same likelihood of being drawn as every other card. As a result, card players should be concerned if the dealer of the cards draws eight aces in a row with a single deck of playing cards and should insist on a new deck and a new dealer. For those players who are blessed with prodigious memories, the odds of winning at the gaming tables can be improved because such players can "count" cards by committing to memory the cards that have been drawn from a deck during the game. This technique, which is frowned upon by all pious casino pit managers, enables the player to calculate in his own mind the likelihood that a particular type of card will show up. If the player knows that all of the aces and kings have been drawn in a game of blackjack, for example, then he may be tempted to "hold" or take a "hit" at a different total than he might otherwise choose. Such a decision would be based upon his assessment of the comparatively low probability that the dealer would draw a card that could defeat the player's hand.

WINNING THE LOTTERY

The prospective lottery player has an unshakable belief that he or she is capable of selecting a winning group of numbers on a card while purchasing a six-pack of beer at the local convenience store. The logic that guides the playing decisions of lottery players can be perplexing and, at times, completely contradictory. The typical lottery player knows in his heart that these contests consist of random drawings of a few numbers (4, 5, or 6) from a much larger pool of numbers (such as 1 through 40 or 1 through 48). Because these drawings are random, there should not be any rhyme or reason as to the order in which they appear. More importantly, no number should be any more likely to be drawn than any other number. If the state lottery officials have a big machine in which forty-eight uniquely numbered balls bounce about from which six balls are selected, then each ball should have the same probability of being selected: 1/48. Once a particular ball is selected, then the probability that any remaining ball will be selected will increase, but the chances of selecting any remaining ball will be the same. If one ball is removed from the pool of forty-eight balls, then we will have a 1/47 chance of selecting any remaining ball. If two balls are removed, then the odds we will select any one of the remaining forty-six balls will be 1/46, and so on.

So the lottery player must face up to the fact that there is nothing he can do to alter the chance that one ball is more likely to be selected than another. The selection of each numbered ball is mutually exclusive and separate from the selection of every other numbered ball. This cruel reality should at least discourage lottery players from insisting upon playing their favorite lucky number more than once on the same ticket because it is statistically impossible for any single numbered ball to be withdrawn more than once during a single drawing. This is not to say that such arguably stupid behavior would ever be discouraged by state lottery officials who are always happy to part lottery players from their hard-earned dollars. But it does remind us that we need to know the basic rules of the lottery game in order to have a chance at winning the jackpot.

The sad fact of the lottery is that it is purely a game of chance. Of those forty-eight balls bouncing around in the machine, only six will be selected by the lovely moving mannequin who is typically hired to oversee such tasks. This is very sad because it underscores that many players waste too much time reviewing previous combinations of winning numbers or playing "lucky" numbers such as the ages of your six best friends or the birthdates of your children or the dates of your previous divorces. With any game of chance, every number has an equal chance of being selected. The fact that the number 7 has been the common winning number in a state lottery, for example, with it showing up in 35 percent of all winning tickets over time, does not mean that it is an inherently luckier number. There is nothing special about the number 7 as compared to any other number in the pantheon of lottery balls. On average, it should appear about as frequently as any other number. But if the 7 ball in a lottery continues to appear with a frequency far greater than that warranted by the laws of probability (e.g., 1/48 in a forty-eight-ball lottery machine), then it may be time to investigate the lottery machine itself. Perhaps the 7 ball is a little lighter than the other balls and therefore much more likely to pop up one of the slots and be selected. Or perhaps the 7 ball is imperceptibly smaller than the other balls and therefore comparatively more likely to be blown up one of the chutes than the other slightly more rotund lottery balls. In short, there should be a logical explanation for any enduring aberration in the laws of chance—other than luck or the blessings of the gods. And while the laws of chance would not preclude a particular ball from appearing over and over again, the odds of such an event continuing to occur over time without more would be astronomical and would certainly cause many to question whether that particular ball was the same as all the others.

People who play a set of lottery numbers, day after day, week after week, month after month, do so with the hope that the laws of chance will eventually swing around in their favor. The logic seems to be a little like the admonishment we were all given as children in that we should stay in one place if we became lost instead of wandering around and complicating the efforts to find us. Perhaps there is some psychological sense that there is a certain degree of safety in sameness which is reflected in the choice, week in and week out, of the same numbers. Moreover, some people fear that if they do not play "their" numbers and "their" numbers turned up, they would never be able to forgive themselves. Players who play the same numbers unceasingly seem to believe that the lottery will eventually "find" their numbers and that it is somehow statistically preferable to stick with the same set of numbers. There is nothing inherently wrong with playing the same numbers but there is nothing inherently right about it either as either situation still requires us to try to outfox the laws of probability. If every number has the same likelihood of showing up every time a lottery drawing occurs, then it really does not make one whit of difference whether we are playing our tried-and-true lucky numbers week in and week out or if we are picking our numbers each week by throwing a dart at a dartboard. Numbers have no memory and the numbers that showed up last week are no more or less likely to show up this week. Similarly, the player who offers his set of lucky numbers each week without change is no more or no less likely to prevail in the lottery.

But someone must win the lottery and it is this belief that anyone can win that compels people to offer significant sums of money to lottery officials each week. But the odds of winning the typical state lottery are still daunting because a lottery in which six out of forty-nine uniquely numbered balls are selected, for example, has winning odds of about 1 in 14,000,000. (The actual odds for this lottery are about 1 in 13,983,816—the odds have been rounded off to 1 in 14,000,000 in order to simplify the calculations in the discussion.) This does not mean that any set of numbers we might select on a lottery playing card—such as 5-12-34-37-40-48—has no possibility of winning but only a very small possibility. For that occasional player who is both a free spirit and an idiot and who insists on adding other numbers to the playing card by hand such as 59, 74, 289, and 564 which do not have numerical counterparts bouncing around the lottery ball machine, the odds of winning are nil. Not miniscule, but nil.

Because of the random nature of these games, all strategies are equally useful and useless in that no single strategy that does not involve outright cheating will give the lottery player a leg up over his competitors. Making a "Christmas tree" pattern, for example, is no more likely to yield successful results in lottery play than it ever did in high-school class examinations. Indeed, it would be difficult to see how any type of pattern on a lottery card would avoid the basic problem of games of chance—there are no magical numbers or tricks.

But how can one explain the fact that some people are able to pick the winning lottery numbers—sometimes more than once? Well, someone has to win the lottery at some point because the jackpots will typically be rolled over and over until someone plays the winning combination of numbers. Even though the jackpot may increase to several tens or, in the case of multistate lotteries, even several hundred million dollars, the odds of winning will not usually change because players will still be able to choose from the same set of numbers. So even if our lottery which has the forty-nine winning numbers rolls over several times, we will still have the same odds of winning—1 in about 14,000,000. What typically happens with most state lotteries whose winning jackpots have climbed into the stratosphere is that public interest is fanned and far more players leap into the fray. Indeed, it is not uncommon in such situations for so many tickets to be purchased that every possible winning combination of the forty-nine numbers is selected.

More than one enterprising individual has sought to purchase every possible combination of tickets in such lotteries, but the states have typically refrained from permitting such massive purchases because of concerns as to how such preemptive ticket purchases guaranteed to win the huge lottery payoffs would affect the continued interest of the playing public at large. Of course, one could go to the neighborhood convenience store and purchase the tickets one-by-one like everybody else but it would take a long time to purchase all 14 million tickets needed to guarantee a winning lottery number. If you bought one ticket every second or sixty tickets every minute or 3,600 tickets every hour or 86,400 tickets every day or 604,800 tickets every week, then it would take nearly twenty-three weeks to purchase the 14 million tickets. Even though spending five months at a convenience store would provide you with many opportunities to make fascinating new friends and perhaps witness a murder or two, it would be a pointless endeavor because you would clearly have missed the desired weekly lottery drawing by about twenty-two weeks. But if you could enlist the aid of twenty-one or more friends, you could fan out among twenty-three or so of the closest convenience stores and each order approximately 600,000 separate lottery tickets. But these would have to be very good friends as they would have to relish the idea of hanging around the convenience store twenty-four hours a day for a week. They would also have to select the particular number combinations assigned to them; any anarchists who felt unduly constrained by your master allocation of lottery number combinations would probably not be reliable partners in this endeavor. It would certainly do no good if some of your partners decided they wanted to play their own winning numbers instead of the ones given to them because that would clearly frustrate the plan to lock up all possible combinations of winning lottery numbers and thus secure the winning jackpot.

Such an approach to guarantee a lottery win is theoretically possible but it would run into some real-world constraints. First, it assumes that we could stand at a lottery ticket machine around the clock without permitting other people the opportunity to play their own tickets. We would have to convince the store owner to put a sign on his door telling other prospective players to go elsewhere because we would not be able to permit any interruptions in our ticket processing. Whether we would get the owner to agree to such a proposal is unclear because she might be very reluctant to stop her regular customers from playing the lottery at her store. After all, it takes a lot of time to develop a loyal clientele, particularly one that is addicted to playing lottery week in and week out. So even though the owner might be tempted to take the money and enjoy the payoff, they would be concerned that many of their regular customers might riot and burn the store down or, at the very least, go to another location, possibly sever their existing loyalty, and buy their beer elsewhere. Second, we would also have to wonder how realistic it would be to suppose that the lottery machines in each of these convenience stores could pump out lottery tickets at the rate of one per second, hour after hour, day after day, for an entire week, without breaking down or clogging up. Even though they are generally durable machines, it seems that it would be unlikely that the machines at all of the convenience stores could hold up to such a steady demand. Third, we would need to question whether each of our partners could truly be relied upon to stand at the counter, watching the lottery ticket machine spit out tickets for seven days and seven nights, standing guard to prevent various miscreants from jumping into the line and interrupting the ticket machine's activities. Some people are strong-willed and obnoxious enough to tell other would-be players to take a hike and go elsewhere, whereas other persons are simply too polite or fearful of their own personal safety to take such an adamant and necessary tact. Finally, there is simply that element of human error that one must always take into consideration in planning such elaborate campaigns that require both focus and the coordination of the actions of many different individuals. One can never be completely sure that one of the partners did not drop his stack of lottery cards on the way to the convenience store or simply failed to fill them out properly so that the winning number was not even fed into the ticket machine. So there are clearly a number of factors that may preclude any attempt to lock up a winning lottery effort. One additional problem is that the winner cannot be sure—even if he purchases all 14 million tickets needed to play every single possible combination of the numbers—that it will win the entire jackpot. A problem with lotteries—particularly ones with very large multimillion-dollar jackpots— is that they attract extraordinary levels of attention from the public, causing many persons who would not otherwise play the lottery to purchase a few tickets in the hopes of hitting it big. So even though we might spend $14,000,000 to purchase 14 million lottery tickets in the hopes of winning a $50-million lottery jackpot, we might find that four other players picked the winning number—thus necessitating that the $50-million lottery was split five ways—so that we would only get a $10,000,000 return on our $14,000,000 investment. Compounding the problem is the fact that many state lotteries do not give the winners their money when they present the winning ticket but instead spread the payments out over twenty or even thirty years. This means that we would get $500,000 per year for twenty years. But we would find our winnings further degraded by the impact of cost-of-living increases over those twenty years. If, for example, changes in the cost of living increase 7 percent a year every year, then they would double in ten years and double again in twenty years. This means that the value of our $500,000 payments would be correspondingly reduced. Our first payment, which would presumably be received soon after we have turned in our ticket, would be worth $500,000. But the second payment of $500,000, which we would receive in one year, would be able to purchase the equivalent of only $465,000 of goods and services in today's prices—thus representing a loss of $35,000 in purchasing power after one year. The third payment would see another 7 percent erosion in purchasing power of $32,550 so that our $500,000 payment would be able to purchase only $432,450 of goods and services in today's prices. Our purchasing power would continue to erode further each year so that our third year's payment of $500,000 would buy only $402,178.50 of goods and services.

The inherent problem here is that we are receiving the same payments each year over time and they are not indexed in any way for inflation. As a result, the purchasing power of our payments from the state lottery commission will continue to deteriorate.

Now some people might feel that 7 percent is too high and they would be correct because the historical rate of inflation in the United States has tended to average around 3 percent each year. But even a constant 3 percent rate will result in the halving of the value of our yearly $500,000 lottery payment about twenty-three years after our winning ticket is selected. Even though we will have already received our twentieth and final payment three years before that point, we will have seen the purchasing power of our $500,000 payment decline by almost half by the time that we received that payment. Regardless of the number used for the rate of change in the cost of living, however, the point remains the same: The passage of time will invariably degrade the present value of money because the cost of living will generally increase over time. The extent to which this twenty-year payout results in an erosion of the value of our purchasing power will necessarily depend upon the rate of inflation in the national economy, but it further illustrates the problems that entrepreneurs seeking to realize a windfall by buying tickets having all the possible numerical combinations of a big jackpot lottery face when they attempt to make a profit in such an undertaking. In short, the cost of money over time necessitates that a lottery player be able to win a lottery jackpot that is several times the size of the $14,000,000 needed to guarantee a winning ticket so as to offset the corrosive effects of a twenty-year payout. If we assume a 3 percent rate of inflation, then we need to win at least a $28,000,000 payoff to come out (marginally) ahead. If we assume a 7 percent rate of inflation, then we need to win at least $56,000,000 to break even. Of course then we will have to deal with the problems that arise from so much public interest in a superlottery payment of $50 million or above in which we will more than likely have to share our winnings with two, three, four, or even more other winners. As a result, the obvious lesson to be drawn is that it is virtually impossible to come out ahead by purchasing all the tickets in a lottery unless the payoff is sufficiently large to offset the corrosive effect of inflation and to offset the likelihood that the jackpot will have to be shared with one or more fellow lottery players.

The other factor that also conspires to dampen the enthusiasm of the winning player is the amount of taxes that are withheld by lottery officials. Because state lotteries are concerned that a lottery winner may simply decide to skip the country instead of paying taxes on his or her winnings, they do the only prudent thing and pull the taxes out before the money is awarded. Although each state has its own rules and procedures, a common rule of thumb is that the state authorities will hold up to 30 percent of the payout for federal income tax and, if it is a state with a state income tax, it will also withhold an additional 5, 6, 7, or even 8 percent more of the winnings to pay for state income taxes. Because this money is pulled off the top from the very beginning, there is no opportunity to have the withheld funds work for the winning player. As a result, the value of the payoff is further reduced.

State lotteries are viewed as an increasingly popular and valuable way to raise revenue. Legislators have never had any real problem spending tax revenues; the tricky part has been to devise ways to raise enough money to fund everyone's pet projects. But the state-sanctioning of games of chance has opened up vast new gambling opportunities to the masses and made it possible for even grandmothers to bet some of their spare change on the random selection of several bouncing balls. Debates periodically occur as to the wisdom of making gambling so easy for the entire adult population, but it does appear as though state-sponsored gambling is here to stay. But for the lucky few who manage to select a winning ticket, it is a wonderful thing. As we have seen, however, even a sure thing such as a guaranteed win of the lottery is actually no guarantee that the player will cover his own costs, let alone come out ahead.

TIPS FOR THE CASINO

Everybody likes to go into casinos because they are opulent palaces laden with rows upon rows of shiny, brightly lit one-armed bandits (slot machines) in which people feed coins in the hopes that the laws of chance will smile upon them and favor them with a jackpot. Casinos are also well known for the arrangements of tables at which players battle against the house in a variety of games including blackjack, craps, poker, and roulette. Because the patrons are routinely plied with complimentary drinks and tasty snacks, they are encouraged to enjoy themselves and indulge in their passion for games of chance. For those who consider gambling to be nothing more than a form of entertainment, it is a very pleasant experience with comparatively low expectations. The recreational gambler has no illusions that she will break even, let alone make a fortune, but she can sit down at the blackjack table or the slot machine and know that she will be able to enjoy herself for a few hours and, hopefully, make a few dollars. Even though nearly everyone who sets foot in a casino is aware that the odds do not favor them competing against the house, they hope that they can be one of the exceptions to the general rule that the house rules.

As with lotteries, games of chance in the casino are governed by the laws of probability. In their most basic form, the law of probability apportions the likelihood that a given event such as the showing of "heads" on a coin toss will occur. We will first look at the probabilities associated with a simple coin toss and move on to those associated with the toss of a die so that we can then plunge back into the topic of casino gambling. But another excursion through probability theory is necessary in order to appreciate the dynamics of the gambling process and the manner in which institutionalized gambling is set up to guarantee that the average gambler will invariably lose his investment.

Because a coin has two sides, each side should have an equal probability of showing up in a coin toss. This statement assumes that the coin is "true" in that it has not been specially designed to favor one side or the other on the toss as might be the case if it was weighted on one side. So we can assume with a true coin that on any given flip, there is an equal likelihood that it will land on "heads" or on "tails." A mathematician would say that there is a probability of 1/2 that it will land on "heads" and a probability of 1/2 that it will land on tails. We know that it is a certainty that it will land on either heads or tails; this certainty is reflected in adding 1/2 + 1/2 to get 1. Not surprisingly, a probability of 0 refers to an event that has no likelihood of occurring, such as the coin landing on its rim. So the continuum of numerical values in our coin example ranges from 0 (no chance of an event occurring) to 1 (100 percent chance of an event occurring). If we toss a coin once, we have a 1/2 probability that it will land on heads and a 1/2 probability that it will land on tails. But what is the probability that it will land on heads two times in a row? We simply multiply 1/2 (the probability it will land on heads on the first toss) by 1/2 (the probability it will land on heads on the second toss) to get a probability of 1/4 for two consecutive heads. Each toss is a separate event and the outcome of each toss should not have any effect on the outcomes of any subsequent tosses. But the odds that a coin will continue to land on the same side over and over again will become correspondingly less with each additional toss. In other words, the odds that a coin will land on the same side three times in a row is 1/8, four times in a row 1/16, five times in a row 1/32, and so on.

The reasoning behind the probabilities associated with tossing a die are identical to those used when tossing a coin. Because a die has six sides, each side should have a probability of turning up equal to 1/6. Similarly, we would expect the probability of two consecutive tosses of the die to turn up the same side to be equal to 1/36 (1/6 × 1/6). In any legitimate casino, the laws of chance should have every opportunity to flourish because no casino wants to be known for having crooked dealers or marked cards or any other type of device that gives the house an unfair advantage. But gambling casinos need to have some type of advantage in order to stay in business because a pure adherence to the laws of probability would mean that the gambler and the house would, on average, break even over the long term. In other words, the casinos would not make any money and would therefore have no way to pay for their opulent faux Greco buildings or their bloated payrolls (especially the gentlemen who watch card counters and other vermin). So there must be some way for the casinos to have a built-in advantage without actually cheating their customers. The answer to this quandary is simple: the payout given to the winning player must always be less than the amount that player could expect to realize if the casino and the player both had an equal chance of winning the game. In other words, the house must have a built-in advantage that will enable it to make a profit over the long term from its gambling operations.

The most obvious example of a setting in which the odds of winning are adjusted in order to favor the house are the slot machines—the so-called one-armed bandits. These machines, which are very popular among novice gamblers who reportedly find them less threatening than the steely-eyed, bow-tied dealers who run the card tables, may be calibrated to skew the odds of winning in favor of the house to any desired degree. In general, the odds of winning on a slot machine are about 8 out of 10. This means that for every dollar we put into a slot machine, our expected return is only about 80 cents. As a result, the player is guaranteed to lose over the longer term because he or she has no statistical likelihood of breaking even.

This bleak conclusion does pose something of a problem for those slot machine players who would like to play but dislike the idea of proceeding headlong into a money-losing proposition. The solution is very simple. If you want to improve your odds, you let other people play the slot machines for you and then wait for them to give up in disgust. At that point, you can then swoop in with your cupful of coins and hope that the calibrations have swung around enough to bestow a jackpot favor upon you. For those who doubt that there are people on the prowl in casinos throughout the world looking for machines that have nearly digested their fill of coins, you should visit any casino and watch the players. While this strategy does not guarantee that you will win, it may help to shore up your chances of prevailing in a game that will necessarily favor the casino over time. But you must be very careful to be sure that the player has in fact left the slot machine for good before you sit down on the stool and begin pulling the handle. Few things will prompt hysterical rantings and even threats of murder quicker than the perception by a cranky slot machine player that a squatter is trying to take over her slot machine—particularly a machine that has been consuming coins for hours without so much as a hiccup of a payout. Compounding the difficulty of ascertaining the odds of winning on slots is the fact that the machines may be calibrated to reflect any desired set of odds so that a player really has no idea as to the extent the house is favored by the machine.

But what about games of chance such as roulette and blackjack in which players and dealers play against each other? Where is the advantage for the house? Here the edge lies in the payout. The dealer and the player are not playing a game of pure chance because there would be no advantage for the house. All things being equal, we would expect the player and the house to win about the same number of games over time. But this is not the case because the payout is not dollar for dollar. A player must correctly guess the number on which the roulette wheel will stop turning in order to win. The house, by contrast, has no such burden. It wins any time the roulette player fails to select the winning number. In short, it is the default victor because it will necessarily prevail when no single player is lucky enough to select the winning number—which will be the vast majority of the time. The house is not required to bet on the winning number; it wins every time the individual players lose. Depending on the game and the individual casino, the house will also win every other losing player's chips even if one player should prevail against the casino.

The same line of reasoning edge holds true in blackjack where a dealer will deal cards to one, two, three, or even more players. The point of blackjack is to accumulate cards whose points come as close as possible to twenty-one without going over. All face cards are equal to ten points; all numbered cards have corresponding point values. The ace can be worth either one or eleven points, depending on the preference of the player. Because each player is dealt two cards, one faceup and one facedown, no one knows the exact number of points in any single player's hand. But skilled blackjack players generally advise that players should stop playing a hand if they have 17, 18, 19, 20, or 21 points. The reason for this strategy is that the odds of being dealt a sufficiently low face card (e.g., a 2, 3, 4, 5) and avoiding "going bust" is sufficiently less than 50 percent. So the cautious player who wishes to marshal his reserves for the evening will not want to take a lot of "hits" when he is at or above seventeen points. But the point is that the casino card game is not like a neighborhood card game in which everyone shows their hands at the same time or players alternate in showing their hands first. In the casino, the players are invariably given the opportunity to decide how many cards they wish to draw before the house. This means that many players will "bust" before the house ever has to deal an additional card to itself or even reveal the contents of its hand. This burden upon the player to show her hand first gives the house an inherent advantage because it will win most of its hands without having to exert any effort at all. This "default" margin of victory is analogous to the unselected slots of the roulette wheel and help to ensure the preeminence of the house over time. This margin is further enhanced at casinos where "ties" go to the house. Of course there may be situations in which the cards are drawn in a way so as to frustrate the advantage enjoyed by the casino as would be the case if the players continued to be dealt hands of 18, 19, 20, or 21 points and the dealer was repeatedly forced to take extra hits to try to catch up (with the many resulting busts that would result from such an approach). But such situations are rare and, in any event, do not last for a very long time. This possibility is made even more remote by the fact that casinos routinely shift their dealers around the tables so that the players who are enjoying a particular dealer who has a flair for dealing better hands to the players than to himself will only get to enjoy the privilege for a comparatively brief time. Shifting the dealers has no effect on probability calculations but it can have the effect of "breaking" a winning streak and also complicating conspiracies by players and crooked dealers to defraud the casino.

The only way to guarantee that you will break even in the casino is to keep your money in your pocket and not play at all. But prudence in the midst of a sea of green felt-covered card tables and highly polished slot machines is not a very entertaining way to spend the evening. So perhaps the best strategy is to recognize that the odds are not in your favor and to view the gambling experience as nothing more than a form of entertainment in which a few dollars will necessarily be spent and a few hours of pleasure will be realized. Gambling is not an investment any more than any other type of expenditure, for entertainment can be considered an investment. But it does provide the lure of instant riches that will be bestowed upon a chosen few. That lure continues to draw millions of persons to casinos all over the world and to tempt them to engage in a wide variety of gambling activities elsewhere such as state lotteries, horsetrack betting, sports gambling, and even Internet games of chance.

6

DANGERS IN THE WORKPLACE

Most of us find our daily office routine to be both tedious and lacking in drama. Few persons would liken nine to ten hours spent each day in a poorly lit, stuffy cubicle as being equal to the excitement of driving a team of sled dogs across the Siberian tundra or diving off a cliff into the ocean or even vaulting over a turnstile at a subway station to avoid paying the fare. Certainly the motivation for going to the office each day is not the spirit of adventure or the desire to be browbeaten by dense superiors who occupy their positions of prominence due solely to accident, birth, family connections, luck, or even the fortuitous choice of sleeping partners who are susceptible to blackmail. Instead most of us endure mind-numbing commutes and poorly ventilated workplaces because we need to make money.

Yes, money is the root of all things that we hold dear in modern society because it is the glue that holds together our materialistic civilization. Whether this primordial importance makes money the root of all evil—as those who typically do not have very much money like to claim—is debatable. But the need to survive, which is met by earning enough money to pay for basic necessities, is the theme that is behind the little voice in our head that urges us not to play hooky from work merely because the local baseball team is playing a doubleheader under a cloudless sky or the local brewery is offering half-priced kegs at its drive-through window. Yet the tensions and frustrations of our modern society have conspired in recent years to add an additional ingredient to the distastefulness of the modern workplace—the epidemic of physical violence. In recent years, the usual reasons that we can cite for not liking our jobs have become overshadowed by the threat of violence in the workplace. One does not have to be a postal employee to spray an office with bullets from a semiautomatic weapon or torch the company-owned cafeteria. The advantage of having arms merchants in every city and town in the country is that we as citizens can fully indulge ourselves in any destructive passion we may have to ease our feelings of frustration and ineptitude about our station in life.

VIOLENCE IN THE WORKPLACE

America's workplaces are becoming increasingly violent with nearly 900,000 workers physically attacked in the workplace each year. Even though a tiny percentage of the victims of such violence may be the hypersensitive types who would consider a paper cut to be akin to a life-threatening wound, the fact that so may people are victims is truly astonishing. As with anything else, the injuries suffered by the victims are diverse and run the gamut from superficial cuts and bruises to physical attacks in which the victim is maimed or even mortally wounded by a perpetrator armed with a gun or knife.

But there may be certain subtle warning signs indicating whether a coworker is a potential candidate for committing a homicide. A worker who spends his break time proudly polishing his pistol and challenging you to a game of Russian roulette is not one with whom you would want to be partnered at the company picnic's three-legged race. Similarly, those people who are continually trying to stab their coworkers exhibit telltale signs of aggression that may hint at the desire to commit heinous crimes. While such disturbing behavior may reflect some underlying dissatisfaction with society as a whole such as the maldistribution of wealth among nations or the depletion of the ozone layer, aggressive behavior may also be rooted in the perpetrator's own mental delusions. Of course there are some people who are perfectly fine except for the fact that they honestly want to see their fellow employees lying on the floor in a pool of their own blood. Some therapists would applaud the efforts of such person to express their true feelings because complete honesty is a characteristic so lacking in our modern transient society. But it is advisable to disarm such individuals before encouraging them to get in touch with their inner selves.

With nearly a million acts of violence occurring each year in this country's workplaces, we might wonder what the odds are that we might become a victim of violence and the type of violence that would most likely be committed toward us. According to the American Bar Association's *The Brief* magazine, nearly three-fourths of all workplace homicides involve a shooting. Now when we say homicides, we are not referring to accidental shootings as might be the case if two postal workers had brought their semiautomatic weapons to work one day to play "show and tell" and one of the weapons had actually discharged, thus killing one of the workers. Instead we are talking about intentional shootings in which one of the postal employees, frustrated at not being able to purchase the same caliber of armor-piercing bullets as his braggart coworker, would finally decide he had had enough of the loudmouth as he squeezed the trigger and emptied a few rounds into his colleague's head. But he would have convincingly asserted his constitutional right to bear arms and, in many cases, shoot arms and legs and any other part of the body he may choose.

To find out the number of workplace incidents involving violence, we would then need to check with the U.S. Bureau of Labor Statistics whose statisticians would tell us that there are about 130 million persons who are employed in the U.S. labor force (versus some seven million who are unemployed but thought to be searching for work). If we divide the number of persons in the labor force by the number of violent incidents (approximately 900,000), then we would calculate that each worker has a 1:144 chance of being a victim of violence in the workplace. But does this figure mean that the sword of fate will come crashing down upon every 144th worker throughout the country? No, of course not. Even though we can calculate an average rate of injury, common sense and our own experiences tell us that the injuries are likely to be more common in some occupations than others. For example, we might expect that a manufacturing plant or a shipyard in which the workers pride themselves on their toughness and their ability to curse in three languages would be a setting more prone to outbreaks of violence than a place such as a convent or the Vatican. Although figures are not kept on the violent acts committed by nuns or cardinals, fairly detailed statistics are available on the types of occupations which have the greatest number of work-related homicides. So we can get some idea as to the likelihood that we will get a bloody nose or a bullet wound in the workplace based on our own profession.

Perhaps the best way to measure the degree of violence in any given job is to check the very cheery statistics collected by the U.S. Bureau of Labor Statistics which measure the risk of work-related homicides. Now you could say that the occupation that has the greatest number of homicides overall would be the most dangerous occupation, but that would really not get at the concept of evaluating the degree of risk one would encounter being employed in a certain occupation. If, for example, we find that ninety homicides occur each year in the bartending business but only forty-five homicides occur in the pool-cleaning business annually, then we might assume that the bartending business is twice as dangerous as the pool-cleaning business. We might assume that bartenders would be dropping left and right having beer bottles and specialty drink glasses smashed upon their heads in drunken

The Most Dangerous Jobs in America

Occupation	Number of Deaths	Homocide Rates (per 100,000 workers)
Taxi Driver	46	22.7
Security Guard	50	6.2
Police & Detectives	54	5.6
Bartenders & Sales Clerks	14	5.5
Managers, Food and Lodging	75	4.4

Source of Statistics: U.S. Bureau of Labor Statistics

brawls whereas only a comparatively few pool cleaners would be shoved into swimming pools with weights tied to their ankles. But we might change our mind if we found out that there were ten times as many bartenders as pool cleaners, which means that the pool cleaners would actually be five times more likely to be killed in the line of duty than bartenders.

The U.S. Bureau of Labor Statistics informs us that driving a taxi is the most dangerous occupation in terms of the number of workplace homicides. In 1996, for example, forty-six cabdrivers were killed nationwide. This may not sound like very many, particularly for those people who ride in limousines and do not have to consider the dangers of sitting in a taxicab. But we find that these deaths occur at a rate of nearly 23 per 100,000 persons employed in the taxi-driving industry nationwide. This high homicide rate is due in part to the fact that taxicabs must pick up fares off the street even though the cabdrivers have no way of knowing in advance whether a passenger wants to commit robbery and/or murder or merely wants to be transported across town.

The second most dangerous occupation in terms of risk of homicide is the comparatively tranquil world of security-guard work. These stalwarts of the private crime-prevention business enjoy a mild rate of violent homicidal death that is only about 6 per 100,000 employed. So the cabdrivers are nearly four times as likely to be murdered as are security guards. But because there are far more security guards than cabdrivers, greater numbers of security guards than cabdrivers die each year at the hands of their fellow humans even though our previous figures show that driving a cab is a far more dangerous occupation. Dealing with the public seems to be a common thread for the rest of the occupations that round out the top-ten list of homicides. They include such occupations as police officers, sales clerks, motel managers, bartenders, cashiers, and truck drivers. Monks and professional hermits do not even crack the top one hundred list in terms of workplace-related homicides, so there does appear to be some merit in not being a "people person" and refusing to deal with the general public.

INJURIES IN THE WORKPLACE

Workplace injuries do not garner the headlines of workplace homicides but it is still important to determine the risk of suffering serious injuries in different occupations.

One very good reason for evaluating the risk of injury in a given job is that one can make a more informed decision whether to pursue a position in that industry or to seek employment elsewhere in a safer line of work, such as game-show hosting where the greatest possibility of injury lies in getting crushed by a bear hug from some overly enthusiastic contestant.

The U.S. Bureau of Labor Statistics also informs us that restaurants and hospitals are in a virtual tie for the honor of most "injury-prone business" with restaurants having 309,700 cases in 1996 and hospitals documenting 300,200 cases. Food preparation coupled with having to deal with the public can pose an enormous challenge to one's personal safety so it is not surprising to see that restaurants would have the greatest number of cases. Moreover, the range of injuries could range from cutting oneself while dicing carrots in preparing the restaurant's famous carrot-flavored sorbet or slipping on a recently mopped floor to burning one's hand on the grill or cutting one's hand on broken glass. The additional element of danger comes in the form of the general public who must actually enter the restaurant in order for the owner to make money. Some members of the general public are very well-mannered and would never think of holding a group of waitresses and cooks hostage and threatening to blow up the building with dynamite strapped to their bodies if their demands for the perfect medium-rare steak, a house salad, and a hearty table wine are not met. However, there are other persons who see nothing wrong with taking a few hostages and maybe killing one or two of them in a robbery to show they mean business in order to obtain a large sum of money.

Hospitals would seem to be an ideal setting for competing for the title of most injury-prone business. After all, nearly every person who stays at a hospital (voluntarily or not) is by definition sick or injured or giving birth. However, the illnesses and injuries suffered by the patients usually occur before they get to the hospital. Otherwise, most of these patients (except for the occasional hypochondriac) would not be there in the first place. Moreover, it would be an unfair advantage to permit hospitals to count the injuries and illnesses that patients incur before they get to the hospital in competing for the title of most injury-prone business. But the government statistics deal with those injuries which occur on the premises of the hospitals and would include everything from a janitor impaling himself on the handle of a mop to a surgeon accidentally cutting himself with a scalpel while trying to trim a wart on his own or his patient's nose to a receptionist suffering a concussion after accidentally striking herself in the face with a telephone receiver to a candy striper running over her toe with a magazine cart. Patient injuries would also be counted to the extent that they were independent events which had occurred on the premises, such as a patient falling out of his bed and breaking his leg or an incompetent surgeon removing his unfortunate patient's good lung instead of the bad one.

As with our discussion of the varying rates of homicides in different occupations, we also need to consider the rates at which injuries occur in different occupations. Even though restaurants have the greatest absolute number of reported injuries, the injury rate at hospitals is nearly double that of restaurants. Of course the quality of the hospital food could play some role in this varied rate of risk if there are significant cases of food poisoning in the injury tally. But the statistics show that a person (employee or patient) has nearly an 80 percent greater chance of suffering an injury at a hospital than at a restaurant. But neither of these businesses are at the top of the injury rate index. Indeed, those who seek a career in the glamorous air transportation business have the highest rate of workplace injuries (a rate which is no doubt enhanced every time a jumbo jet falls out of the sky) followed closely behind by nursing homes. Air transportation offers the promise of an injury rate of more than three times that of restaurants whereas the likelihood of injury in nursing homes is almost two and one-half times that of restaurants. One explanation for the high rate of injuries in nursing homes is that most of the people who live in nursing homes are elderly, frail, and in poor health. These individuals are more likely to suffer serious injury from a fall than a younger person who is in good health. But nursing home patients are also given various types of treatments that can pose some risk of injury, including physical therapy. After all, one can get seriously injured if he is smacked in the face by a medicine ball or slips in a whirlpool bath. Elderly men are also particularly susceptible to violent injury when they attempt to maintain intimate relationships with more than one elderly woman at the same time —particularly if two or more of the affected elderly women find out.

Following closely behind nursing homes are workers in two types of retail stores—grocery stores and department stores. Grocery stores boast row after row of gleaming products, some of which are housed in very breakable containers that can be dropped on very slick and hard floors. Once these containers hit the floors and shatter into a thousand pieces, it is a very simple matter for a small child, older person, or enterprising scam artist to slip on the mess and fall to the ground, thus creating vast new opportunities to effect redistributions of wealth from powerful grocery-store chains to downtrodden individual shoppers. But the U.S. Bureau of Labor Statistics is concerned solely with occupational injuries—not those suffered by customers venturing onto the premises. We can certainly imagine a number of situations where employees working at grocery stores could be injured by workplace hazards such as slicing a finger off while cutting a pound of "thinly sliced" roast beef or suffering hypothermia after being accidentally locked in the meat freezer or being buried alive after a fifteen-foot-high pyramid of two-liter cola bottles collapses or severing a foot in a particularly powerful automatic sliding glass door or being attacked by a crazed crowd on "Lottery Night" which had decided that it had waited long enough to get its winning tickets. Grocery stores are also dangerous because of the sheer number and variety of products that must be continuously stocked and restocked. Any employee can drop a one-gallon bottle of apple juice on their foot or get their hands stuck on the frozen-food bin racks while loading stacks of frozen pizza. The element of risk is further enhanced by the sheer numbers of employees who are involved in the preparation of food on the premises such as cooking baked goods (hot ovens) and cutting up meat (sharp knives, psychotic coworkers). Whenever an employee finds it necessary to fire up an oven or wander into a freezer or unload a truck, there is a risk of injury which cannot be eliminated— no matter how many precautions the employer may take.

Government statisticians in the U.S. Bureau of Labor Statistics note that department stores have about the same rate of injuries as grocery stores but report about thirty thousand fewer occupational injuries in a given year. The obvious reason for the smaller number of injuries in department stores may be attributed to the fact that more people visit grocery stores more frequently than department stores. In short, we would rather eat than be assured that we are wearing the latest in fine European designer wear. But we do not know whether the phrase "department stores" includes only those stores which carry overpriced brand names in clothing and fine household goods or if it encompasses all nonfood stores. If the broader definition is the accurate one, then it is less clear that we can explain the differing number of injuries on the relative popularity of food versus dry-goods stores. But department stores clearly have their own unique hazards ranging from the periodic stampedes for sale to the temporary blindness that can result when one is sprayed by an overly eager perfume salesclerk.

Of course one can go on about the number of injuries in any occupation but most injuries are comparatively minor and rarely, if ever, life-threatening. It is difficult to attract the attention of the local television news station if one has a bruised shin or a paper cut. But it is much more dramatic when one can boast a gaping wound or a limb hanging by a thread or, better yet, a gruesome death. Because death sells and gory, hideous death really sells, it is incumbent upon us to stride from those occupations that promise the greatest chance of injury to those occupations that provide the greatest opportunities for self-annihilation. This is not to say that the persons who work in these industries actually enter them with the idea that they may have a better-than-average chance of shortening their lives. But it is certainly the case that some jobs pose a greater risk of death than other jobs and it is prudent for us to consider those occupations if only to know which ones to avoid before making our own career choices.

The most dangerous occupation in America in terms of the odds that a worker will die on the job is—the fisher. We used to call fishers "fishermen" in those simpler times when the language police were not running amuck through the halls of the nation's colleges and universities. But there is another reason other than "political correctness" for adopting a more gender-neutral term—the growing number of women who are actively involved in commercial fishing operations both as captains of their own ships and members of fishing crews. But this change in the rank and file of commercial fishers should not obscure the fact that you are more likely to die while working on a fishing boat than working as a guard in a maximum security prison or walking the beat as a police officer in the nation's most dangerous neighborhoods. Now this fact is somewhat surprising because most of us think of fishing as a zenlike activity in which the fisher goes out on a boat and floats on a lake or ocean and waits for the fish to bite his hook. But the life of the commercial fisher is not the peaceful, tranquil life that is suggested by a casual review of the "fishing channel" on cable television where "Vern" and "Dave" stand waist-high in a mountain stream and try to catch fish with a fly rod. Instead it can involve clinging for dear life to a tiny boat being tossed by raging mountains of water and howling winds amid the unforgiving black vastness of an ocean storm. Although this kind of setting can provide a very compelling dramatic backdrop for a disaster movie, it is not an environment for persons who are faint of heart or queasy of stomach.

We know that we can describe the odds that an event will occur in terms of probabilities. But there are different ways in which we can express the probability that one will die while on the job that will illustrate the differing risks inherent in the more dangerous jobs in America. We can speculate, for example, that the odds a fisher will die on the job are 10,000 to 1. Or we can illustrate the comparative danger of commercial fishing by determining an average rate of death on the job for all workers and setting that equal to a single value such as 1.0, as was done by the *Wall Street Journal Almanac 1999*, so that occupations having a greater-than-average risk can be reflected in a proportionately higher number. In other words, a job that is ten times as risky as the average American job in terms of the likelihood of suffering a hideous death would have a "death index" of 10 and a job that is thirty times as risky would have a death index of 30, and so on. Although this does not tell us the actual probability of suffering death while doing a given kind of work, it gives us a yardstick whereby we may govern our discussions with career counselors.

So if we are assuming that the average index for all workers in all occupations throughout the United States in terms of the rate of risk of on-the-job death is equal to 1.0, then we find that the noble fisher has, according to the *Almanac*, a death index of 37.5. This means that the fisher is 37.5 times more likely to die on the job than is the average American worker. Of course this average reflects a mix of high-risk occupations such as construction workers and lower-risk occupations such as clergymen, so there may be no single line of work which has the exact death index of 1.0. But we do know that the fisher has a very dangerous occupation in that he is almost thirty-eight times more likely than the average American worker to die on the job.

Now what could account for such a high rate of fatality in an industry in which the overriding goal is to catch fishes? It seems unlikely that sunstroke would play much of a role in the hazards of the job, particularly for those fishermen who spend their days plying the cold waters of the North Atlantic. Nor does it seem that fishers would die from gluttony as there are not very many buffets available on the decks of most trawlers. So that leaves getting hit by a broken mast and falling overboard and getting bitten by a big angry shark as the most logical reasons for suffering a premature demise on the high seas. According to the government statistics, however, the primary cause of death for fishers is—drowning. Nearly three out of every four fisher deaths result from falling overboard. And while it would appear to be a fairly simple task to avoid falling overboard, this is not always so simple when forty-foot waves are crashing onto the deck and hurricane-force winds are whipping across the waters. Indeed, many of the deaths suffered by fishers occur during violent storms. Very few commercial fishers fall overboard while wandering up and down the deck of ocean-going yachts wearing swimming trunks and sandals on a sun-drenched afternoon and carrying a glass of wine in each hand.

Next in line for the title of deadliest job in America is the glorious timber cutter, with a death rate of about thirty-three times that of the national average. Timber cutters spend most of their time cutting down big trees with chain saws and axes. They also get to shout "Timber!" and to wear flannel shirts and eat pancakes whenever they please—or so we are led to believe. The danger with being a timber cutter is that you have to cut down timber. In general, falling timber is very heavy and very hard on the head of the person who happens to be standing in the wrong place when it hits the ground. So while timber cutters are fairly adept at cutting down even the most massive trees, these trees do not always land in the exact spots for which they were intended. The result can be severe headaches at best and death at worst. Hopefully, this high death rate will not quell the aspirations of would-be lumberjacks who want to breathe the cold clean air of the Pacific Northwest while wielding their enormous chain saws to clear the land of unsightly 200-foot-tall trees.

For those who are not fond of the great outdoors but who still aspire to enjoy the thrill of working in a dangerous occupation, our next occupation—airplane pilot—offers both the thrill of working in a job in which the likelihood of death is more than eighteen times that of the national average as well as the comfort of a cushy "indoor" job in which you will not get your hands dirty. It is also the only occupation among the elite "top ten" of America's deadliest careers in which 100 percent of all deaths may be attributed to a single cause—airplanes dropping out of the sky and smashing into the ground.

The fourth most dangerous job is another outdoor job—structural metalworker—which naturally appeals to people who like to walk on narrow metal beams high above busy city streets. This job has the additional benefit of breathtaking views and extensive work involving welding torches. This labor gives the worker a sense of satisfaction as he works with his hands attaching beams of steel together and building a gigantic steel skeleton. Structural metalworkers make their living in an industry in which the death risk is slightly less than that faced by airplane pilots (at about eighteen times that of the average American worker). However, they must deal with two types of problems: (1) falling off the beams and plummeting to their deaths and (2) being struck on the heads by those very same beams. So structural metalworkers must deal with both of the primary dangers faced by timber cutters and pilots—falling to earth and falling objects. However, more than three-fourths of all deaths suffered by structural metalworkers involve falling to earth so the major concern is being able to walk a straight line while strolling along a beam three hundred feet above the streets.

Finally, the *Wall Street Journal Almanac* informs us that the fifth deadliest job involves working in the great outdoors in the loosest sense of the word—if you consider a mine running several thousand feet below the surface of the earth to be the great outdoors. But those tenacious workers who help to bring minerals, coal, and jewels to the surface of the earth have the unfortunate distinction of working in a job that is both one of the most physically demanding of all as well as one in which they are about fourteen times more likely than the average American worker to die. Certainly the hazards due to cave-ins are obvious but the government statistics suggest that this obvious hazard is not the most prevalent cause of workplace fatalities for miners. Instead vehicular accidents account for about one-fourth of all mining deaths and thus constitute the biggest single cause of death. It is unclear, however, as to the kinds of vehicular accidents which are included in this tally as they could include surface vehicles as well as those operating in the mines themselves.

DRINKING AND DRUGS IN THE WORKPLACE

Having brought some fellowship and cheer to our readers who are considering changing their careers, we now need to shift our focus from injuries and death that arise from third parties or independent causes such as man-made accidents and natural disasters to look at self-inflicted injuries—specifically the incidence of drugs and alcohol in the workplace. The statistics are provided by the Substance Abuse and Mental Health Services Administration and present a disturbing picture of the rates of illicit drug use and heavy alcohol use by industry. Of course if you are a heavy drug or alcohol user in search of fellow users with whom you can share a few smokes or a snort or two, then this type of information could be invaluable. After all, it is difficult enough to meet persons with whom one can share common interests and so it may be useful to know the industries in which the greatest percentage of workers are engaged in such behavior.

As drug use is rampant throughout America, we might want to begin by considering the industries in which such activities are most common. What are the odds that the person who serves you at your favorite restaurant or the contractor putting a new roof on your house or the smiling gas station attendant who is filling your tank while taking a drag on his cigarette is a user of illicit drugs? The likelihood that any or all of these people may have a hankering for cocaine, heroin, or even hard candy varies widely from industry to industry. But it is not to say that working in a specific industry necessarily creates or otherwise encourages a predisposition toward illicit drug use because nothing could be further from the truth. The occupation is not the causal agent; it is instead the fact that certain industries attract persons who are predisposed to engage in illicit drug use.

Why might the drug use among employees vary from industry to industry? One obvious answer might be the average pay given to employees in a particular industry is extremely low and would tend to attract only those persons who are living on the edge of society's mainstream. But this is not a very convincing argument because the vast majority of employees in the industries which have the greatest proportion of employees engaging in illicit drug use do not use drugs. Another possibility might be that the type of work may create such stress in employees as to encourage a higher-than-average rate of drug use. But the same argument regarding the previous "living on society's margin" applies in that most employees in even the most stressful industries do not use illicit drugs. A third possibility might be the opportunity theory in that we could argue employees in those industries having access to drugs will engage in an above-average rate of drug use. This reasoning would suggest that pharmacists, doctors, and nurses would be those who are most inclined to engage in the consumption of illicit drugs. Such a conclusion would not be of great comfort to those persons waiting to undergo elective surgical procedures or, indeed, those being moved to the operating table for an organ transplant.

But we find, surprisingly enough, that the greatest percentage of workers who consume illicit drugs are found in the restaurant industry with 16.4 percent of all workers reporting some kind of drug use. We can put a more human face on this statistic if we imagine that sixteen out of every one hundred restaurant workers we meet stick things up their nose or smoke substances or ingest pills which are not given the "Good Housekeeping Seal of Approval." Now this may give a traveler some pause when he or she considers whether to stop for a meal at a restaurant because you never know when a worker may have accidentally dropped a few pills in the "soup of the day" or sneezed some cocaine into the cognac by mistake or confused the lye with cooking oil. As far as a stress factor is concerned, one does not necessarily think of food-service workers as being subject to extraordinary levels of stress, so it is unclear as to whether there is a satisfactory explanation for this problem. The fact that the restaurant industry consists primarily of lower-paying jobs with a comparatively high rate of turnover might give some insight as to the reason for the high rate of drug use. But we also need to be careful before we start forming images of kitchens manned by crazed heroin junkies, because the type of drug use is not specified. Indeed, it may be the case that the majority of persons in the restaurant industry reporting some type of illicit drug use are referring to their occasional or habitual use of marijuana. Although we may not like the idea that our double-decker stack of pancakes is being cooked by a chef who may have been smoking a "reefer" prior to coming to work, we may be somewhat comforted by the fact that our chef was not "popping" vials of crack cocaine while grilling our bacon. Fortunately, most people who engage in illicit drug use do so on a part-time basis because they cannot afford to be full-time addicts. Many of them also view their drug consumption as something akin to entertainment and probably do not see their indulgence as a harmful activity. Of course these points will be of scant comfort when we are served pancakes that have been deep-fried in a vat of hot grease and served with a generous topping of coffee grounds, radishes, and catsup.

Furniture and appliance retail sales constitute the next most common area of employment for drug users with more than fourteen out of every one hundred workers engaging at least some of the time in the consumption of illicit drugs. One advantage that furniture salesclerks enjoy over most occupations is that there are plenty of plush chairs and comfy sofas to plop onto in furniture showrooms so that a drug trip can be more fully enjoyed without having to worry about maintaining one's balance. There is nothing so annoying as falling through a plate-glass window and suffering massive cuts all over one's body when one is trying to experience a hallucinogenic meeting with God. Appliance salesclerks are at a comparative disadvantage because they must steady themselves by climbing on top of a washing machine or dishwasher. However, the tumble-dry action of an electric dryer can bring some straddlers pleasures that they never imagined could exist in an appliance store.

The next two likely areas in which one can find employees who indulge in pharmacological hobbies are the entertainment and recreation industry (13.7 per 100 employees) and the advertisement and consulting industry (13.1 per 100 employees). These industries are viewed as being more glamorous than most because they involve many prominent celebrities and have a very visible presence in the mass media. But it does not automatically follow that the presence of movie and television stars, for example, leads to a higher rate of drug use in those industries because most of the persons using the drugs probably have very little contact with movie stars and do not typically travel in such exalted social circles unless, of course, they work as gardeners, butlers, chauffeurs, or chambermaids. So there is really no easy way to explain the widespread use of illicit drugs in these industries because the vast majority of the persons involved do not use such drugs.

What about those industries which rank at the bottom of the drug consumption scale? Well, it is childcare services in which only about 1.3 out of one hundred workers report that they consume illicit drugs. This should make us feel pretty good that nearly 99 percent of all childcare services workers do not use drugs. Of course we would not be pleased to find that we had hired a member from that top 1 percent group which knew that spoons and candles could be used for things other than formal dinner parties. But this extremely low incidence of drug use might also make us wonder about the accuracy of the survey itself, particularly when it involves admissions of an activity such as illicit drug consumption. Can we expect people to accurately report the extent to which they engage in an activity that is not only illegal but is viewed unfavorably by society at large? It may be that childcare workers would be more principled than most people due to the concern they have for children in general and would not surprisingly be more ashamed for using drugs. But one can also argue that some children are so difficult that they could prompt even the hardiest caregiver to be tempted by narcotics.

As far as alcohol consumption is concerned, there is surprisingly little overlap with those occupations reporting the highest levels of drug consumption. According to the Substance Abuse and Mental Health Services Administration, computer and data processing workers have the highest incidence of heavy alcohol consumption. Nearly 16.2 out of every 100 workers admit to engaging in excessive alcohol use. That it would be the industry in which computer programmers and software engineers would work is surprising because this is not the traditional group that most of us associate with beer consumption in general. Indeed, a review of most beer and alcohol commercials in the broadcast and print media respectively shows rugged he-man types banging huge foam-covered mugs together. Seldom if ever do you see an advertisement in which a group of software developers wearing black-rimmed glasses and pocket protectors hurry down to the corner bar to indulge in a round of manly self-intoxication. (Notice the avoidance of any stereotypes here!) But there must be something about the very long and grueling hours peering at a computer screen and perhaps the man (and woman) versus machine atmosphere that pervades the computer industry to prompt so many people who are obviously intelligent to engage in heavy alcohol consumption. Some might suggest that this industry attracts a disproportionate share of people who have difficulty relating to other people and who, as a result, must find solace in mechanical devices. But such a view appears to be overly simplistic. As with our leading drug-consuming occupations, there is probably no completely satisfactory explanation for the high rate in which alcohol is consumed in the computer industry. We can surmise, however, that there are many people who work very long hours in this line of work and they may naturally seek some type of refuge in drink to ease the pressure that they feel to compete with their colleagues who are trying to work as many hours as them.

But the folks who serve meals and drinks do show up as the second-highest rate of consumers of alcohol, with nearly 15.4 per 100 workers admitting to heavy alcohol use. Of course it is easy to engage in heavy alcohol use if you work in a restaurant with a liquor license or a bar because relief is just a few feet away. You do not have to worry about driving your car to a tavern because your workplace is your tavern. Some people would find this to be a very satisfactory state of affairs but these are probably the very same people to whom you would not want to turn for your childcare needs. It is quite possible that many of the same drug-abuse overachievers in the food and drink business also enjoy the occasional bottle of liquor or fine wine. But it is probably pointless to speculate as to the reasons why this industry attracts persons who are predisposed to heavy alcohol consumption, let alone illicit drug consumption.

It is only when we move to construction workers, the third-highest-ranking group of heavy alcohol drinkers (with a rate of 13.4 out of every one hundred users), that the perceptions created by the media (e.g., beer commercials with swarthy ex-football players who like to pat each other on the bottom) begin to coincide with our survey results. We can visualize construction workers going to the neighborhood bar after a long day of erecting steel girders and pouring concrete and whistling at any woman. This is the popular image of the beer drinker and it is likely that construction workers themselves feel some pressure to live up to that macho image. Whether many of them get together with the local software programmers group to spend a delightful evening playing darts and seeing who can find the largest prime number is less certain.

SOME CLOSING THOUGHTS

Certainly no one would disagree that a worker's death in the workplace is a tragedy, particularly when it occurs to one who has not done anything to bring about his or her own demise. Accidental deaths often prompt us to think profound philosophical thoughts such as wondering why the decedent had to be the one who died, as well as the deep sense of loss that often accompanies the passing of one who failed to pay back a hundred-dollar bet on a football game. Those of us who mourn the death of a colleague or a friend can usually list four, five, six, or even more persons who were more deserving of a premature ending. But such are the mysteries of our universe that bad things sometimes happen to good people and good things continue to happen to some absolutely rotten people—such as repeated reelections to high office.

Yet one can argue that those deaths that result from the conscious desire to engage in reckless behavior—whether it be ignoring workplace safety standards or consuming enormous quantities of alcohol or drugs—are nearly as tragic in that they result from people compulsorily proceeding down a very dangerous and obvious path. Accidental deaths are often random events that cannot be predicted beforehand; they often occur when people happen to be in the wrong place at the wrong time. But the victims of accidental deaths are innocent; they usually have not engaged in conduct evidencing a desire to assume the risk of death other than the fact that they have chosen to engage in an occupation that, like all occupations, has some risk of death. In contrast, those persons who deliberately push the envelope of risky behavior are less sympathetic and seem to "get what they deserve" when their conduct leads to the predictable result. This is not to say that the tragedies of the workplace should not be viewed with concern. Private employers and public entities should endeavor to reduce workplace fatalities and injuries and drug use as much as possible. At the same time, however, there is certainly an issue of free will here that may frustrate the best-intentioned efforts of employers and government to minimize the dangers of the workplace.

Statistics are tools and they are admittedly of limited effectiveness, particularly when used by persons of limited effectiveness. These numbers cannot tell us everything we want to know about a subject; they instead provide us with certain limited insights. Statistics cannot tell us why some job occupations have much higher rates of death or injury or drug use than other types of careers. Indeed, we have to admit that we really do not know how accurate our statistics may be in situations where the respondents are talking about engaging in conduct for which they may have feelings of shame or embarrassment. Perhaps the best we can do is to acknowledge that statistics are tools for measuring the prevalence of certain events and that the value of our statistics ultimately depends on the accuracy of our data. Because statistics are dependent on information which may or may not be completely accurate and verifiable, we need to accept the fact that they are limited means to limited ends. They will not necessarily provide us with deep intuitive revelations or profound psychological insights.

7

WORKING ON THE CHAIN GANG

Everybody likes to work. Well, maybe "like" is too strong a word but it is true that nearly every adult in the United States has some type of occupation by which he or she makes a living. Some people have what we would consider more traditional occupations such as electricians, teachers, grocers, chefs, doctors, lawyers, and waiters. But there are also more exotic occupations such as table dancers, image consultants, entourage members, and studio-audience members which have become more common in recent years. Some people do not appear to work at all but they still do have occupations of one form or another. A vagrant, for example, is not a nonworker because he must do something in order to scrounge up enough coins to buy the occasional bottle of fine wine with a screw top or a pack of unfiltered cigarettes. As a result, he might stand on the street corner with a cup in hand asking passersby for change or he might run a dirty rag over the windshields of cars stopped at intersections and then ask for a cleaning fee. In this case, he could be said to have an occupation as a self-philanthropist because he would be seeking monetary support for a charity case (himself). Or he could be regarded as an automobile-service worker even though the quality of his service might be unappreciated by the majority of his clients who would find themselves unable to peer through the grease-streaked, spotted windshields of their automobiles. Similarly, the often-maligned pimp is another person who is viewed as not really working for a living even though his job requires substantial administrative skills and the ability to match clients in search of "personal" services with the appropriate supplier of those services. Indeed, the pimp is a sort of professional "matchmaker" who is able by persuasion or threat of force to bring together lonely people who can enjoy an intimate twenty-minute relationship with each other crouched over in the front seat of an automobile. If the pimp is unable to provide the appropriate quality of urban hostess to prospective clients, then he does not make any money and his hostesses do not make any money and the local neighborhood economy suffers accordingly. So the pimp plays an important behind-the-scenes role in helping to facilitate mutually beneficial relationships which, through trickle-down economics, adds to the nation's gross domestic product. Of course, while lacking legal sanction in most states, drive-by matchmaking has proven to be impossible for law-enforcement officials to stamp out.

Working—whether at a one-man magazine stand or a vast multinational corporation spanning the globe with hundreds of thousands of employees—is not only the way in which we earn the money needed to put food on the table and clothes on our backs but it is also the way we define ourselves and the basis for much of our self-esteem. As such, the self-approval that comes from working cannot be "learned" but instead must be earned through the dint of one's own effort. And it is because of the efforts of millions and millions of American workers that statisticians have been able to construct a composite of the American labor force that can provide us with a great deal of information—some of which is actually useful to people who specialize in arcane occupations themselves—such as economists and political scientists.

Employment itself is a tricky concept. We may find it difficult to get a handle on the way in which we define the level of employment in this country because one can be defined as being unemployed only if one is out of work but actively searching for work. If we want to determine such things as the odds that we will be unemployed at a given time, we certainly need to be acquainted with the traditional concept of unemployment. Otherwise, we may find ourselves sloshing around a semantic riverbank and not getting very far in any one direction. Statisticians are certainly very concerned that the concepts they use in their analyses be as straightforward and as precise as possible because a concept that is mushy or ambiguous provides correspondingly less analytical value. For those of us who are unconcerned about the plight of statisticians forced to deal every day with the conceptual messiness of the real world, however, we would still find ourselves forced to admit that there is value in the logical organization of data and measurements.

Having provided ample introduction to our subject matter, we know that we are now going to deal with certain probabilities associated with employment in the labor force. Because we are all so concerned about the status conferred upon us by our jobs, the first and most obvious question would be to try to determine the probability that we might find ourselves unemployed at any given time. How one tries to make such a determination depends in large part on the manner in which one defines the problems and utilizes the existing numbers at hand. But the first step in the process would be to take a look at the general unemployment levels in the American economy and examine the levels of unemployment on a national level. The Bureau of Labor Statistics of the U.S. Department of Labor informs us that the rate of unemployment in the United States has, through most of the past century, been less than 10 percent—except for that period of time in the 1930s and early 1940s known as the Great Depression. Although younger persons might be tempted to ask what was so depressing about this time in American history that could not be cured with a few doses of Ritalin, this was a time in which the national economy almost ground to a halt and the level of unemployment rose to include one-fourth of the entire labor force. Fortunately for economists and policymakers who had encountered great difficulty figuring out how to jump-start the economy for most of the decade, World War II intervened and the nation was forced to enter a life-and-death military struggle against Japan and Germany that helped to put its idle millions back to work for good. But the government statistics show that unemployment has tended to range from 5.0 percent in 1900 to 14.6 percent in 1940 to 7.1 percent in 1980 to 4.2 percent in 1999. So for most of the last century, more than nine-tenths of the working population searching for gainful employment has been able to find work. Of course not everybody has been able to find the job of their dreams. After all, there are only so many television game-show host jobs to go around and not everyone can realize their dreams to test the limits of their thespian talents on the silver screen. For the rest of us who simply lack the talent to carry on meaningless banter on talk shows or flipping oversized playing cards or reminding players to phrase every answer in the form of a question, we have to settle for less-than-perfect careers in more mundane occupations where each of us can rise to our own level of incompetence.

So we see that the odds of our becoming unemployed really depend on whether we actually care about finding a job in the first place. If we are happily lying on the beach every day without a care in the world and cannot even remember what we did in our last job and are quite happy to pass each day squandering our trust fund, then we would not be considered unemployed because we obviously are not concerned about trying to find gainful employment. However, if we occasionally got up from our beach blanket to go drop a résumé in the mail in response to the classified ads seeking lion tamer, magazine recipe testers, or even statistics book writers, then the fact that we were actually trying to get employment—regardless of how little we might want to work—would cause us to be tarred with the label of "unemployed." Of course we would be able to lose that label by actually taking a job and becoming a productive member of society, but that would mean having to cut back on our days at the beach. On the other hand, we could simply shelve any idea of having a job and resume our busy schedule watching the beautiful people meander up and down the shoreline, turning ourselves over every so often to ensure even tanning. By giving up our search for employment, we would no longer be considered as unemployed and so our deciding to seek the perfect tan on the beach would result in a brighter unemployment picture and thereby lend to the collective cheer of the government statisticians who collect such figures.

UNEMPLOYMENT NUMBERS

But in considering the statistics regarding unemployment figures, we see that most people who have actually desired to work are extremely likely to find work. If we look at the unemployment figures provided by the U.S. Department of Labor, we would find that in 1999, for example, there were 133,488,000 employed and 5,880,000 unemployed persons, giving an unemployment rate of 4.4 percent—about the lowest level of unemployment in the post–World War II era. In the aggregate scheme of things, a person in the 1999 American economy would have about a 1-in-25 chance of becoming unemployed. However, this figure has to be considered in light of the wide variety of occupations in the American economy as well as the fact that there are literally millions of business owners who are employees only in the sense that they work for themselves. They cannot be "fired" in the traditional sense that a boss can terminate a worker; the business owner's career will last as long as the business itself is able to last. So they do not have to worry about getting a "pink slip" as does the traditional employee. However, they do have to worry about a variety of other matters including snooping government officials; employees who believe that life, liberty, and the right to purloin their employer's property are inalienable rights; costly business regulations; taxes; and meeting the company payroll. So the unemployment figures may greatly understate the probability that the employee may soon be searching for gainful employment elsewhere. The *New York Times Almanac 2001* tells us that "small businesses account for 99 percent of the 24.8 million nonfarm businesses in the United States" with "sole proprietorships (including artists, freelance writers, actors, and other self-employed people who are not technically businesses) mak[ing] up the vast majority of the businesses; the remainder are divided between partnerships and corporations." If we assume that about twenty million of these 24.8 million nonfarm businesses are owned by one person, then we would automatically see a reduction in the employment figures noted above to about 113 million persons—which would cause a nominal rise in the unemployment rate to 5.2 percent. If we assumed that these same 20 million businesses were owned by an average of 1.5 persons, then the unemployment rate would rise even higher to 5.7 percent. Because these figures are being derived from a time in which the unemployment rate was extraordinarily low, however, it stands to reason that the probabilities that one will be rendered unemployed may be somewhat understated. But such a sweeping generalization does not provide a great deal of insight because, as with everything else, there are some people who will never lose their job even though they may be grossly incompetent, morally repugnant, and, fortunately for them, extremely personable and perhaps even a little lucky. And then there are the hardworking, ethical, shy, and extremely unlucky persons who get caught in one corporate downsizing after another and must scramble over and over again to restart their careers. So even though the nation's unemployment rate may tell a story of sorts, it is very limited in the sort of information that it can provide to the statistician. It does not say which industries subject workers to repeated layoffs and shutdowns and which industries are so dynamic that people seldom lose their jobs. Moreover, it may paint a rosier picture of the odds of losing a job because it lumps together everyone who works for a living—whether they are self-employed sole proprietors or the principals in a two-person partnership or one of two hundred thousand employees in a gigantic conglomerate.

Despite its imperfections, the unemployment rate does provide us with a benchmark of sorts that we can use to gauge the health of the national economy and, in our spasms of jingoistic chest-pounding, compare our economy to those of Europe and Asia. And what we find is that the unemployment figures in the United States have been steadily declining over the past two decades from 7.1 percent in 1980 to 5.6 percent in 1990 to 4.2 percent at the dawn of the new century. The Bureau of Labor Statistics points out that many of the industrialized democracies have seen their unemployment rates rise during that same period even though the labor movements in these nations are comparatively stronger and the governments of these countries have consciously pursued policies to minimize unemployment. For example, 1980 saw unemployment rates of 6.5 percent in France, 2.8 percent in Germany (then West Germany), 2.0 percent in Japan, and 7.0 percent in England. By 1990, the unemployment rates in those countries had generally risen to 9.1 percent in France, 5.0 percent in a united Germany, 2.1 percent in Japan, and 6.9 percent in England. By 1999, despite massive efforts to reduce unemployment in these European nations, the unemployment rates for most of these countries had edged upward even more, with France at 11.1 percent, Germany at 9.0 percent, Japan at 4.7 percent, and England at 6.1 percent. Of the four countries, only England had seen its unemployment rate steadily decline over the preceding two decades. But as it had started off in this time period in double digits, it admittedly had to play "catch up" so that any improvement was bound to represent a noticeable upturn in the nation's fortunes. So even though American workers who have been caught in corporate downsizings or terminated through no fault of their own might despair as to how long it will take them to get back on their feet, they should take some comfort in the fact that the U.S. unemployment rate has continued to trend downward while Europe and Japan have seen their rates continue to rise and seem powerless to reverse the situation. If the American economy is proving to be a more dynamic entity in creating jobs, then American workers who suddenly find themselves forced to look for work should be grateful that they are not living in Paris or London or Berlin or Tokyo despite the fact that Paris has the best food and wine. Even though the social assistance programs offered in these foreign countries may be more generous than those found in the United States, the fact that it is probably much easier to find meaningful employment here as opposed to overseas should be of some comfort.

HOW OLD ARE YOUR WORKERS?

Many companies like to advertise about their willingness to hire older Americans as employees—a move that makes sense due to the lifelong training and disciplined work habits typically displayed by the nation's senior citizens. Very few seniors working as chefs in restaurant kitchens drop their teeth into pots of soup or fall asleep while garnishing entrees at a cafeteria or talk at great length on the telephone with their main squeezes. As a result, the participation of seniors in the workplace has been embraced by most American companies—even though some seniors find they must still combat certain prejudices in some industries regarding the value of the contributions that they can make to the workplace.

Because of the attention devoted to age-discrimination legislation over the past several years, one would think that all senior citizens are determined to fill out employment applications with fast-food restaurants so that they can pull down the big money that they were unable to earn during their careers as corporate managers and business professionals. Certainly the popular perception is that older Americans want

Labor Participation Rates of Elderly (65+ Years of Age) Workers in the U.S. Labor Force

Year	Men	Women
1890	68.3	7.6
1900	63.1	8.3
1910		
1920	55.6	7.3
1930	54.0	7.3
1940	41.8	6.1
1950	41.4	7.8
1960	30.5	10.3
1970	24.8	10.0
1980	19.3	8.2
1990	17.6	8.4

Source of Statistics: Bureau of the Census, U.S. Department of Commerce

to work long hours for low rates of hourly pay with few benefits so that they can better enjoy their golden years. As a result, we would expect that the rate of senior participation in the workforce would reflect a steady upward trend over the past few decades. After all, do not all senior citizens want to give up their leisurely vacations and their weekdays on the golf course and their stress-free days in order to fry hamburgers and clean public restrooms? Although the popular perception would indicate that seniors are lining up to take even the most vile job, the actual statistics that have been collected regarding this matter point to a very different conclusion. According to the Bureau of the Census, U.S. Department of Commerce, 41.4 percent of all men 65 years of age and older worked in the labor force in 1950. By 1960, the share of senior men in the workforce had dropped to 30.5 percent. In successive decades, the rate of senior men participation in the labor force continued to decline with only 24.8 percent in 1970, 19.3 percent in 1980, and 17.6 percent in 1990. This documented trend certainly does not appear to jibe with popular perceptions that older men are lining up to work the cash registers and mop the floors and clean the grills at hamburger stands.

But why are fewer and fewer old men going to work? Could it be the attraction of spending the day wandering around in a daze at the local mall with their wives? Who would not want to spend four or five hours each day sitting forlornly in front of a dressing room watching your spouse try on outfits? Perhaps that is one reason that there are some men who are still choosing to work beyond their retirement age. But it does not help to explain why more than four out of every five senior men have chosen to retire from the workforce. One obvious reason is that many companies have mandatory retirement ages (typically 65) that are imposed upon everyone from the chief executive officer to the vegetable dispenser in the company cafeteria. Another reason is that many people simply want to retire from their careers and have more time to spend with their loved ones as well as their spouses and to indulge in travel, hobbies, and amorous neighbors. Government programs such as Social Security and Medicare also provide retirees with certain minimal levels of financial benefits which, when combined with company pensions and savings, make it possible to leave the workforce. Retirement makes it possible to get around to doing those things you never had time to do before, like doing errands for your spouse and meeting all of her widowed friends for bridge.

The lack of any government assistance programs for persons of retirement age prior to the 1930s also explains why the rate of participation of older men in the labor force was so high in the past as compared to today. In 1890, for example, the Bureau of the U.S. Census reports that 68.3 percent of all men 65 years of age or older worked in the labor force. This era predated the creation of Social Security and other governmental assistance programs by some four decades, so for those few men who actually lived to the age of 65 there was really little meaningful opportunity to think about a placid retirement. Instead, the more common retirement was to be wished a happy 65th and then head back down to the coal mines and risk being killed in a cave-in or finally succumb to black lung disease. This participation rate of older men in the labor force began to decline throughout the course of the 20th century, dropping to 63.1 percent in 1910, 55.6 percent in 1920, and 54.0 percent in 1930. At the same time, however, the average life expectancy of the American male continued to increase, meaning that more and more men were actually living past the age of 65 (almost eight years on average from 65.6 years in 1950 to 73.6 years in 1997 per the U.S. Department of Health and Human Services) so that there was actually an opportunity to retire in the first place. So the odds that you (assuming you are a male worker of retirement age) will get to enjoy retirement are better than ever before as the probability is greater than 80 percent that you will leave work at age 65—whether you want to retire or not.

It would be nice to say that the advent of government assistance programs, more generous company pension plans, longer life expectancies, and a greater variety of leisure activities all helped older men to enjoy wonderful retirements with their families. But for many of these retirees, all of this added leisure time and increased quality time with their families brought on added stress of a type they had never known in their working lives and, sadly, caused many to suffer great aggravation, ulcers, and heart attacks. But there was a silver lining for the widows of those retired workers who were thoughtful enough to obtain big life insurance policies, because it made it possible for their bereaved spouses to get through their periods of mourning and enjoy a lifestyle that would not have been possible without their husbands' untimely, heavily insured deaths.

As far as women in the workforce are concerned, their rate of retirement at age 65 has been very different than that of men. The

Bureau of the Census statistics show that the percentage of females in the workforce above the age of 65 has remained fairly constant over the past century. In 1890, for example, 7.6 percent of the women in the female workforce continued to work beyond age 65. This figure rose slightly to 8.3 percent in 1900, fell to 7.3 percent in 1920, and remained the same in 1930. In 1940, the rate of labor force participation dropped a little to 6.1 percent but, by 1950, had risen to 7.8 percent. By 1960, 10.3 percent of working women continued to remain in the labor force after age 65; this number declined a little to 10 percent in 1970, 8.2 percent in 1980, and 8.4 percent in 1990. But it is striking that the rate of older female participation in the workforce has not really varied very much at all even though they have been subject to many of the same factors that we would assume have caused such dramatic declines in the rate of older male participation—Social Security, Medicare, increased life expectancy, and, in some cases, company pensions.

We should also point out that the number of women workers as a whole in the labor force has steadily increased over time so that there are now eighty-seven female workers for every one hundred male workers in the year 2000 according to the U.S. Department of Labor Bureau of Labor Statistics. This represents an increase from 1980 when there were seventy-three female workers for every one hundred male workers and 1960 when there were fifty female workers for every one hundred male workers. Given the fact that the number of females in the labor force has continued to increase steadily over the past several decades, it is not difficult to imagine a day when the number of female workers actually exceeds the number of male workers in the labor force. How long it will take for this female majority in the labor force to translate to a female parity in the upper levels of corporate America, however, remains to be seen.

WORK STOPPAGES

One of the perks of being an employee in a labor union is that you have the opportunity to participate in organized strikes to try to compel your employer to increase your wages and improve your conditions of employment. The logic behind participating in a labor union is simple: a union controls the workers and can thus counteract the immense power that an employer can wield regarding any individual employee. The union can therefore negotiate on behalf of all employees and thus exert far greater leverage than can any employee. The downside of participating in a labor union is that all the members must be willing to engage in collective action against the employer should the need arise. Because workers do not get paid when they are on strike, there are obvious disadvantages to such a situation. Moreover, companies may try to hire substitute workers to take the place of the striking workers so that they do not go out of business while the strike negotiations are progressing. Most factory workers are not independently wealthy except for one or two self-made tycoons who prefer the camaraderie of their fellow assembly-line workers to the stuffiness of the local yacht club. As a result, a prolonged strike can be financially devastating for most striking workers—even those who belong to the larger unions.

In general, the number of workers who belong to unions continued to increase in absolute terms from the 1930s to about 1980, going from about 3,401,000 members in a 1930 labor force of 29,424,000 to 19,843,000 members in a 1980 labor force of 90,564,000. Although this fivefold increase in fifty years was very impressive, the percentage of the labor force that was unionized actually peaked in 1955 when unionized workers constituted fully one-third of the labor force and then began to decline. In 1980, union membership had declined to about 21.9 percent of the total labor force. Sadly for labor-union organizers, however, this decline in the union membership has continued to the present day in both absolute and percentile terms. By 1999, the

Bureau of Labor Statistics reports that union membership had stabilized about a little over 16 million members and 13.9 percent of the labor force. Although a variety of factors such as the vast expansion in the service sector of the economy and the decision by many companies to move production facilities to offshore nations with cheap (non-unionized) labor have been blamed for the decline, it may also be true that the shift from a smokestack economy with its large centralized production techniques (which facilitated union-organization efforts) has also hurt efforts to attract new members. Perhaps there is also an increasing reluctance of workers—who are increasingly less likely to spend more than a few years let alone an entire working career with the same company (let alone the same industry)—to join a union that they believe may not really be able to help them in any meaningful way in the short term. For today's worker who feels no more loyalty to his company than his company has traditionally felt toward him, the union may not be a part of the solution unless he is working in an office in which union membership is mandatory. So the probability that you as a worker will belong to a union is little more than 1 in 9 and, if the existing trends of declining membership continue to hold, the odds will increase to 1 in 10 in the not-too-distant future.

But even though organized labor is not as dominant a force in the American economy as it was a generation ago, strikes do occur but admittedly with less frequency than in the past. Does this mean that we are entering a new age in which enlightened management and altruistic labor unions have forged a new alliance to promote the common good of workers? The answer is not very clear. It is true that work stoppages have—according to the Bureau of Labor Statistics—declined greatly in the past few decades, dropping from a peak of 381 strikes in 1970 involving 2,468,000 workers entailing the loss of 52,761,000 workdays to just thirty-four strikes in 1998 with 387,000 workers losing a total of 5,116,000 workdays. Such a precipitous decline is astounding and may reflect that senior management and organized labor have become united in brotherhood. Or it may mean that there are other factors that have come into play to ensure an apparently placid if still unsettled labor-management relation. One argument is that the American economy has enjoyed unprecedented prosperity through most of the 1980s and 1990s and more Americans—including unionized workers—have been able to share in this new prosperity. Another argument is that the vast expansion of non-union (particularly service) industries in the past few decades has simply diluted the power of unions in general and, given the widespread recognition of increased global competition in almost every industry, made them much more reluctant to try to use strikes for fear that management would try to insulate itself from future work stoppages by such measures as hiring non-union workers or shifting production facilities offshore.

What are the odds that you will be involved in a strike? Well, the answer depends on whether you are management or labor. If you are the president of a multibillion-dollar company, you are by definition management and no amount of persuasion will enable you to be included in the ranks of the union that organized your employees. It simply would not make any sense because your interests are considered to be adversarial to those of your workers because you want to hire their labor for the lowest amount of money possible whereas they want to get the highest wages possible . . . and reserved parking and on-premises childcare services and nondeductible medical coverage and free orthodontia care and frequent flyer points and company-contributed pension plans and—well, you get the picture. So presidents of corporations are typically excluded from participating in strikes.

What if you are a member of the urban proletariat—a poor soul who has been oppressed by the greed of your capitalistic warmongering manager? What would be the probability that you will be nailing signs together that call for the overthrow of the corporate oligarchists who have made it impossible for you to earn a decent salary or to afford a new automobile or to send your children to college? You do need to be working in a unionized workplace to have any chance of being called upon by the union to take to the streets and raise your fists in anger at the faceless bureaucrats who have tried to work you to the bone and refused to give you that fourth week of paid vacation this year. But as the sheer drop in work stoppages has shown, the likelihood that you will be called upon to go out into the streets and storm the Winter Palace is increasingly remote.

In 1998, there were approximately 16,211,000 union members of which, according to the Bureau of Labor Statistics, 387,000 union workers went on strike. In terms of aggregate statistics, this would suggest that each unionized worker had a 1-in-41.8 chance of going on strike. Of course the fact that only about 2.3 percent of all workers went on strike illustrates the increasing irrelevance of strikes in the calculations of most unions and management representatives. Certainly it is great fun to threaten to shut down an employer with a crippling strike but it seems as though this weapon is used so little anymore that it may become virtually irrelevant. After all, the threat of a strike is only viable so long as the employer believes that a strike is actually possible. But it may be that the political landscape has changed so that unions are reluctant to risk engaging in work stoppages except in the most desperate of situations. Or could it be that most workers were so happy with their wages and benefits that they did not feel particularly compelled to consider going on strike? The answer is not altogether clear but it may be that many workers, having seen millions of jobs move overseas and millions of workers suffer through repeated layoffs or downsizings, are very reluctant to rock the boat. During recent years, however, the job markets for skilled workers have become extremely tight and employers have found it more and more difficult to fill certain types of skilled positions. So it may be that this comparative labor peace has resulted from the desires of both labor and management to take steps to try to minimize work stoppages by acting in a conciliatory manner and by avoiding extreme positions that might provoke damaging responses by the other side. And while this relative calm may not make for great newspaper copy, it does help to ensure that fewer companies will be shut down and fewer numbers of workers will find themselves standing alongside highways and in front of company buildings, holding signs and chanting antimanagement slogans.

8

DOCTORS AND
LAWYERS

Americans—like most other people in the world—have a love-hate relationship with their jobs. In short, they love to hate their jobs—or at least complain about their jobs. But those very same people would be at a loss if they did not have their jobs because they would have to channel their energies and leisure into their relationships with their spouses and children. This dreary prospect would, of course, be unpalatable to most people who would find themselves forced to communicate with persons with whom they had formerly been content to toss an occasional "hello" to or "how was school today?" No, the stress of greater intrafamily communications would doubtless prove to be too much for most people and would probably contribute to record numbers of heart attacks.

Instead we should be grateful for the fact that we have jobs to which we can hurry after yet another interminable weekend of family togetherness has finally ended. But we are all aware that we go to work for reasons beyond those of avoiding family meetings and your neighbor's child's birthday party. Indeed, it is our jobs that define who we are and create the image that we project to society as a whole. But there is a more fundamental reason that causes us to get up each day and trudge to our windowless cubicles: the need to earn money and—more pointedly—put food on the table and clothes on our back and lottery tickets in our pockets. Even though we may all derive some sense of personal satisfaction from having careers and places to go during the 9-to-5 workday so that we will have something to talk about when we see our friends, relatives, and neighbors, there are a few people who might—dare we say it—be content to leave their jobs behind. But those persons are few and far between because a number of them have already been arrested and thrown into jail for being lazy malcontents.

But for those of us who must work in order to survive, we must necessarily be concerned with our careers and the rate at which we are advancing—both in terms of our movement up the corporate ladder as well as our ever growing rate of compensation. If money is a concern, however, we may want to try to find out how we are doing as compared to the average workers in our particular occupation. In other words, we can look at the average salaries for computer programmers, for example, and determine if we are in fact woefully underpaid and should in fact consider selling company secrets in order to supplement our income. But the U.S. Bureau of Labor Statistics collects huge amounts of data on hundreds and hundreds of occupations to try to determine the average rates of compensation so that most of us can feel inadequate and underpaid. But the bureau's ongoing efforts to collect such data does have a positive effect because it can show us some of the career opportunities we should consider if we wish to increase our earning power. For example, I might currently be working as a cashier at the Greasy Piggy barbeque earning $5 an hour and decide that I want to earn more money as a surgeon.

Leaving aside the fact that I had not completed high school—let alone college or medical school—I would first want to check the U.S. Bureau of Labor Statistics to see if it would be worth my while financially to become a surgeon. After all, I would not want to have to go to the trouble to complete high school, college, and medical school—as well as a few internships and residencies—in the next year only to find that I would not be able to earn more than $4.50 an hour as a surgeon. So it is clear that one should take the trouble to at least scout out whether it is truly worthwhile to undertake a particular career path before expending the time and energy and money necessary to obtain that objective.

MY CHILD, THE DOCTOR

But if money is our objective then we want to focus on those occupations which yield the greatest return and make it possible to buy big houses, fancy cars, and hideously gaudy huge chunks of jewelry. If we like the idea of being a surgeon, then we have made a good choice as we find that physicians as a group enjoy one of the highest median weekly earnings of full-time workers, with more than $1,200 per week. But surgeons are among the elite of physicians and are able to command much higher salaries than would presumably be far greater than those enjoyed by the more run-of-the-mill physicians who prescribe pills and say magic words to make children's boo-boos feel better. Indeed, the American Medical Association reports that the median pretax income of surgeons had climbed to nearly $230,000 per year by 1996. As the median pretax income of surgeons had been about $129,000 in 1985, the surgeons as a group by 1996 had seen a dramatic rise of their pretax income of $101,000 per year, an increase of about 78 percent.

But what are the odds that one can become a physician—let alone a surgeon who is able to reap a yearly income that would feed a small town? Well, we should point out that doctors have been proliferating almost as rapidly as attorneys in the past few decades. Indeed, the American Medical Association reports that the numbers of physicians in the United States has increased from 219,997 in 1950 to 260,484 in 1960 to 334,028 in 1970 to 467,679 in 1980 to 615,421 in 1990 to 737,764 in 1996. This proliferation was prompted by many factors including an

The Number of Doctors in the United States

Year	Number of Doctors	Number of Doctors Per 100,000 Persons
1950	219,997	142
1960	260,484	142
1970	334,028	161
1980	467,679	202
1990	615,421	244
1996	737,764	278

Source of Statistics: American Medical Association

expanding population coupled with growing affluence. Many people decided it would be a good idea to take up doctoring instead of more physically demanding occupations such as ditch digging and welding because one could work inside most of the time but still leave the more unpleasant tasks such as talking with the patients and changing the dressings and administering enemas to nurses and other persons who enjoy the glamour of the medical profession.

But the increasing numbers of physicians practicing in the United States do not really give us a clear idea as to the odds of becoming a physician because one also needs to consider how the ratio of the number of doctors to the population at large has changed. The American Medical Association reports that the number of physicians per 100,000 persons in the population has increased from 142 in 1950 to 142 in 1960 (admittedly, not much of an increase) to 161 in 1970 to 202 in 1980 to 244 in 1990 to 278 in 1996 to 352 by the year 2000. This statistic suggests that there are now more than twice as many doctors for a given number of persons as there were in 1950. Whether this increase in the number of physicians was prompted by a greater desire to serve humanity is subject to debate. But it does suggest that more persons are able to make a living as physicians now than ever before which is good news for people who desire a career path that is replete with social status, monetary rewards, and choice tables in fine restaurants.

With more than 350 physicians for every 100,000 persons, we can now have a physician in every neighborhood in the country if we so desire. The problem with trying to spread out our physicians evenly is that there are some neighborhoods that can boast incredible wealth and extraordinary homes and other neighborhoods where you are safest crawling around on your elbows when crossing the floor of your living room for fear of being gunned down through the picture window. Most physicians, not surprisingly, do not want to live in neighborhoods in which they fear for their lives and cannot risk parking their Mercedes on the streets for fear that they will have only a set of axles upon their return. People do not want to spend many years in medical school and incur massive personal debts to pay for their education only to end up living in a war zone. So what we find is that there is a very uneven distribution of physicians in America with most tending to settle down in the most affluent regions of the country and comparatively few choosing to set up shop in the poor urban and rural areas where there is the greatest need for their services. As a result, some of the wealthiest communities in America are overwhelmed with physicians, much in the same ways that the nation's political parties are overrun with rats and other vermin. You cannot walk more than a few feet down some of the nation's ritziest neighborhoods without passing by someone who specializes in diseases of the overinsured and obnoxiously wealthy where the symptoms can be whatever the patient with an infinite pocketbook can dream up.

There is also a pecking order among the states themselves as to the ratio of the number of doctors to the population as a whole. Not surprisingly, the states with the highest concentrations of doctors include Massachusetts (426 doctors per 100,000 population), New York (395 doctors per 100,000 population), New Jersey (306 doctors per 100,000 population), Pennsylvania (303 doctors per 100,000 population), Florida (277 doctors per 100,000 population), and California (276 doctors per 100,000 population). These states typically boast higher per capita incomes than most of the other states. The wealthier populations found in these states also include many older persons who require greater levels of medical care than the average person and therefore support more extensive hospitals, greater numbers of physicians, more diagnostic tests and interminable visits to doctors' waiting rooms, and, ultimately, more fees.

Many persons have wondered whether America is becoming overdoctored due to the concentration of physicians in the nation's cities. While it is comforting to know that you cannot walk more than a few feet in any direction without passing a doctor's office, one cannot help but wonder whether the continuing proliferation of doctors is actually providing a better quality of health care to the population as a whole. The quality of care and health insurance in general are topics that can usually be counted upon to provoke heated debates among any gathering of persons, particularly when most people believe that any efforts to contain medical costs such as managed-care plans will lead to reduced healthcare quality or doctors who learn their trade by video or mail. Certainly you could not arouse the same passions that would accompany a discussion regarding health maintenance organizations (HMOs) with a subject such as the quality of apples for sale at the grocery store. While people may not like the fact that some of the apples they purchase at the store are "woody" in texture, they will not bother to air their feelings to the point of coming to blows with each other. But pity the poor fellow who ventures into a crowd and claims that managed care is the greatest invention in the history of humanity and he will more than likely be set upon as though he were a piece of meat thrown to a ravenous pack of wild dogs.

But to return to our analysis of our odds for becoming a physician, we can first look at the previous figures we discussed which show that there is about one physician out of every 350 people in the United States. With any statistical figure, one has to be careful as to the conclusions one can draw, and the ratio of physicians to the general population is no exception. The fact that only one out of every 350 persons in the United States is a physician does not mean that you cannot be a physician if one of your neighbors is already a physician. This figure does not have an element of determinism or predestination; it is merely an averaging of the number of physicians relative to the population as a whole. If you desire to be a physician and determine that you can add an additional dollar or two to the hourly wages to be earned at the Greasy Piggy, there is nothing other than your own mental and physical limitations and tolerance for financial indebtedness to stand in the way of your becoming a physician. Of course physicians also need to have a tolerance for peering inside gaping wounds and finding their way through the body cavities of their patients without fainting, laughing, or vomiting. So not everyone has the fortitude to be a physician and, quite frankly, not everyone wants to spend all of their time with sick people—particularly those who do not have a lot of money. But the point of the matter is that the statistic is merely a reflection of the decisions of persons throughout the country to pursue or not pursue a medical career; it does not determine in any way whether you can pursue a medical career or not. So even if you live on a block that is choked with physicians of all types, you can still decide to pursue a medical career—even though your block may be far and away the most highly concentrated center of medical talent in the country.

But what are the odds that you could find yourself working in a particular specialty in the medical field? The American Medical Association reports that the distribution of leading specialties among physicians in 1999 was as follows: anesthesiology (4.3 percent), family practice (8.6 percent), general practice (1.9 percent), general surgery (4.9 percent), obstetrics/gynecology (4.9 percent), pediatrics (7.4 percent), and psychiatry (4.8 percent). These figures do provide some interesting insights into the distribution of specialties in the medical profession and suggest that family doctors are the most common type of doctor, although those who actually make housecalls are doubtless the rarest kind of physician. But these figures also make it possible for us to discern the extent to which there is a demand for each of these types of physicians and, possibly, the extent to which physicians themselves wish to make their living in each of these specialties. On the face of it, we might draw the conclusion that there are more people (general surgeons) who like to cut into the side of a human being like a butcher carving a hind quarter than there are people (anesthesiologists) who are content merely to knock patients out with gas. But it is extremely risky and indeed reckless to use statistics by themselves to make inferences about the motivations that cause people to go into medicine. Indeed, we might use such logic to infer that obstetricians/gynecologists are more likely to develop unique ways to meet women merely because they like to place their patients on examination tables with their feet in stirrups. But the reality of it is that there are a myriad of reasons that compel a physician to choose a certain occupation, including the perceived intellectual challenges, the expected financial renumeration, the opportunity to wear those cool-looking surgical scrubs, and the opportunities to see attractive people in various states of undress. Of course some persons such as proctologists probably do not view the "naked" factor with quite the same enthusiasm.

We hear a lot about how more and more women are joining the ranks of all professions and the same is true of the medical profession. In 1975, only about 9.1 percent or 35,636 women out of a total of 393,742 licensed physicians in the United States were in the medical profession. By 1985, there were 80,725 women out of a total of 552,716 licensed physicians; their ranks having swelled to more than 14.6 percent. This trend continued onward for the following decade so that by 1999 nearly 23.3 percent of all physicians or 186,606 out of 797,634 of all physicians were women. This movement toward a more equal representation of the sexes in the medical business was especially pronounced among physicians under 35 who had seen the percentage of female physicians rise from 12.5 percent in 1975 to 24.2 percent in 1985 to 35.6 percent in 1996 to 39.3 percent in 1999. So the prospects for women physicians appear increasingly brighter with time as they move to a more equal representation of their gender in the medical profession. Unfortunately, this very same medical profession is beset by all sorts of cost-containment pressures which will continue to make it progressively more difficult for physicians to enjoy a lifestyle of conspicuous consumption. In short, the rise of managed care—particularly HMOs, PPOs, and many other Os, has put what may be a permanent crimp in the ability of most physicians to earn the dollars that formerly were considered to be a birthright. But we do not see many physicians standing on streetcorners holding signs such as "Will Give Physicals for Food" or "Will Perform Angioplasty for Clothes," so any concerns about physicians being unable to make a living and having to live in flophouses and cardboard boxes are premature. Moreover, government assistance programs such as Medicare and Medicaid coupled with the private health insurance coverage enjoyed by most Americans plus the strength of the American Medical Association will help to ensure that we will not have thousands of physicians pressing empty tin cups in the paths of passersby in the hopes of receiving a few pennies or perhaps selling a pencil or two.

But the difficulties of earning a huge income as a doctor may pale when compared to the obstacles that face applicants seeking admission to medical school. In *Getting into Medical School*, Sanford J. Brown points out that 41,064 applicants filled out a total of 481,336 applications (about twelve per applicant) in 1999. Of these applicants, approximately 16,221 or 39.5 percent ultimately took their seats as the members of the newest entering class. These are not terribly good odds and underscore the fact that there is a far greater demand by students for admission to medical school than there are seats in the nation's medical schools to meet this demand. This imbalance has resulted in many persons who would make excellent doctors ultimately being left out in the cold.

Yet an applicant's admission to medical school may represent only the beginning of his headaches. Most students will have to borrow a lot of money to finish their medical studies; these amounts may range up to $150,000. If the applicant has the good fortune to be born into a wealthy family, this will not be an issue as "Mommy" or "Daddy" can write a check to cover the tuition and not give it a further thought. But most students will have to confront the following question: Is a medical education a sound investment? There is no single answer to this question because it ultimately depends on (1) whether the student plans to practice medicine; (2) the amount of dollars that the student can earn practicing medicine; and (3) the actual cost of the education. Because any or all of these factors change almost constantly, it is impossible to devise a single chart that can apply to all persons in all other situations.

LAWYERS, LAWYERS, LAWYERS

Although the medical profession offers prestige and handsome incomes to most of its practitioners, particularly those who venture into private service, not everyone has the desire to be a physician. Does this mean that those people who do not like dissecting cadavers in medical school have no hope of making big dollars and donning rubber gloves at cocktail parties and daring fellow patrons to cough? Well, there are other avenues to wealth and power—perhaps none more direct or in the crosshairs of public hostility than attorneys or, as they are more commonly known, mercenary barbarians. But the hostility toward lawyers has always been common among the population as a whole and this may stem from the unique positions lawyers or persons who have a legal background have occupied in the halls of government throughout history. But whether you see lawyers as shining soldiers of democracy who are bulwarks of freedom or as dirty thieving bastards who are interested only in lining their pockets, it seems as though attorneys are lightning rods of controversy because of the central roles they play in political and legal matters. But the public perception is often at odds with the everyday reality. Few lawyers would consider themselves to be power brokers even though the very few who occupy such positions in our nation's great cities often come disproportionately from the legal ranks.

But for those who would like to pursue a legal career and become the butt of endless numbers of jokes, there is much good news. Many law schools have opened over the past few decades and enrollments have swelled. As with physicians, lawyers have been featured in numerous television shows and movies and, as a result, have rightly or wrongly acquired something of a glamorous image. This idea that lawyers always dine in fancy restaurants and drive fancy cars and spend their weekends traveling to exotic places is, sadly for most lawyers, more of a perception than a reality. Indeed, most lawyers would be quite happy to live the glamorous life they see portrayed in the media and would probably be less concerned about the barbs they endure if they could live in such a fast lane. But lawyers are also seen as enjoying extraordinary incomes; this belief has prompted many tens of thousands of persons to endure the often mind-numbing tedium of three years of law school only to find that very little of what they had learned had anything to do with the actual practice of the law.

How have the numbers of lawyers increased over the years? The American Bar Association notes that the legal ranks numbered a mere 326,842 in 1970 but grew to 574,810 in 1980 and 755,694 in 1990 and, more recently, 985,900 in 1997. You would think that Americans as a whole would be profoundly grateful for the prolific output of newly minted attorneys over the past few decades but the continued torrent of lawyer jokes suggests that the general public has yet to recognize the good fortune that has been bestowed upon it by the nation's law schools.

Any profession that can boast a tripling of its ranks in a generation from 1970 to 1997 must have something going for it because the growth of the legal profession has certainly outstripped the growth of the population as a whole. Indeed, the U.S. Census Bureau informs us that the population of the United States was 203,302,000 in 1970 but increased to 226,546,000 in 1980 (an increase of 11.4 percent) and then increased to 249,398,000 in 1990 (an increase of 10.1 percent) and then increased still further to 268,922,000 in 1998 (an increase of 7.8 percent). These numbers show that the general population is increasing at a rate of about 10 percent per decade or about 1 percent per year. At the same time, however, the ratio of lawyers to the population of the whole has increased from one lawyer in 622 people in 1970 to one lawyer in 394 people in 1980 to one lawyer in 330 people in 1990. As of 1997, we were fortunate enough to have one lawyer for every 272 people. The obvious point is that the number of lawyers is growing far faster than the population as a whole which means, of course, that in the not-so-distant future, every family will have a lawyer and, ultimately, every person shall be a lawyer. (Just kidding!) Nevertheless, how long will it take for this happy event to occur when every schoolchild can file a complaint against his teacher for the intentional infliction of emotional distress? If we play a little game and extrapolate the two trends of population growth in general and the growth in lawyers in particular, then we find that the trends would tend to converge if the ratios continued to decrease. The increase in the ratios of lawyers to the population (an increase of 228 [one in 622 to one in 394] from 1970 to 1980, an increase of 64 [one in 394 to one in 330] from 1980 to 1990, and an increase of 58 [one in 330 to one in 272] from 1990 to 1998) show that the profusion of lawyers was slowing in relative terms but was still resulting in a national landscape increasingly clogged up with persons educated in the "wheretofores" and "hereinafters" of the legal world.

Most lawyers say they are generally content with their lot in life. Part of their satisfaction stems from the challenges of their jobs and, in more than a few cases, the amount of compensation they receive. But lawyers, like everyone else, cast covetous eyes at other professions which seem to have certain advantages, such as the medical profession. Why would lawyers be envious of doctors? Well, there is the advantage that doctors seem to be more highly regarded than lawyers in the eyes of most persons—even some lawyers. Doctors are viewed as healers whereas lawyers are typically viewed as "hired guns" or, in some quarters, "agents of Satan." But lawyers do play major—indeed dominant— roles in politics, business, and, yes, the nation's courthouses. However, they are not very good at carrying out even the most routine surgical procedures—never mind complex medical operations—and therefore have not much opportunity to appear as gods in their clients' eyes. This admittedly remote likelihood of deification is usually squashed altogether once the clients receive their invoices for services rendered and thereby lose any remaining warm and fuzzy feelings about their legal representatives. On the other hand, very few lawyers can actually kill their clients by accidentally severing an artery or removing the wrong organ or even using the wrong anesthesia. Lawyers are quite capable of costing their clients a great deal of money if they should mishandle a transaction but they are not usually responsible for the loss of a client's leg or arm or any other appendage.

As the ratio of lawyers to the general population as a whole is now about one in 270, we have reached the brave new world in which the legal population is about to cross the one million mark and thereby signify the onset of the end of the world. As the national population is about 270 times the size of the nation's legal population, there is still much work to be done by the nation's law schools to enroll and graduate the other 269/270ths of the population which has not had the fortune of enduring three years of indoctrination as to the elements of contracts, torts, property law, civil procedure, constitutional law, and criminal law. Then every man, woman, and child can obtain a license to practice law and engage in complex litigation and sue all of their neighbors, friends, and relatives.

But the real issue of this digression into irrelevance is to discuss the odds that a person can become a lawyer. As with physicians, the odds are merely the dividing of the total number of persons who actually become attorneys into the total number of persons who live in the population. But any one person may choose to enroll in a law school without regard to whether any of his relatives, friends, or neighbors make a similar decision. The statistics surrounding the pool of lawyers in the nation's population are thus devoid of any determinism, and any single individual is free to pursue his or her dreams of glory in the courtrooms. Whether every person on your street or no one within a mile of your house has studied law is really of no consequence as to whether you decide to pursue such a career.

But deciding to initiate a legal career is not the same as actually applying to a law school, being accepted by a law school, graduating from a law school, passing the state licensing board exam, and actually beginning to practice law. There is a certain amount of attrition at each stage of this process in that more people apply to law school than actually get in, more people matriculate at law school than actually graduate from law school, more people graduate from law school than actually pass the state licensing board exam, and more people pass the state licensing board exam than actually practice law. So there is a certain degree of "leakage" throughout the legal educational system with which anyone who wishes to study law should probably be acquainted. But we can better understand the probability that law school applicants shall become practicing lawyers by looking at the numbers that are generated by these would-be attorneys in any given year.

According to the *Kaplan-Newsweek Law School Admissions Adviser*, the nation's law schools received applications from an estimated 67,500 applicants in 1999 from which about 44,000 students were ultimately selected. Of course the joy of entering law school was quickly muted by the actual law school experience that consists of Socratic lectures and enormous amounts of dry reading. On the plus side, however, no one has to cut open a cadaver—which many law students consider to be quite a compelling reason to study law instead of medicine. The important point, however, is that 65 percent of all applicants to law school were actually accepted to a law school—an acceptance rate that is nearly twice as high as that of the nation's medical schools. Whether some of these applicants who were unsuccessful in the applications process had a change of heart midway through the process and decided to pursue careers elsewhere or simply lost interest in a legal career altogether does not detract from the fact that fewer people enrolled in law school than had originally applied. But this is not the end of the story because the National Association for Law Placement's (NALP) *Jobs and JDs* tells us that about 6 percent of those who enroll will ultimately decide to drop out before they graduate. So the cumulative effect between application and graduation will be to see the original applicant pool reduced by some 61.1 percent.

But that is not the end of the obstacle course that greets all would-be attorneys. The first barrier is the bar exam itself which, in most states, is a two-day ordeal that tests the ability of newly minted graduates to regurgitate legal theories and concepts and apply them to hypothetical situations. The passing rates of these bar exams can vary dramatically from state to state and from summer to winter. But the bar exam is the last real obstacle to any person's desire to practice law and, eventually, an estimated 80 percent of all takers will receive a passing grade. But some of the persons who sit for the exam will, despite their best efforts and their promises to God to attend church or synagogue regularly, be unable to pass the exam and thus be forced to look for some other avenue of employment. These persons, who will swear their undying hatred for the state's bar examiners, will further reduce the numbers that are able to navigate the rocks and shoals inherent in the legal educational process so that less than one-half of the original applicant pool will actually obtain a license to practice law.

But not all persons who are licensed to practice law will actually choose to practice law. Some will meet the heir or heiress of their dreams and immediately drop any plans to worry about getting a job with a company or law firm. Others will find that the rough-and-tumble world of courtroom jousting or the piles of paperwork that accompany most transactions are not to their liking. Still others will be surprised to find that their first legal job will not invariably be accompanied by the offer of a complementary Mercedes-Benz or a low-interest loan on an estate home or even a corner office with a view of the harbor. The reality that becomes immediately apparent to most new lawyers is that there is a glaring discrepancy between the law business as it is portrayed on television and in the movies and the real world of legal practice. The salary will not seem so generous after the lawyer is forced to work nights and weekends (even though the starting salary may be in excess of $100,000, which in a work year of 2,500 hours will equal to $40 per hour). Moreover, the attorney may be surprised to find that the supply of free Mercedes-Benzes has run out and that any low-interest loans would probably not even be adequate to purchase a cold-water flat. But the job of the lawyer is like any other job in that most of it involves routine, often monotonous tasks. Very few lawyers get to jet off to Washington, D.C., to argue before the U.S. Supreme Court or meet with corporate leaders to discuss international trade policies—at least not in the first year of their careers.

But the odds of becoming a practicing lawyer, while not forbidding, are significant and do need to be considered by anyone who is thinking about going to law school. Law school, like medical school, is a significant investment of time, energy, and money and those who go forward should have at least some desire to follow it all the way through or otherwise make alternative plans to start dating well-to-do people with bad hearts, big trust accounts, and trusting natures. But whether one chooses a career in law or medicine is less important than an understanding that there is an attrition process involved in getting to the beginning of the career itself, which in turn underscores the fact that the odds of

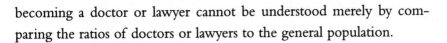

becoming a doctor or lawyer cannot be understood merely by comparing the ratios of doctors or lawyers to the general population.

9

WHO WANTS
AN AUDIT?

All red-blooded Americans consider it a sacred duty to pay their taxes because we trust that our government has the interests of the general population in mind and will allocate our tax dollars to pay for those programs that provide the greatest good to the greatest number of people. Indeed, we consider the payment of taxes—whether income, estate, excise, sales, or otherwise—to be a privilege of citizenship. For many, it is troubling that our tax burden seems to be too low in view of the wondrous bounty that is given to us by the wise leaders who run our country. We can only marvel that the funds taxed from each of us are collected together and disbursed in ways that fund a wide variety of programs that only the most narrow-minded among us would characterize as "bloated boondoggles." The simple fact is that taxes are necessary to provide for a government that can ensure the general welfare and promote the common good. But there are still many persons who think that they should not have to pay any of their hard-earned dollars to the government because they believe that they alone should prosper from the fruits of their labors. Of course these are the very same people who complain about the decimation of the nation's military forces or the poor quality of public schools or even the conditions of the highways and thereby conveniently ignore the critical role government taxation plays in funding the continued upgrading of the nation's economic infrastructure.

There is an old saying about not being able to avoid death and taxes. Of course there are some persons who believe that old sayings are not always 100 percent accurate and that one can avoid taxes if one employs high-powered lawyers and accountants and keeps two or three sets of books. Doing business in cash only is one way that go-getter entrepreneurs who have philosophical difficulties with the concept of paying income taxes can shelter their income. Cash transactions have no real paper trail and would-be income shelterers may create very imaginative schemes for hiding their income or, at the very least, underreporting the receipts from their businesses. Of course this is an approach that has never been used by legitimate cash businesses but there is always the possibility that one or two rascals might be tempted to try to shirk his or her fair share of the tax burden. But certainly that would never occur to the rest of us who despair that our leaders do not have enough of our revenues to allocate to their pet programs. How many times have each of us lay awake at night, wondering whether we should have tossed a few extra dollars into the government till to help make ends meet?

But this book is geared toward educating all segments of society as to certain odds and probabilities—including that segment which is interested in tax avoidance or even tax—dare we say it—evasion, a felony. Indeed, Al Capone, perhaps one of the most sinister gangsters of the 20th century, was finally sent to jail not for racketeering or murder but for tax evasion. But we should not be so quick to condemn those who would seek to minimize their tax burdens but should instead stand up for their right to hide their hard-earned gains in their mattresses, their front yards, or wherever else they may choose to conceal their dollars. In seeking to play a constructive role, it remains for us to examine the mechanism that prods us to pay our taxes in the first place—the fear of being audited and, if successfully prosecuted for tax evasion, the very real fear of spending twenty or thirty years in a federal prison sharing a cell with a sweaty gentleman named Alf who insists on your combing the hair on his back.

But is the fear of an audit so real for most individuals? The answer depends in part on the nature of the entity filing the return (individual versus corporation) and the amount of income claimed on the return. It also varies to some extent from year to year—even though the total number of returns continues to climb each year due to the natural increases in the population of the tax-paying public. According to the Internal Revenue Service, the total number of tax returns processed in 1990 was 201,715,000 but rose to 205,747,000 in 1995 and increased still further to 224,453,000 in 1998. Of these totals, individual returns totaled 112,492,000 in 1990, 116,298,000 in 1995, and 123,000,000 in 1998, respectively. In a country of about 275,000,000 persons, nearly one out of every two American citizens—regardless of age, race, gender, or ethnicity—filed personal income tax returns. What is truly heartening, however, is that recent efforts to create a "kinder, gentler" Internal Revenue Service have greatly reduced the frequency with which returns are audited. The *New York Time Almanac 2001* reports that the Internal Revenue Service audited 2.13 million returns of a total number of 155 million tax returns filed, a rate of 1.3 percent. In 1998, however, the Internal Revenue Service had reduced its enforcement efforts to such an extent that it audited only about 1,360,000 returns out of nearly 161 million returns filed—thus representing an aggregate audit rate of only about 0.8 percent. This means that individuals who wished to test the patience of the government and the actual odds that they would get audited by very angry, underpaid civil servants was not very high at all and certainly not of a sufficiently high likelihood to strike fear into the hearts of most taxpayers. Indeed, many Americans were saddened to see that the Internal Revenue Service has evolved from a beastly bureaucracy that once terrorized the wealthiest citizens and the largest corporations alike into a much more "touchy feely" organization that seems to be more concerned with the rights of taxpayers and not playing the federal "heavy." It is hard to fathom why anyone would want to live in a country in which the Internal Revenue Service was not viewed as the equivalent of an organizational Antichrist. Indeed, we should be concerned that our society may be softening too much when we do not break into a cold sweat at night worrying about having our financial records reviewed in painful detail by an auditor who is bent upon climbing up the corporate ladder using our carcasses as a sturdy first rung. Can an America that no longer fears the petty excesses of its most overreaching agency truly consider itself a superpower?

The answers to these daunting philosophical questions are not easily ascertained but it does appear to be the case that Americans are less likely to be audited now than they have ever been in recent memory. Although this would appear to be a good thing, this increasing laxness on the part of the government may have some unintended consequences because it may encourage people to do anything they can to avoid paying taxes. Although this may seem to be a perfectly healthy attitude, it will probably lead to greater taxes for those of us who continue to file our returns every year because we will have to make up for the shortfalls resulting from the nonpayments of our fellow tax revolutionaries.

But there is more to the story than merely the aggregate numbers because they only tell us that there has been a general downward trend in the rates at which individuals and corporations have been audited in the past decade. Although the Internal Revenue Service has begun to chant the mantra "Love thy taxpayer" and treat taxpayers as human beings, we taxpayers want to know what factors will affect the probability of being audited. The fact that fewer of our fellow citizens will receive the dreaded notification letter from the Internal Revenue Service is not very much comfort. As a result, we should also consider the various factors that affect the probability that a taxpayer will be audited—namely, income and entity status. Indeed, these are the only two factors that appear to figure into the decision by the Internal Revenue Service to audit a return and the odds of being audited can vary greatly depending on these facts.

Internal Revenue Service Audit Rates for U.S. Taxpayers

Income	Number of Returns Filed	Number of Audited Returns	Audit Rate
$0.00–25,000	58,266,600		
	45,343,300 (1090A)	515,015	0.0113
	12,923,300 (non-1040A)	104,050	0.8
$25,001–$49,999	28,292,600	165,168	0.58
$50,000–$99,999	19,443 3,700	121,384	0.062
$100,000+	6,044,700	100,079	0.016

Source of Statistics: *Internal Revenue Service 1998 Data Book*

If we consider individual returns, we find that there is no hard and fast rule as to predicting the likelihood of an audit because the statistics show that increased income does not necessarily lead to increased probabilities of being audited. According to the *Internal Revenue Service 1998 Data Book*, there were 58,266,600 taxpayers who filed individual returns reporting total personal income (TPI) of less than $25,000 (excluding schedule C returns but including both 1040A and non-1040A returns). Of the 45,343,300 1040A returns with TPI of less than $25,000, the Internal Revenue Service examined 515,015 for a total of 1.13 percent. Of the 12,923,300 non-1040A returns with TPI of less than $25,000, the IRS audited 104,050 for a total of 0.8 percent. Although we might want to impute some sinister motive to the different audit rates between the 1040A and non-1040A returns such as a government-wide conspiracy, there is actually very little difference statistically—one-fifth of 1 percent—between the two numbers. So if the differing audit rates result from the existence of a vast right-wing conspiracy, then it is admittedly not very much of a conspiracy. Suffice it to say, the taxpayers in this particular income class have about a

1-in-100 chance of being audited overall. This is not the sort of odds that will cause most people to begin keeping notebooks of daily expenditures and receipts or even reporting all of their cash earnings.

But what happens as we move higher up the income ladder? Do the scofflaws get their due and get audited or do they simply laugh in the face of threats of federal prosecution and go on their merry way? If we return to the Internal Revenue Service's own statistics and look at the 28,292,600 returns filed by persons making between $25,000 and $50,000 each year, we find that the auditors snagged 165,168 returns. This represented a slight decline in the audit rate to 0.58 percent. Certainly the notion of conspiracies to defraud working-class families of their hard-earned tax dollars must be considered because the audit rate drops by nearly one-half of a percent when the taxpayer crosses the $25,000 income threshold! But the statistican would likely scoff at such an idea, arguing that a decline of one-half of 1 percent in the audit rate is hardly reflective of a conscious effort to hammer lower-income families with a disproportionate number of audited returns. But it does seem strange that there would be a higher rate of audits among returns below $25,000 than those reporting between $25,000 and $50,000. But as with every other politically charged argument, there are other reasons that should be considered as to why a counterintuitive result would occur. First, those making less than $25,000 are probably the least likely income group to hire a professional tax preparer to assist them with their taxes. As a result, these taxpayers could inadvertently make errors in their return which would trigger an IRS inquiry. Moreover, it may be that many of these audits were prompted by the occupations of the taxpayers themselves—those working in cash businesses, for example, would appear to be primary candidates for review by the federal government. In occupations where underreported income is a mantra, there is likely to be a tendency by the auditors to focus in on businesses (e.g., restaurants, services) in which there is no trail of income receipts. Of course cash businesses can be found at all income levels but it would not be surprising to find that certain occupations such as food servicers would report very little income due to their reliance on tips and fall in the under $25,000 income level.

If we move up to the $50,000 to $100,000 income level, we find that the Internal Revenue Service processed 19,443,700 returns and decided, for the sake of fun, to audit 121,384, for a rate of 0.62 percent. Though this rate means that roughly three more out of every thousand taxpayers in the $50,000 to $100,000 category are being audited than in the $25,000 to $50,000, it is still about half the rate of our lowest income bracket. As far as those fortunate taxpayers who make above $100,000 per year are concerned, they filed 6,044,700 returns and saw 100,079 of them audited by the government—a rate of 1.65 percent. This is truly puzzling because it is the first true sign of any type of progressivity in the audit rate with rising reported incomes—so that about one out of every sixteen taxpayers who reports in excess of $100,000 in income can expect to hear from the IRS.

But are the taxes and penalties that are obtained by the IRS commensurate with the taxpayers' respective income brackets? One would naturally be inclined to think that the bigger the return, the bigger the amount of taxes and penalties collected per return. At least that would be the logical and rational conclusion to draw. But we are admittedly dealing with the issue of taxation and the IRS, a subject in which logic and straightforward thinking often go out the window. And so it is the case that the expectation of increasingly larger collected amounts of penalties and interest with progressively larger incomes.

What is the average tax and penalty for each of these income brackets? For those taxpayers reporting less than $25,000, the average tax and penalty return was equal to $11,241 for 1040A returns and $10,049 for non-1040A returns. When one considers that these amounts were on average equal to more than 40 percent of the reported income, it is clear that these persons are subject to a very high nominal tax rate and probably in need of some tax advice. This thought is borne out by the fact that those taxpayers who earn between $25,000 and $50,000 pay an average tax and penalty equal to $9,544. So increased income and lower taxes suggests that the tax system has some regressive aspects which the government would rather not publicize. If we move up to the next income level ($50,000 to $100,000), then we find that the average taxes and penalties move back up to $10,048—one dollar less than the average taxes and penalties charged our most downtrodden income group. But before we give up in despair of ever seeing any sense in our tax system, we are relieved to find that those taxpayers who earn more than $100,000 per year paid an average tax and penalty equal to $31,053. This is clearly much more than the $10,049 being exacted from the hides of those earning less than $25,000 each year. But our temporary jubilation at the idea that the rich people have rolled into town to rescue the tax system from its own inequities is tempered by the realization that some of these rich persons earn millions, tens of millions, or even hundreds of millions of dollars a year. The fact that a centimillionaire who has homes on three continents and travels in a private jet plane paid $50,000 in taxes may be of small comfort to those less fortunate even though we could argue that $50,000 is indeed greater than $10,049. But also affecting the amount collected is the availability of deductions, most notably home mortgages and self-funded retirement plans such as IRAs and business expenses. The lower the income, the less likely that persons are able to take advantage of most tax shelters and reduce the amount of taxes owed. But this is of less comfort to those persons who find that the tax code is so riddled with exceptions, exemptions, credits, deductions, and all sorts of policy-driven devices that there the idea of a progressive tax system in which the wealthiest pay the greatest amount of taxes is undermined. Of course you may not lose very much sleep if you are fortunate enough to enjoy inherited wealth and a high income, because it really does no good to get aggravated over matters of social injustice. Indeed, one can scarcely enjoy a glass of Dom Perignon 1992 when riding in a charter jet plane if one has to think about all of the inequitable distribution of wealth in the world.

10

CRIME AND PUNISHMENT

Americans like to view the United States as an overachiever in all fields of human endeavor—whether it be industrial production, military prowess, athletic competition, wealth creation, or popular culture. But we should be pleased to learn that the United States is also the leader in violent crime and incarceration rates among the industrialized nations. Our citizens commit more murders, rapes, robberies, and burglaries than any other modern country and clearly stamp the United States as a country not to be trifled with due to the huge number of persons with obvious antisocietal and psychopathic tendencies. Although there are some persons who fret about the high rates of crime undermining the very fabric of our society, most of us would rather see our citizens err on the side of exuberance than act like mild-mannered mice and scurry away at the slightest sign of trouble. Indeed, violent crime can serve as a valuable safety-valve release because highly publicized criminal trials and the occasional execution can permit the general public to vent any feelings of revenge and anger and thus distract their attention from other issues such as the mismanaged economy and failing public schools.

In talking about crime and punishment, we really need to look at

181

A Comparison of Murder, Rape, and Robbery Crimes Rates in the United States and Great Britain 1981–1996

	Murder		Rape		Robbery	
	U.S.	England	U.S.	England	U.S.	England
1981	9.83	1.13	70.59	4.19	258.75	40.86
1985	7.95	1.24	72.83	7.19	208.54	54.94
1990	9.42	1.32	80.86	12.04	257.03	71.15
1995	8.22	1.44	72.73	18.90	220.95	131.37
1996	7.41	1.31	70.79	21.77	202.44	142.35

Source of Statistics: U.S. Bureau of Justice Statistics,
Crime and Justice in the U.S. and England and Wales, 1981–1996.

two types of probabilities: that of becoming a victim and that of being caught and locked up in prison or—in rare instances—executed. But we should begin with a broad review of the rate of serious crime in the United States which is provided to us by the Federal Bureau of Investigation, *Uniform Crime Reports: Crime in the United States 1998*, which examines the rates of change in serious crimes in the United States from 1975 to 1998. The good news is that most types of violent crime (murder, rape, robbery, assault) have steadily declined as have most types of property crime (burglary, larceny, motor vehicle theft). For the violent crimes, there has been noticeable declines in the past decade with murders declining from 23,440 to 16,910; rapes dropping from 102,560 to 93,100; robberies falling from 639,270 to 446,330; and aggravated assaults slipping from 1,054,860 to 974,400 in that very same time period. Property crimes have also declined significantly from 1990 to 1998, with burglaries falling 3,073,900 to 2,330,000; larcenies dropping from 7,945,700 to 7,373,900; and motor vehicle theft declining from 1,635,900 to 1,240,800. But these numbers, as pointed out by the *New York Times Almanac 2001*, only tell part of the story because crime rates are typically measured in terms of numbers of crimes per 100,000 persons. The fact that the rates of crime have continued to fall over the past quarter century while the population as a whole continued to increase understates the true decline in the crime rate. But this is not to say that you can now go through the most run-down neighborhoods in the country bedecked in jewelry and daring people to rob you because such behavior will almost invariably result in your getting robbed and probably beaten up—no matter how low the rate of crime. People have speculated as to the reasons behind this decline in the rate of crime but some of the more plausible factors include an aging population that is seeing proportionately fewer persons in their teens and early twenties (the age group most likely to engage in criminal behavior), an exploding jail population which has left fewer people on the streets to rob and kill the rest of us, greater numbers of police officers who have guns and billy clubs with which to subdue the aforementioned criminals, and a generally improved economic environment which has enabled many who might have otherwise been predisposed to criminal behavior to go into arguably related careers as stockbrokers and lawyers.

But these numbers are admittedly global in scale and they are not detailed enough to provide us with information as to the prevalence or absence of crime in a given city. If we were interested in deciding where to live and we were concerned about the crime rate, we might automatically rule out cities such as New York and Los Angeles that are the butts of jokes about criminal activity. But is the popular image accurate? Would we be better off moving to a smaller city or even out into the country where people greet each other by name and let their dogs and their children share the watering dish? Well, we can always speculate about the joy of living in a given area with reference to its level of criminal activity, but the only reliable way to arrive at a decision is to look at the Federal Bureau of Investigation's statistics for particular cities which are calculated as numbers of crimes committed per 100,000 population in given metropolitan areas. A review of these figures reveals that some of our perceptions about the most dangerous cities in the country may need to be revised.

New York City reported that the number of violent (murder, rape, robbery) crimes per 100,000 population declined from 1,865 in 1993 to 1,037 in 1998—a drop of almost 55 percent in five years. Those persons interested in sandy beaches, beautiful girls, and the tropical nightlife might be surprised to find that the city of Miami, Florida (also famous for its political machinations), had 2,136 violent crimes per 100,000 population in 1993 but that it had dropped to 1,281 by 1998 for that same 100,000 population. The point of this exercise (which could have been sponsored by the New York Chamber of Commerce) is that Miami had nearly 9 percent more violent crimes per 100,000 population than New York in 1993 and that gap did not narrow appreciably by 1998 when New York could still claim a lower incidence of violent crime (8 percent). Of course New York posted higher absolute numbers of violent crimes but that was due purely to its having a much larger population than Miami. The moral of the story is that being surrounded by bikini-clad supermodels and palm trees does not necessarily protect you from having your wallet taken or your car stolen or your life snuffed out. However, getting to sit in a beachside café in the middle of January with nothing more than shorts and sandals on and tossing back a few drinks may help to ease the angst that one might feel vacationing in one of America's most dangerous cities. However, one could still enjoy the beaches of Honolulu, Hawaii, which saw a comparatively lower violent crime rate drop from 285 per 100,000 population in 1993 to 267 per 100,000 population in 1998. If one could live with the long transoceanic flights to the Hawaiian Islands, then Honolulu might be just the thing for the person who desires both fine weather as well as relative freedom from criminal acts—about one-fifth the probability of being a victim of violent crime in Miami.

If you would like to minimize your chances of becoming a victim of violent crime, you might consider leaving the country altogether. But because you would probably prefer a country where the natives speak English, you might consider putting down roots in Merrie Olde England. A study by the U.S. Department of Justice—*Crime and Justice in the U.S. and England and Wales, 1981–1996*—offered an eye-opening comparison of the crime rates in the United States and England. In 1981, for example, the United States had a murder rate of 9.82 per 100,000 population whereas England had a rate of only 1.13 per 100,000 population. By 1997, the U.S. rate had fallen to 7.41 per 100,000 population whereas the murder rate in England had crept up slightly to 1.31 per 100,000. Now statisticians could offer a variety of reasons for the continuing differences in the murder rates in the two countries, such as the relative scarcity of guns in England or the poor phone manners exhibited by many Americans. But the most significant difference may be the fact that the British take their tea every afternoon. Tea, as most people know, is a ritual which necessarily imposes both civility and good table manners on the observers and it allows its participants to relax from the hustle and bustle of the day. While this is not a scientifically based conclusion, it seems to be as good as any explanation for the comparatively low murder rate in Britain. Even though we could offer other explanations such as the fact that the British gun-wielding criminals might have much worse aim in addition to poorer teeth than their American counterparts, it seems that there is something more fundamental in a societal and cultural sense which continues to ensure that American society will remain more violent and, to some extent, more primitive.

What about other crimes? What if the British are simply more squeamish about taking lives but revel in committing other violent crimes such as rape, robbery, and assault? We find that the British are slowly but steadily closing the "crime gap" in most other violent crimes and, in the case of assaults, actually passing their American colleagues in crime. In 1981, 70.59 rapes per 100,000 population were committed in the United States as compared with 4.19 rapes per 100,000 population in England. By 1996, however, the rate of rapes occurring in the United States had barely changed to 70.79 rapes per 100,000 population while the British criminals had apparently gone on a rampage (from their standpoint) and committed rapes at the rate of 21.77 per 100,000 population.

What has played a role in the continuing disparity between the two countries' rates of crime is unclear but one must wonder whether other factors such as poor economic circumstances in Great Britain might have contributed to the virtual explosion (a fivefold increase) in the number of rapes in Britain. The problem with cross-border comparisons is that the numbers by themselves provide only a snapshot of the frequency that a particular event (in this case, an illegal act) is occurring but they cannot really provide any definitive qualitative insights into the reasons for these differences. As a result, the social scientist must necessarily grasp for any qualitative explanations which will not neatly account for the quantitative discrepancies.

A similar argument would apply in trying to understand the differences in the rates of robberies, assaults, burglaries, and motor thefts in the United States and Great Britain. Although the 1981 robbery rates were quite different with 258 per 100,000 persons in the United States and only 40.86 in Great Britain, this difference was reduced considerably by 1996 at which time the United States saw its robbery rate drop to 202 per 100,000 while Great Britain witnessed almost a quadrupling of its robbery rate to 142 per 100,000. From the British perspective, the robbery rate had skyrocketed so that it was not even safe to go outside to tend the garden. For Americans, however, the crime rate had dropped by nearly 20 percent so people felt much freer to wander through Times Square late at night.

In this situation, the starting points of the two analyses would greatly affect the way in which the public would view these trends and very likely would be manipulated by politicians for their own ends.

American leaders would want to point to the decline in robberies as evidence of the success of their policies whereas British political candidates seeking to unseat some scruffy or dusty incumbents might point to that very same explosion of robberies in England to underscore the poor job performance of their opponents. In either case, the perception of the direction the trends were taking would be as important—if not more important—than the actual numbers of robberies themselves.

As far as assaults are concerned, the stories are somewhat more difficult to understand because the rate of assaults in the United States in 1981 was 289 per 100,000 population whereas the rate of assaults in Great Britain was 197 per 100,000 population. Obviously, the British criminals were not such laggards in the assault category and by 1996 had pulled ahead, committing 439 assaults per 100,000 population to the comparatively paltry totals of 388 per 100,000 population posted by the American miscreants. But the increase in assaults seemed to buck the general downward trend in crime in America over the past two decades and forced the social scientists to consider other explanations for the increase in assaults in the United States and the virtual doubling of assaults in Great Britain. Perhaps too many tea drinkers in England were substituting stronger drinks such as coffee or even hard liquor and thereby finding themselves literally compelled to go out and assault the mail carrier or the local grocer.

The image of a manicured, mannered Great Britain suffers additional blows with the examination of the burglary and motor vehicle theft rates in the two countries. In 1981, there were 1,649 burglaries per 100,000 population in the United States and 1,447 burglaries per 100,000 in Great Britain. By 1996, however, the British had raced ahead of the Americans in their efforts to loot their neighbors' homes in committing an incredible 2,239 burglaries per 100,000 population to the anemic 942 burglaries per 100,000 population committed by an American criminal element that, by comparison, appeared to have lost its drive to succeed and had become "soft" and listless. Of course,

Americans may not have bothered to report some of the burglaries because they knew that it was unlikely that they would recover their possessions; they may have also worried that filing a theft report with their insurance company would cause their insurance rates to increase over time. Why the British should take such joy in sneaking into other persons' houses and stealing their possessions while they obviously did not have the same enthusiasm for murder, for example, as their American counterparts is puzzling, and the explanation for this difference is not obvious. Perhaps the British are naturally more friendly toward their neighbors and, as a result, think nothing of wandering into their neighbors' homes, regardless of whether anyone is at home or not. This very same explanation, though one which might be dismissed by most statisticians, might also explain the apparent British attitude toward motor vehicle theft. We find that in 1981, American criminals stole 474 motor vehicles per 100,000 population whereas their British colleagues in crime drove off with 670 motor vehicles per 100,000 population. By 1996, the American motor vehicle theft rate had increased to 525 per 100,000 population whereas the British motor vehicle theft rate had jumped to 948 per 100,000 population. Again, these discrepancies might be accounted for by a peculiarly permissive British attitude toward the theft of motor vehicles. But if one considers this question in greater detail, it becomes less obvious as to why the British would be such overachievers in motor vehicle theft. After all, Great Britain is a small country and there are fewer places to hide a stolen motor vehicle as compared to the United States which occupies nearly half of the North American continent and offers numerous places to hide stolen motor vehicles. But perhaps the British view motor vehicle theft as something of a "sport" much like cricket and rugby. In any event, the comparison of various crime rates in the two countries shows the risks one necessarily assumes when trying to draw quantitative conclusions about a purely sociological phenomenon.

When talking about the crime rate and the direction in which law-enforcement trends are moving, we often overlook the fact that every crime has a victim. Moreover, we forget that those who are most in danger of becoming victims of crime are often those who are at the lower end of the socioeconomic strata. According to the Bureau of Justice Statistics bulletin's *Criminal Victimization 1998* report, 63 of every 1,000 persons making less than $7,000 per year were victims of crimes whereas only 33.1 of every 1,000 persons making $75,000 or more per year were victims. Obviously, much of this discrepancy is explained by the fact that poorer persons live in impoverished neighborhoods where drug usage is more rampant. But it is difficult to make any definitive conclusions about why this rate of crime should be disproportionately higher in poorer neighbors than wealthier ones. Why would there not be higher rates of crime in wealthier neighborhoods? After all, the rich have far more things to steal than do most poor people. But the rich also live in exclusive communities that are often patrolled by security guards who can toss would-be perpetrators out on their rear ends. Most poor neighborhoods do not have roving security squads that will descend upon suspicious-looking riffraff at a moment's notice. Moreover, very few rich people commit violent crimes; most seem to lean toward "victimless" white-collar crimes such as embezzlement. Indeed, the biggest risk faced by most embezzlers (other than actual capture) is getting a paper cut from a hundred-dollar bill or perhaps dropping a bag of gold bullion on one's foot. This is not to say that some wealthy people do not commit violent crimes, but it is a less common occurrence because they spend so much more time bullying their servants and hiding their jewelry from larcenous houseguests.

Regardless of the reason for the comparatively high rate of criminal victimization rates among poorer persons, it is surprising to find that the rate does not flatten out precipitously because the rate drops to 49.3 per 1,000 population for families with incomes between $7,500 and $15,000 and 39.4 per 1,000 population for families with incomes between $15,000 and $24,999. Although it spikes upward a little to

42.0 per 1,000 population for families with incomes between $25,000 and $34,999, it continues its general decline to 31.7 per 1,000 population for families with incomes between $35,000 and $49,999. But the decline in the rate of victimization ends there and bumps upward slightly to a rate of 32.0 per 1,000 population for families with incomes between $50,000 and $74,999. The final tally shows a victimization rate of 33.1 per 1,000 population for families with incomes greater than $75,000. The fact that victimization rates level off and do not continue an inexorable decline with increases in income is very surprising because we somehow think that the wealthier citizens would have a negligible criminal victimization rate. However, we can appreciate the fact that wealthier Americans might have unique concerns that would not necessarily occur to poorer Americans, such as the possibility of kidnapping and becoming accidentally trapped in the family vault.

But an examination of the very same statistics at both ends of the income scale (family incomes under $7,500 and those in excess of $75,000) shows that even though the incidence of victimization declines by about 50 percent as we move up the income scale, no one is really safe from becoming a victim of crime. In looking at the rates of violent crime for these two income groups, we see that those with a family income of less than $7,500 per year have 3.2 rapes per 1,000 population, 6.5 robberies per 1,000 population, 54.2 assaults per 1,000 population, and 1.7 thefts per 1,000 population. Those at the other end of the income spectrum—with family incomes in excess of $75,000—have 1.2 rapes per 1,000 population, 2.9 robberies per 1,000 population, 29.0 assaults per 1,000 population, and 1.0 thefts per 1,000 population. The differences in the incidences of these crimes vary from almost twofold (theft) up to nearly threefold (rape). So there is something to be said for being rich as it does seem to reduce the likelihood that one will become a victim of violent crime—even though a high-flying lifestyle will not provide any absolute degree of protection from crime.

For those persons who are unfortunate enough to be the victims of crimes, there is some disheartening news in store for them as they wait anxiously for news from the police that the perpetrators have been arrested: The criminal justice system is a very leaky, very inefficient mechanism and only a fraction of the perpetrators of most crimes of violence are actually arrested, let alone convicted of their crimes. Even though the United States boasts more than 600,000 uniformed officers who are able to carry guns and shoot out the tires of speeders—about one for every five hundred American civilians—most criminals have a very good chance of getting away with their crimes.

You can better understand the problems associated with the criminal justice system by considering a situation in which a man getting off a subway is robbed at gunpoint by two young thugs of his wallet and watch. Once he reports the crime to the police, he would become a member of a group of nearly 537,000 persons who reported a robbery crime during the calendar year. There are no special privileges or perks associated with this group whose common thread is that they were robbed and placed in fear of imminent bodily harm. But the affront to our victim's dignity would be significant if he were left unharmed, so he would run down to the local precinct and fill out the necessary reports to enable the detectives to solve his case right away. Whether they would even arrest an alleged perpetrator would be anyone's guess because only 106,178 adults are actually arrested—or about one arrest for every five robberies committed. This does not appear to be very good odds but it underscores the difficulty that the authorities—no matter how numerous and well armed—encounter when they attempt to track down criminals after the crimes have taken place, if indeed they make the effort. We can only hope that those persons being arrested are committing most of the other robberies so that the statistics are not so grim as they may appear. But if only about one-fifth of all robberies end in arrests, then it does not bode well for the number of convictions.

Why do we say that? The number of arrests for any crime is always significantly larger than the number of convictions because the criminal justice system is like a leaky bucket. Because both the police and the prosecutorial authorities have limited resources and attention spans, they are physically incapable of prosecuting every single robbery case. So they must select the more compelling cases—particularly those that are newsworthy, such as ones involving robberies of famous persons that will ensure extraordinary media attention and accelerated career advancement—as well as those that are simply stronger from an evidentiary standpoint. No prosecutor wants to take the time to prepare a case that he or she does not expect to win. But even most of the cases which involve arrests will not go to trial but will instead be resolved by plea bargain because there are simply not enough judges and courts to hear all of these cases.

So our robbery victim, already dismayed by the low rate of arrests for robberies, will be further upset to find that only about 42,831 of the 106,178 persons arrested for robbery will actually be convicted. This means that only about two out of every five persons arrested will actually be convicted of robbery—leaving the other sixty-four thousand or so free to get back out on the streets to engage in charitable works and good deeds. Given the fact that more than half a million robberies were reported, the fact that only about one in twelve actually resulted in convictions does not inspire great confidence in the nation's abilities to battle crime.

But maybe robbery is an isolated incident, you say. Perhaps it has an usually low conviction rate relative to other types of crimes because the victims are too traumatized to provide enough assistance to police and prosecutors or because there are not enough witnesses in most such cases. Perhaps there is some merit to this argument. Maybe the robbery statistics paint an unusually dim portrait of the leakiness of the criminal justice system. Maybe we should look at a crime such as motor vehicle theft; one for which American criminals share a special fondness—having committed nearly 1,400,000 such thefts in 1996. But fewer than one in ten of these thefts (actually 102,578) resulted in arrests. So with less than an 8 percent arrest rate for motor vehicle thefts, there is even less cause for optimism among motor vehicle theft victims than their robbery victim counterparts that the perpetrators will be caught and tried.

Given that motor vehicle theft arrests number about 102,578, we may be reluctant to ask about the number of convictions that are actually secured, and our reluctance would be well-founded. Indeed, only about 17,794 persons were actually convicted of motor vehicle theft— about 17 percent of those persons arrested but only a little more than 1 percent of all reported motor vehicle theft crimes. The only solace one can take is that most motor vehicle thieves are repeat offenders and that it is very probable that those 17,794 convictions were, by and large, repeat offenders who were not fingered for every single motor vehicle theft they committed. After all, there is some skill involved in hot-wiring automobiles, and the enterprising hoodlum does not study the techniques of motor vehicle theft with the idea of stealing only one car. Motor vehicle thieves are technocrats compared to robbers—who have not received any technical training other than some advice on how to point a gun or knife at a prospective victim. Motor vehicle thieves, by contrast, must know a little bit about hot-wiring the ignition system of a car, and some have knowledge about local chop shops and the ways in which stolen vehicles can be dismantled in a matter of hours. But even though we can probably safely assume that most motor vehicle thieves have stolen more than one vehicle in their lives, the dismal conviction rate of 17 percent of those arrested suggests that many of their brethren are managing to escape the grasp of the long arm of the law.

Given the unsettling news about the low conviction rates of robbers and motor vehicle thieves, we might be ready to throw up our hands in disgust. How does our criminal justice system deal with the crown princes of the criminal hierarchy—the murderers? Fortunately, there are fewer murders reported (19,650 in 1996) than motor vehicle thefts (1,395,200) because our society would truly epitomize the Hobbesian image of life being "nasty, brutish, and short." Yet there is some good news to be told about the extent to which law-enforcement officials are able to track down murder suspects because the Bureau of Justice Statistics bulletin *Felony Sentences in State Courts 1996* reports that 16,161 persons were arrested for crimes of murder. This arrest record—which is equal to some 82 percent of the total number of reported murders—is far and away the most impressive arrest record for any category of crime. Of these 16,161 persons arrested, about 11,430 were convicted of murder—a rate of almost 71 percent of those arrested and more than 58 percent of the total number of reported murders. This does not mean that murder is somehow magically different from other crimes. Instead it seems that murder is a crime in its own category because there are far fewer murders than almost any other type of crime one can imagine. More importantly, murder is viewed as the most serious or heinous crime and consequently the police and the courts devote disproportionate resources toward apprehending murderers. After all, there is no crime greater than ending the existence of another human being, and the act of murder is an event that cannot but help to attract the attention of even the most caustic person. Moreover, we feel more threatened by cold-blooded killers than we do by people who on a lark rob a bank without shooting anyone. It would be hard to imagine an instance in which an entire town was terrorized by a serial motor vehicle thief even though a few persons who love their cars more than life itself might break into a cold sweat at the prospect of having their beloved collectible stolen. But serial killers can paralyze entire cities with fear and cause people to feel an exaggerated sense of vulnerability. As a result, we punish murderers more severely than any other criminals and we devote extraordinary amounts of resources to the apprehension, conviction, jailing, and, in some cases, the execution of them.

Although America is a land of entrepreneurs, we do not place a high value on criminal creativity—particularly creative murderers. In fact, some of the most creative serial murders are rewarded by a seat in an electric chair or an injection of poison or a firing squad or a hanging or a trip into the gas chamber. As there were forty-five convicted criminals executed in 1996 and there were nearly 11,430 convicted of murder in 1996 that year, we can assume for the sake of this learned discussion that the average convicted murderer had a 1-in-254 chance of actually being snuffed courtesy of the state. Now very few street criminals have backgrounds in advanced statistics and it is reasonable to suppose that comparatively few know anything about basic statistical concepts such as standard distributions, means, and variances. But it is a safe bet that most persons who are thinking about committing their first murder do not spend very much time worrying about the possibility of going to the gas chamber because they know that the odds of their being executed are fairly remote. One does not have to engage in detailed statistical calculations to draw this conclusion but can instead read the newspapers about the endless court appeals involved in capital cases and talk with other people who have been in prison and watch television reports on the many years that will often pass before a prisoner condemned to die is actually put to death. Quite simply, there is not very much deterrence value in a death penalty when less than one-half of 1 percent of all convicted murderers will actually pay the ultimate price. Many persons will question the morality of the government being in the execution business. But we are admittedly spending a great deal of time viewing this issue from the perspective of the victims—many of whose families will want to see every convicted murderer strapped to an electric chair. If we look at the issue from the viewpoint of the convicted murderers themselves who are naturally very much in favor of not being put to death for engaging in a little bit of mischief and taking a few lives, then the very remote odds of being executed are actually a very good thing indeed. You will not see many convicted murderers sitting around a bar bemoaning the relatively low odds that they will be put to death at some point during their criminal careers. So there is something to be said for having the proper perspective about an issue.

Although crime in America has been studied by platoons of sociologists and psychologists, we still find ourselves unable to explain why people commit crimes. After all, we live in a country in which few people are driven to steal in order to feed their families because there are various assistance programs as well as private charities able to provide food and drink to the nation's poor persons. Most people receiving government housing now live in or formally lived in an apartment or house. Despite all of our studies and statistical analyses, the scheme for trying to tackle the root causes of criminal behavior remains largely anecdotal.

11

TO YOUR HEALTH!

Very few people relish the idea of going to visit the doctor's office because they know that they will have to spend an hour or even more waiting for a nurse to usher them into another room where they can wait for an additional half hour or so in private before being seen by a nurse who will then leave the room so that they can wait a few more minutes before finally seeing the doctor who will spend at least four or five minutes with the patient before leaving the room. Then the patient gathers his things together and straggles out to the front desk where he will be presented by a clerk (who lacks any visible sense of humor) with the bill totaling more money than the patient will make in the next three weeks. Although one can almost feel like one has been sucker punched after visiting a doctor's office, the impact following a visit to the local hospital can be likened to being run over by a steamroller because there is probably no other event that can have such a dramatic impact upon the physical, emotional, and financial well-being of an individual.

Hospitals are viewed in very stark terms by people because, quite frankly, they are often the place in which many people draw their last breath. But they are perhaps the most obvious symbol of our healthcare system and most Americans will spend at least some time in a hospital at some point in their lives.

Hospitals exist, first and foremost, to help sick people get well. They are often affiliated with university medical schools (hence the term "teaching hospitals" which sounds much more appealing than "learning-curve hospitals") that serve as centers for research. Hospitals also play an important role in advancing the frontiers of medical science by virtue of their being the focus of new medical techniques such as transplant operations.

ORGAN TRANSPLANTS

In considering any decision to undergo an organ transplant, you need to be cognizant of the fact that the supply of organs is limited and there is a waiting list that can last for years before the appropriate organ is found for a recipient. The demand for organs obviously affects the probability that one will receive the desired organ. But what are the probabilities that a person in need of an organ will actually receive that organ? The United Network for Organ Sharing reports that as of October 2000, there were 4,114 persons waiting for hearts; 219 persons waiting for hearts and lungs; 3,648 persons waiting for lungs alone; 968 waiting for pancreas; 46,817 persons waiting for kidneys; and 16,399 waiting for livers. Given this staggering pent-up demand and the comparatively lower rate of organ transplants carried out each year, it seems unfortunate that one cannot merely go to the local grocery store and snap up a vital organ and take it over to one's doctor and have the failing organ replaced. One could even imagine sleek do-it-yourself kits whereby you could replace that failing kidney with a few simple deft strokes of the scalpel and the pulling of a staple-gun trigger. But we can safely assume that the American Medical Association will never allow such a democratization of the organ transplant business to occur and the AMA will no doubt offer the usual empty excuses for continuing to require that organ transplants be done in hospitals such as patient safety and risk of infection. But consumers need to let the medical establishment know that we are on to their self-serving game to keep the organ transplant business to themselves and continue propping up the prices of such procedures.

If we consider the waiting lists for organ transplants to be the population and the number of transplants taking place in a given year to be the sample, then we can estimate the probability that a member of the waiting list will receive an organ donation. But there will be some inherent inaccuracies because we will be using the current number of transplant procedures and comparing them with aggregate totals for waiting lists that will admittedly require many years before all of the current prospective recipients have been given an organ donation or, in some cases, died while waiting for a transplant.

If we take the 4,114 persons who have been patiently waiting for heart transplants and compare it to the fortunate 2,340 who actually received such transplants in 1998, we find that the odds of any given persons on the waiting list receiving a heart transplant that year were about one in 1.75 or, expressed as percentages, about 56.8 percent. Such waiting lists are generally "first come, first serve" but may also consider other factors such as the recipient's age and general health—unless, of course, you make a generous donation to the cardiac department of the local hospital to help speed up the transplant approval process. But the rate at which heart transplants take place means that it would take almost two years for the entire current waiting list roster to be exhausted, during which time many new waiting list recipients would have been added. Waiting in line for a heart transplant is obviously not something that Type A personalities would relish because there is a significant time delay involved and there is no guarantee that you will live long enough to receive a new heart. But it seems to be the best that can be made of the situation given the understandable reluctance of most people to offer their heart (literally, not poetically) while they are still alive to a recipient. In fact, it is a pity that so few people donate their organs.

What if you have a very good heart but you find that your liver or kidney is starting to fail? If the massive donation to the appropriate hospital is not a viable alternative, you may find yourself with no other option but to get in line with the other prospective recipients and hope for the best. In the case of a liver transplant, there were 16,399 persons on the 2000 waiting list. With approximately 4,450 liver transplants taking place each year, the prospect transplantee might find himself having to wait for up to four years because the probability that any one person on the transplant list will receive a liver in a given year is only about one in 3.6 or 27 percent.

If these liver numbers discourage you, then consider kidneys. After all, most people have two kidneys and can certainly be counted on to spare the extra one to better the lot of their fellow humans. With 46,817 persons on the waiting list and 11,990 transplants being performed per year, the potential recipient has about a 1-in-3.9 or 25.6 percent chance of getting the desired kidney. So the odds are not particularly good of getting a timely transplant if you need one in a hurry, particularly if you have no way to get moved to the head of the line. Of course there are other, more unorthodox sources of supply such as Internet auction sites and secret journeys to poor countries to try to purchase the desired organ on the black market, but these are not measures that are either available to most persons or ones which pass the "smell" test. After all, most people get upset about having another person touch their hotdog bun while at a ballgame. Why would they go to some poverty-stricken country where the medical technology and sanitation and hygiene are poor and have an organ transplant? Fortunately, few persons are willing to undertake these additional risks.

Now very few people want to get an organ transplant when they are perfectly well because their existing organs work just fine and they feel a little squeamish about having Joe's heart or Billy Bob's kidney or Maggie's liver implanted in their own body. But their attitudes change as soon as a vital organ begins to give out and their health is threatened. Once a failing organ begins to threaten one's own ability to carry out major life functions, however, then a trip to the operating room starts to look a little more enticing. And what person would not want to be laid out virtually naked on a steel gurney under an array of bright lights surrounded by a group of masked and gowned doctors and nurses with a few tourists peering down from the arena seats overhead? Certainly it is an experience that should not be missed by anyone who prizes their dignity and privacy.

So what are the odds that you will have the dubious privilege of receiving a truly rare kind of organ transplant? First, we need to understand that the process by which one goes about getting an organ transplant is both involved and expensive. Quite simply, there are more persons who need organs than there are unfortunate accident victims to supply that demand. Even though we could try to increase the supply of organs by encouraging people to drive their cars without putting on their seatbelts or to use their hair dryers while taking showers or even using chain saws to give back massages, we would probably still find that we could not satisfy the demand due to the inherent difficulties in matching donor organs with recipients whose bodies will not reject the implanted organs.

So if you are fortunate enough to be accepted for a transplant and a matching donor organ is found, then you will be in very rare company indeed. For example, the United Network for Organ Sharing reports that there were 2,340 heart transplants in 1998 and that the 79 percent of the patients who received heart transplants in 1995 survived for at least three years. This rate of success is good news for everybody except those 21 percent who, for whatever reason, went to that great outpatient clinic in the sky and the spouses of some of the survivors who were counting on receiving an early inheritance. Given the fact that there were more than 5,382,000 cardiovascular operations in the United States in 1997, as reported by the American Heart Association, heart transplants represented by far the least commonly performed cardiovascular procedure, with fewer than one in 2,300 of all cardiovascular procedures involving heart transplants.

But what if you were interested in having a more unusual transplant operation because all of your friends had heart transplants and you could not stomach the idea of being just another heart recipient? You might opt for a lung transplant, a procedure that was performed 849 times in 1998 with a 61 percent survival rate. Too mundane? Then you could consider a pancreas transplant, an operation that sounds very exotic because it involves an organ that few people can spell let alone locate on an anatomy chart. Only 215 pancreas transplants were performed in 1998. As a result, this is a procedure that would put you in the upper echelon of transplant warriors and, in the vast majority of cases, give you bragging rights at the Rotary Club meeting when you and your fellow club members decide to compare surgical scars. Although your scar might not look as interesting as Ray's vasectomy or Fred's colostomy, you could still boast that your operation was far less common and, hence, far more prestigious.

Imagine the anger and jealousy that you would feel, however, if your tennis doubles partner, Edgar, announced that he had just undergone a heart-lung transplant, a delicate operation that was performed just forty-five times in 1998 and boasted a 65 percent survival rate. In a fit you might call your doctor and demand an intestine transplant in a pique of anger only to later find out after coming out of surgery that a whopping sixty-nine intestine transplants were performed in 1998 so that Edgar could still claim to have received the rarest form of transplant operation. Of course you could consider a brain transplant but there is no record that any such procedure has ever been attempted on humans or that such a procedure would even be survivable—even though we all know of people who seem to have defied the odds of surviving without a brain for many decades. Alas, your search for any other exotic transplant operations would take you to the comparatively common liver transplant of which 4,450 were performed in 1998 or the comparatively proletarian kidney transplant for which 11,990 procedures were performed in 1998. However, you could consider suggesting a rare combination transplant that would make the heart–lung transplant obtained by Edgar seem positively commonplace. As a start, you could opt for a heart–lung–intestine transplant or, if you were feeling particularly lucky, a heart–lung–intestine–kidney transplant. But if you wanted to set the mark so high that no one would dare try and top you, you could go for the world transplant record and propose to your squadron of surgeons that you wished to have a heart–lung–intestine–kidney–liver–lung–pancreas transplant. Not only would you make medical history as well as the top column of the local obituary page but you would also create a logistical nightmare for the organ banks that would have to supply organs that would not be rejected by what was left of your body. But such complex procedures are currently beyond the skill levels of our most gifted surgeons and will undoubtedly have to wait until further advances in medical technology occur.

COMMON SURGERIES

Not everyone is eager to undergo a rare surgical procedure because not everyone needs to have a rare surgical procedure. Not all of us are so unfortunate as to be able to contract a disease that will require the transplant of three or four organs at the same time. Indeed, the vast majority of surgical procedures do not involve transplants at all but instead comparatively straightforward cutting and suturing procedures. Oh, the doctors will have you believe that one must have many years of training in order to hack up a lung or spleen or liver even though a course or two in cross-stitching or rug-hooking would probably provide enough "real world" experience to enable an enthusiastic novice surgeon to do a serviceable job. As very few of us wish to be touched by a doctor, much less drawn and quartered, we would probably like to know the odds that

America's Most Popular Surgical Procedures

Type of Procedure	Number of Procedures Performed
Endoscopy	1,423,000
Cardiac Catheterization	1,202,000
Repair Lacerations from Delivery	1,093,000
Removal of Artery Blockage	926,000
Cesarean Deliveries	900,000
Hysterectomy	645,000
Coronary Artery Bypass	553,000
Removal of Ovaries	491,000
Removal of Gall Bladder	439,000

Source of Statistics: U.S. Department of Health and Human Services, National Center for Health Statistics—1998.

we as Americans will need to undergo a surgical procedure in a given year. Although some persons will be genetically predisposed to having certain conditions, we will limit ourselves to making purely numerical analyses so that we can determine the general probabilities that we will meet our very own surgeon in the operating room.

As we know, we live in a nation of about 280 million persons, many of whom we can each claim as friends. In 1998, the U.S. Department of Health and Human Services, National Center for Health Statistics 1998 Summary, *National Hospital Discharge Survey* (June 30, 2000), determined that there were a total of 41,500,000 operations in the United States in 1998—16,188,000 of which were performed on males and 25,312,000 of which were carried out on females. This means that an American would have a 1-in-6.7 chance of undergoing a surgical procedure in a given year. Of course this statistic makes an assumption which is probably not true—that no American underwent more than one surgical procedure. The reality, however, is very different because there are some patients who must undergo many operations in a comparatively short span of time whereas there are some Americans who will never set foot in a hospital until the day they are brought in on a stretcher with a tag tied to their big toe. For those patients for whom trips to the emergency room are as common as drives to the local fast-food restaurant, these statistics are obviously wrong because they would greatly understate the number of operations that these patients could be expected to incur. Certainly if they were to read this chapter after having already undergone two, three, four, or even five operations this year, they would be quite angry to find that they were being carted off to the operating room yet again despite having been assured by the immutable laws of statistics that they should not need another surgical procedure. But the statistics would not necessarily be wrong; its predictions regarding the average number of surgical procedures would be accurate for the population as a whole. However, it would not be capable of offering predictions as to which individuals would have no surgical procedures and which individuals would have two, three, four, or more operations because it has no predictive value on the individual level. It is the same analysis used when describing the odds that a slot machine will pay out. Statistics can be used to calculate the probability that a payout will occur over time but cannot tell which pull of the lever will be the winning event.

What are the odds that you will undergo a surgical procedure this year? Perhaps the easiest way to look at this problem is to consider several of the more common procedures. The endoscopy of the large or small intestine ranks as the most popular of America's surgical procedures although sales of the home version have reportedly not matched expectations. But any type of procedure which involves the insertion of any type of foreign object into the large or small intestine is not one which causes men to break into cheers—most of them will instead cross their legs and press their buttocks together with enough force to turn a lump of coal into a diamond. However, the endoscopy was still administered to 1,423,000 persons (794,000 of whom were females) in 1998, meaning that any one person in the United States had a 1-in-197 chance of being probed.

The next most common procedure, which is probably more appealing to those who are squeamish about rectal examinations at all, is cardiac catheterization, which was performed on 1,202,000 persons (716,000 of whom were men) so that any one person had a 1-in-232 chance of going through such a process. The third most common operation involved the repair of lacerations caused during the delivery of a baby, which occurred in 1,093,000 cases, none of which involved men! This is the type of statistic which can cause an obvious error when one does not adjust the aggregate statistic. Because men do not deliver babies—even though there are a few particularly sensitive men who would feel much more complete if they could deliver a child—we would want to exclude the male component of the national population when calculating the probability that a person would have to undergo postdelivery surgery to repair lacerations. (However, some prospective fathers have been known to trip and injure themselves in the operating room.) If there are an estimated 145,000,000 women in the United States, then each woman would have a 1-in-256 chance of undergoing such a procedure. But this statistic by itself would obviously have its own inherent inaccuracies as we know that not every woman in the United States is of childbearing age or even able to bear children if she is of such an age. To get a truly meaningful statistic regarding the probability of a woman undergoing such a procedure, we would want to further screen out those persons who were not of the appropriate age. Statisticians generally describe women of childbearing age as being between the ages of 18 and 44 years—even though we know there are women who are both younger and older than this age group who have children. But for the sake of argument, we will focus on the 18- to 44-year-old group which numbers, according to the National Center for

Health Statistics, about 60 million women. If we then compare the 1,093,000 postdelivery procedures to the female childbearing-age population, we find that the likelihood someone in that population will undergo this procedure increases to 1 in 54 or about 1.85 percent. But there may be a flaw in our reasoning here because we are presuming that these lacerations occur regardless of whether women deliver normally or by cesarean section. However, it is more logical to assume that the lacerations occur primarily with vaginal births which would, of course, result in a correspondingly greater probability that a woman delivering vaginally would have lacerations.

The removal of arterial blockages represented more of an equal opportunity procedure with nearly 926,000 being carried out in 1998— 594,000 on men and 332,000 on women. The numbers for this procedure rebuked the notion that heart disease is a male illness only, but it showed that men were still overachievers in eating too much fatty foods and not getting enough exercise. In one sense, however, these numbers had a positive aspect because they represented the number of persons who had cardiac procedures before they would have likely suffered the heart attacks that almost invariably develop in the absence of such treatments. Even though this procedure is not overly pleasant as the attending surgeon must essentially thread a tube through the patient's artery, it is far more preferable to having one, two, three, or even four arteries cut out of one's legs and arms to replace the clogged arteries that must be removed from the patient's gaping chest cavity. While such a setting can provide a festive backdrop for shooting the family holiday card with the patient's spouse and children standing around the operating table, it is a situation that most persons would rather avoid.

As far as the next most common operations are concerned, the U.S. Department of Health and Human Services informs us that there were approximately 900,000 cesarean sections and 645,000 hysterectomies— both procedures which are exclusive to women as they both relate to the female reproductive organs. Using our 60 million childbearing population, a member of that group has a 1-in-66 chance of having a cesarean section. Of course some of these women will never have a cesarean whereas others will have two, three, or even more, but we are only concerned with the probabilities for the group as a whole. As far as hysterectomies are concerned, we must enlarge our group to include all females in the United States because any female could undergo a hysterectomy even though the risks that any given individual will have to do so will vary based on a variety of factors including age, cancer history, and the like. With about 145 million women in the United States, any single one of them, without any further qualifications, would have a 1-in-224 chance of having to undergo a hysterectomy.

Although some women believe that men secretly wish they could give birth, the fact of the matter is that the vast majority of men are acutely aware of the pain involved with repairing lacerations caused by childbirth as well as the pain associated with both vaginal and cesarean deliveries and quite frankly have no desire at all to play any greater role in the delivery process than they do at present. Most men believe that they are very fortunate to play the role of "egg fertilizer" and are quite content to remain on the sidelines until the day they must accompany their wife/partner to the hospital for the delivery. Whether the human race would have died out centuries ago had men been responsible for child-bearing is open to debate, but the fact remains that the female physiology is far better suited to the carrying, delivery, and nursing of a child than the male physiology which is somewhat clunky and utilitarian by comparison.

Although there are many other surgical procedures which can be discussed, we should limit ourselves to the next four most common surgical procedures—coronary artery bypasses, the removal of one or both ovaries, gall bladder removal, and the destruction of or closing off of the fallopian tubes. Once again, the males may feel as though they dodged a bullet, or two or three, because two of these procedures are exclusive to female patients. Because males are generally so worn out from having fertilized the egg, it is probably just as well that they are not subject to additional demands on their fragile bodies. But the coronary artery bypass may be viewed as being largely a "male" procedure in that 396,000 of the 553,000 procedures or 71.6 percent of all procedures are performed on males which, in a population of 135 million males, boils down to an aggregate probability of 1 in 340. Here, we are interested in finding the more specific probability of males undergoing a coronary artery bypass so we are using only the male members of the general population. Undoubtedly, some of this preponderance on this affliction on the part of the male population is due to the lingering effects of the strain caused by the male's role in the fertilization process. If we wanted to determine the probability that a female would undergo a coronary artery bypass, however, we would take the female population of 145 million and divide it by the 158,000 female cases involving coronary artery bypasses to determine that a woman has a 1-in-917 chance of undergoing such a process. As with most other types of surgical procedures and operations, there is an inherent mushiness to these numbers because we are not necessarily dealing with onetime procedures on given individuals as occurs with the removal of particular organs. Instead, some persons may never undergo the procedure, some may undergo it once, and still others may go through it two or more times. So the idea that any given individual will have a definite probability of going through this procedure is not entirely true. Moreover, heart disease is one which occurs most frequently in older persons even though people in their twenties, thirties, and forties can suffer heart attacks or strokes. This calculation probably understates the older person's chances of undergoing a coronary artery bypass and similarly overstates the risks faced by younger persons even though heart disease knows no generational bounds.

Of the remaining procedures that we discussed, the removal of one or both ovaries occurs in about 491,000 patients which, in a population of 145 million women, would entail a probability of 1 in 295. Similarly, 439,000 gall bladders are removed each year, 311,000 of them from female patients and 128,000 of them from male patients. A female would have a 1-in-466 chance of undergoing a gall bladder procedure whereas a man would have a 1-in-1,054 chance of having to submit to the same procedure. Finally, there are 364,000 procedures each year to remove or otherwise close off the fallopian tubes, which no males have ever undergone. For those females who must have this procedure performed, they are the one in every 398 women who undergo this procedure annually.

These statistics do not prove that it is a "man's world" as some females might insist because females generally have a longer life expectancy at every stage of their lives than their male counterparts. The U.S. Department of Health and Human Services reports that the life expectancy of males in 1997 in the United States at the time of birth is 73.6 years whereas the life expectancy of females in 1998 in the United States at the time of birth is 79.2 years. But for those men and women who reach the age of 65, the life expectancies rise to 80.8 years and 84 years, respectively. So any male who hopes to get in the last word will find himself swimming up-river against a statistical tide—regardless of whether he makes it to age 65 or not. This is not to ignore the fact that some men do live longer than some women but merely to point out that such occurrences are more the exception than the rule.

INFECTIOUS DISEASES

We have talked a great deal about organ transplants and surgical procedures but it remains to delve into the wondrous area of infectious diseases. As our knowledge about diseases as well as our formulation of treatments for diseases have evolved, the types of diseases that most heavily plague our people continue to change with the passage of time. Some diseases appearing repeatedly throughout history such as cholera, leprosy, malaria, rabies, and typhoid fever have all but been eradicated in the United States—even though epidemics do break out from time to time in poor countries around the world. But other diseases have taken their place—such as cancer, tuberculosis, gonorrhea, AIDS, Alzheimer's disease, and viral hepatitis. The prevalence of these diseases does not mean that they have just sprung out of the ground but merely that they have assumed greater prominence due to the demographics and lifestyle of our population—as well as the success of our medical technology in controlling, or at least moderating, the effects of the more traditional diseases.

"Cancer" is an umbrella term for a variety of diseases of the body that are all characterized by the explosive growth of cells. According to the U.S. Department of Health and Human Services, cancer ranks second as the leading cause of death in the nation after heart disease with 541,532 deaths in 1998. Heart diseases themselves accounted for 724,859 deaths in 1998. Because these two groups of diseases account for more than half of the 2,337,256 deaths reported in 1998, one almost gets the feeling that if one can somehow avoid being struck down by cancer of one form or another (e.g., lung, liver, pancreas, skin, breast, stomach), that one will probably die from heart disease. It would probably be almost impossible to find a person in the United States who has not lost a relative or friend to either heart disease or cancer.

But what are your options for exiting this world if you somehow manage to make it through the gauntlet of cancer and heart disease? Sadly, the government does not include a category in its collection of statistics that allows one to die by simply standing up and clicking one's heels three times and then painlessly ascending upward to heaven amidst a choir of angels and synchronized gymnasts. No, we instead have an array of unpalatable endings that we must contemplate even though we have very little control over which of these endings we will follow unless, of course, we are of the mind to snuff out our own lives. But we find that suicide is a choice that is selected by comparatively few people because most people, quite frankly, are simply not brave or crazy enough to drive off a cliff or put a gun to their head. Indeed, only 30,575 people chose to take their own lives which, in an annual death toll of 2,337,256, amounts to a percentage of only 1 in 76 or 1.2 percent. If we want to know an aggregate probability that any single person in the country would take his or her own life, we would divide the entire population of 280 million by the number of suicides to get a probability that one out of every 9,150 citizens will end his or her life intentionally this year. More than half of all suicide victims shoot themselves but other popular means of killing oneself include drug overdoses, stabbing oneself, jumping from great heights, hanging, and drowning. As with many other types of statistics we have considered, there is a certain amount of self-selection here because suicide is a voluntary act of self-annihilation. It is certainly a different situation than one in which the victim is struck down by influenza or septicemia or Alzheimer's disease, all of which are diseases that very few persons would voluntarily contract. Also, some people who are suffering from an irreversible painful illness may opt for suicide. But statistics provide snapshots of aggregate figures and essentially ignore the voluntary or involuntary nature of individual situations. On the plus side, it is surprising that, given the depressing conditions in many persons' lives, we do not see tens of thousands of people jumping out of skyscraper windows or throwing themselves in front of speeding trains or even getting married without a prenuptial agreement.

But to return to our lively analysis of death by disease, we should point out that heart disease and cancer are followed by cerebrovascular diseases (e.g., strokes) which claim 158,448 victims per year and pulmonary diseases (lungs) which in turn killed 112,584 persons. If you were one of the persons who died in 1998, then you had a 1-in-14 chance of dying from a cerebrovascular disease and a 1-in-20 chance of dying from a pulmonary affliction (and a zero chance of purchasing this book). As a member of the general population, your odds of death from cerebrovascular disease are 1 in 1,772 and your odds of death from pulmonary disease are 1 in 2,500. This should make you feel pretty good because you know that you have eaten the right foods and exercised and stopped smoking and cut down your drinking and greatly reduced your consumption of heroin. Besides, you live next door to very overweight people who practice every type of vice imaginable and who should be easily found by the actuarial gods when they decide they need to add another cerebrovascular or pulmonary victim to their tally.

If you manage to avoid the big four of heart disease, cancer, cerebrovascular disease, and pulmonary disease, what other diseases will be slithering about trying to grab your attention? The next most popular cause of death (perhaps popular is not the best choice of words here), which claimed 97,835 victims, is not really a medical condition but instead the category of all accidental deaths—whether they resulted from drowning, being crushed during an orgy by the collapse of a flesh pile, being killed in a car accident, or any other type of situation in which lives were unexpectedly and artificially cut short. This accident category was followed closely by pneumonia and influenza with a 1998 toll of 91,871 victims and diabetes mellitus which claimed 64,751 victims. Although pneumonia and influenza ranked as the leading killers of people at the beginning of the 20th century, they have fallen on hard times and simply do not strike fear in the hearts of most persons. Of course they do manage to strike down their fair share of victims but you cannot impress your friends today as easily as you might a century ago if you had announced you had pneumonia and influenza. One reason for the more lackadaisical attitude is that there are a number of effective treatments that can be used to treat both of these diseases. The same is true for diabetes, which, while not having a cure, can be managed by the great majority of its victims. Moreover, the fact that all of the diseases discussed in this chapter do not invariably result in death but instead may be treated removes some of the terror from their names. By contrast, people are much more fearful about contracting AIDS because there is no known cure, despite recent advancements in the control of the disease, and even though it claimed fewer victims in 1998—10,198—than kidney diseases (26,182 deaths), liver disease and cirrhosis (25,192 deaths), atherosclerosis

(15,279 deaths), and hypertension (14,308 deaths). So even though it ranks fairly far down the roll of honor in terms of deadliness, AIDS scares people because a cure has not been found.

Statistics is used in the medical world to help track the spread of diseases and any progress made in treating these very same diseases. It provides scientists and medical professionals with benchmarks whereby success against a particular disease or illness may be measured. As in all other areas of human endeavor, it is not an end unto itself but merely a tool to assist in the collection, organization, and analysis of raw data. The absence of a useful knowledge of statistics would make it impossible to draw any meaningful conclusions about information relating to such things as organ transplants, common surgeries, and infectious diseases.

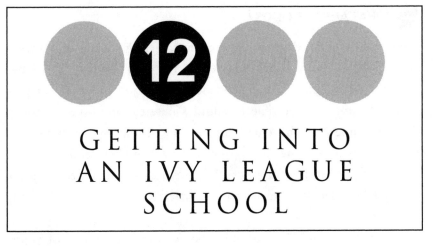

GETTING INTO
AN IVY LEAGUE
SCHOOL

Many of us must one day contemplate the fact that our children will eventually leave the house and seek their fortunes in the world. But in today's modern society in which people amass undergraduate and graduate degrees like baseball cards or cleaning rags, it has become more difficult for a "self-made" person to rise to the top of society. Instead, most of the desirable positions require a college degree before the interviewer will even bother to set up an interview— let alone seriously consider the applicant for a position. Many parents do want their children to eventually leave home so that the kids can get started with their own careers and their own families and rush ahead and make the same mistakes made by their parents and their parents' parents back to the beginning of history.

Young people need to continue their education beyond high school in order to have a fighting chance at securing high-paying jobs in which they can scramble over the backs of their fellow corporate ladder-climbers. Consequently, we have colleges that take 17-year-olds and 18-year-olds who have no idea what they want to do when they grow up and, after four years of intensive courses, exams, and seminars, graduate 21-year-olds and 22-year-olds who have no idea what they want to do when they grow up. However, these graduates do possess a college degree that will help to open up the doors leading to lucrative jobs and a new sense of independence. A new job and a regular paycheck also makes it possible to afford a new car and a new place to live—meaning that the child can now move out of the house. Of course most parents are unhappy when their children leave home for the final time but they are secretly grateful that their gifted offspring will not be celebrating his thirtieth, fortieth, or even fiftieth birthday under their roof.

So college is sort of a breaking point in the maturation of young adults because it not only provides them with some of the skills and analytical techniques that they will use in their careers but it also marks the first time that many young people will venture from home for months at a time. These young folk will arrive at college with visions of sold-out football games and fraternity-house parties and challenging discussions with professors and students alike; they will also meet people with whom they will develop warm, lasting friendships and, in some cases, loving relationships that will last a lifetime or at least one night. But their setting foot on campus will mean that they will have overcome the single biggest obstacle to realizing their dreams of meaningful career choices and the prospects of at least a modest fortune.

But all colleges are not perceived equally and there are definite differences in the academic pecking order. After all, the United States boasts a great variety of institutions of higher learning—ranging from vocational and technical schools to two-year community colleges, four-year private colleges, and great universities offering master's, doctoral, and postgraduate programs in almost every area of human knowledge. Not surprisingly, there are also great variations in the perceived quality of the faculties of these various institutions. The great universities can boast scholars with worldwide reputations as well as being able to attract recruiters from the most prestigious corporations. Not surprisingly, these connections with the elite sectors of commerce and industry become more fragmented as one moves toward the less well known schools and community colleges. After all, corporate recruiters are essentially looking for brand-name prospects and they will confine their interviews to those schools which seem to be able to attract the best and the brightest. Of course not every job requires a valedictorian but it is certainly true that there is a greater likelihood of getting a job on Wall Street or in Washington if one has the necessary stamp of approval in the form of a college diploma from the "right" school. This does not mean that the upper-echelon schools have a monopoly on talent or ambition or drive or even results; many persons who attended less-celebrated institutions have gone on to enjoy remarkable success in both government and industry.

Yet people are always in search of a guarantee or at least a leg-up on their competitors and graduation from a snobby school appears to many to be a surefire route to a personal entourage of sniveling toadies and money and power and all the good things in life. Of course there are two issues that one must confront when considering an undergraduate career at one of these preeminent universities: cost and the admission process itself. Of course the odds of being admitted to any one of these schools may be fair to poor for most students and so they may not give much thought to the cost side of the question as it may never be anything more than a purely academic consideration. But for those who believe that they can resolve the cost issue through either the timely death of a wealthy relative or the selection of a winning lottery ticket, then the remaining issue becomes one of being selected by the admissions staff of the desired school.

How does one go about securing admission to an esteemed university? Well, you can fill out an application; take the college board exams; forward your transcripts from your high school; obtain glowing recommendations from leading political figures, industrial tycoons, and your high-school gym teacher—and cross your fingers. The truth of the matter is that there are so many good students competing for a limited number of slots at a very select group of colleges and universities that there is no single process that will guarantee admission. As very few of us can afford to offer to build a new gymnasium or purchase an armored limousine for the dean of students, we have to resort to other means—beyond glowing recommendation letters and heartrending essays about time spent working with airline pilots who suffer from vertigo—to secure an advantage in the application process.

As this is a book about probabilities, however, we need to look at some cold hard facts culled from recent admissions offices at some of the nation's most elitist institutions of higher learning and indoctrination. The oft-repeated refrain that it gets more difficult each year to gain admission does seem to be true because the entering classes do not increase much if at all from year to year, but the applicant population does appear to be going up along with the general population itself. Indeed, the U.S. Department of Education reports that as of 1999, there were 11.6 million students in public colleges and universities and 3.3 million students in private colleges and universities or a grand total of 14.9 million students carrying on with varying courses of study in higher education. This compares with 10.8 million students in public colleges and universities and 3.0 million students in private colleges and universities or a total of 13.8 million students in 1990, and represents an increase of about 9.2 percent in the past decade. If we assume that the United States had about 280 million persons in 1999, this means that about 5.3 percent of the population was enrolled in a course of study of higher education. This is a very impressive statistic when we think of all of the many hundreds of thousands of persons who are learning about the philosophical arguments denying their own existence and mathematical formulas that they will forget as soon as they complete their final exams. But it also illustrates the huge number of individuals who are continually enrolling each year in the nation's colleges and universities which suggests that there is a great deal of competition for admission to the most prestigious universities.

But the job of calculating the odds that a student will get into one of the nation's top universities is not completely straightforward because the admissions process is not a science or an art form but some sort of mysterious process in which students with perfect board scores and straight As can be denied admission to the very same institution that accepts a student who is not quite so perfect in terms of test scores and grades but who is able to write a compelling essay on why he would commit murder in order to go to that school. Of course one can improve one's chances of success if one is a world-class sprinter or a star running back or an outstanding point guard because even the snobbiest of schools have wealthy alumni who like to root their teams to victory. Therefore, schools cannot confine themselves to stuffing their entering classes with "geeks" because geeks do not usually make very good football or basketball players. And if the football and basketball teams are perennial losers, then the prestige of the university itself will suffer accordingly. In fact, one of the quickest ways for a school to improve the quality of its student body may be for it to field a national championship team because the increased visibility of the program on national television will generally cause the number of applications to rise and, in general, provide the admissions office with a greater number of applicants from which to select.

But we should try to tackle this question using a few examples, beginning with one of the most famous schools in the world, which straddles the banks of the Charles River in Cambridge, Massachusetts, basking in the reflected glory of nearly four centuries at the pinnacle of American education—a school so well known that one needs only to mention the "H" that begins its name to ensure its identification. We are of course talking about the mythical Hirschfield School of Taxidermy—which has been training taxidermists for centuries in the fine art of skinning fish, birds, mammals, and all sorts of other animals and then rewrapping the skins around plaster molds to make them look almost alive. Graduates of Hirschfield have gone on to stuff passenger pigeons, dodo birds, blue whales, and many other species that have either become extinct or been threatened with extinction. How many times have you looked at the bare wall in your bedroom and thought that it could be considerably brightened with the addition of a rhinocerous head or a pair of moose antlers? Many people think similar thoughts, bemoaning their lack of quality taxidermic products, and never realize that their dream of hanging the head of a defenseless animal on their wall is only a matter of money and time.

Although the school cannot claim to have an American president among its alumni, it does continue to deny allegations that it has "treated" some of the more "rigid" or "wooden" political figures such as Al Gore and George Bush. The problem with trying to get a handle on the prospect of getting into Hirschfield is that no one will provide any statistics regarding the number of applicants it receives each year or the number of persons it admits or the number who eventually enroll because the school itself does not exist. For this reason, we cannot really utilize Hirschfield as a case study. But we can consider a school just a few miles away which has also managed to build for itself something of a reputation as an education mecca in America—the school, of course, being Harvard University (pronounced 'Hah-vahd when discussing one's university affiliation at dinner parties). Harvard is the oldest and arguably the most prestigious university in the country—ranking right up there with Hirschfield, although Harvard, regrettably, does not offer a program in taxidermy. On the plus side, however, Harvard does boast a world-class faculty that is so distinguished one can hardly walk very far in any direction without tripping over a Nobel laureate or an internationally recognized scholar. Indeed, so luminous are the intellectual stars that burn so brightly that many persons—students and faculty alike—believe that the world does revolve around Cambridge, Massachusetts. And while we give little credence to the joke that you never see two Harvard professors together in the same class because their egos are so bloated that they cannot fit into the same room at the same time,

Admissions Rates to Selected Prestigious Public and Private Universities

School	Applicants	Admitted	Enrolled	Admission Chances
Harvard	18,160	2,055	1,652	0.11
Yale	13,270	2,135	1,375	0.16
Princeton	14,875	1,694	1,165	0.11
Virginia	16,461	5,588	2,924	0.34
Berkeley	31,108	8,044	3,735	0.25

Source of Statistics: *Barron's Guide to Colleges 2000*

there is undoubtedly something to be said for the idea that Harvard is as much a state of mind as it is an educational institution.

Because Harvard has always figured so prominently in the landscape of American politics and culture, it is viewed—rightly or wrongly—as a gateway to power and money. Not surprisingly, it attracts many more qualified applicants than it can possibly accept and is certainly one of the most selective schools on anyone's list. And so we will use Harvard College as an example so that we may carry out our analysis of the probability of getting into a top-notch school (unless, of course, you are interested in taxidermy, in which case you should contact the director of admissions at Hirschfield). In any event, the application process to Harvard begins with the taking of college board exams—either the SATs or the ACTs. Although Harvard likes to pride itself on admitting free spirits and independent thinkers, this desire for diversity does not extend to people who believe that they should get the lowest possible score on these standardized tests in order to create a perfect bell curve of test scores among incoming freshmen. Instead the admissions office will not look very kindly upon such bad-faith gestures since they do want to believe that they are admitting the most talented class possible.

Because Harvard can afford to be very selective in whom it admits, a student who has perfect college board scores and who graduated as valedictorian of his or her class is not necessarily guaranteed admission. But it is also the case that students with such outstanding academic records do have a better chance of admission than those students who have mastered the popular "Dick and Jane" series of books. Such students typically do not have the mettle for a Harvard education and must instead settle for an undergraduate career at Yale or Columbia.

But we must deal with the question at hand which relates to the probability that one will be able to gain admission to the hallowed halls of Harvard University. In 1999, the *Barron's Guide* informs us that 18,160 students applied for the freshman class and 2,055 were accepted. Of the students who were accepted, 1,652 actually enrolled at Harvard. Now this is a fairly straightforward calculation in that we can determine the odds that any single applicant will be admitted to Harvard are about 1 in 9 or an 11.3 percent chance. But this does not tell us a great deal of information because it lumps together every applicant ranging from those who can barely sign their names and who offered a stick-figure picture in lieu of an essay to those students who might have had a decent shot at formulating the theory of relativity in a different era. Unfortunately, Harvard does not release statistics which indicate the number of students admitted who scored between 600 and 700 or 700 and 800 on their math and verbal SATs, for example, so that one can get an idea of the percentages of applicants admitted who scored within a certain test-score range. Similarly, Harvard is equally unhelpful informing applicants of the percentages of successful applicants who had a grade-point average (GPA), for example, between 3.0 and 3.5 or 3.5 and 4.0, or 4.0 and 4.5. As a result, we have no way of knowing the probabilities that applicants who have a certain combination of grades and test scores would be admitted to Harvard. Although we can safely assume that the candidates having the higher test scores and grades are more likely to be admitted, such a general conclusion is not really of great help to a prospective applicant who wants to know with some degree of certainty the likelihood that he or she might be admitted based upon his or her respective test scores and grades. So the prospective applicant is really left with no choice but to try to dazzle the admissions office with news of every imaginable accomplishment he has achieved until a definitive decision is made. He will thus want to pass on the news of his having started a high-school stamp-collecting club or having performed the title role in Shakespeare's *Hamlet* in pig Latin or having managed to date three women in one evening without getting caught because he will have no choice but to act on the worst-case assumption that he will have to pad his applicant file as much as possible.

What does Harvard have to say about this lack of clarity regarding the guidance it provides to prospective applicants? The undergraduate admissions Web site states the following: "With students applying from close to 5,000 different secondary schools from around the world each year, there is no single path we can expect all students to follow. . . . Generally, successful applicants are at the top of their class—but we do not have rigid requirements and high marks do not guarantee admission." As far as providing any concrete numerical guidelines, the Web site offers the following insights: "Harvard does not admit students by the numbers. Most of our successful applicants have SAT scores ranging from 600 to 800, but high test scores are no guarantee of admission and low scores do not necessarily mean exclusion. Some students with perfect scores are not admitted while other students who may have more modest scores are [admitted]. There are simply too many other factors to consider in making admissions decisions." If one reads between the lines, one may justifiably conclude that Harvard would prefer to admit a high-school student who had penned the Great American Novel while never receiving a grade higher than a C rather than admit a student who had never received anything other than straight As but whose idea of socializing was to play Dungeons and Dragons with three other players and their alter egos via the Internet. But the admissions office does point out that some 98 percent of all admitted applicants are in the top fifth of their class and all 100 percent of all admitted applicants are in the top two-fifths of their classes. Unfortunately, Harvard, like most of the other elite universities in the country, is loathe to give out very much information about the percentages of applicants who are admitted with certain grade-point averages and certain test scores.

As we have no individual statistics on the entering class, we cannot ascertain the range of values (grades and test scores) in the population being studied (successful students). This measure is the standard deviation of a population. If we had access to the grades and test scores of each individual, then we could use our statistics to calculate the range of grades and test scores of the successful Harvard applicants. This calculation would enable us to determine the uniformity or consistency of all the values in the population. Statisticians know that the greater the standard deviation, the more the values within the population being considered will vary from each other. In other words, the greater the standard deviation, the bigger the difference between the grades of the persons gaining admittance. What we can glean from the few scraps of information that the information gatekeepers at Harvard have provided us with is that the standard deviation of the successful applicants' grades and test scores are not likely to be huge because Harvard is such a selective institution in the first place. They do not like to admit students who are challenged by the task of making change in the lunch line; they would instead prefer to admit geniuses and near geniuses whose grades and test scores will likely be in the very upper end of the spectrum. Indeed, we are more likely to find a much greater standard deviation among grades and test scores if we consider a less competitive institution such as a local agricultural college in which you may have successful applicants who have a wider variety of test scores and grades—the students with the lower GPAs applying to the school because they cannot get into a more selective institution such as Hirschfield and the better students applying to the school for a variety of reasons, such as being the children of former alumni or perhaps having a fondness for riding a tractor through fields of grain.

Because statistics is vitally dependent upon the information that is available for analysis, we cannot really give any single applicant to Harvard a clear idea as to the likelihood he or she will be accepted. We do know that extremely high grades and test scores are an obvious plus as are significant extracurricular activities such as negotiating an end to the arms race or creating a multibillion-dollar software empire while in high school or even promising to stop dating the precocious daughter of the dean of admissions in exchange for the coveted admission letter. But must we accept this conspiracy of silence or are there certain resources that can at least help us get a handle on the probability of getting into an Ivy League university? One publication attempting to fill in some of the information gaps permeating the admissions process of many leading universities is the *U.S. News & World Report: America's Best Colleges—2001*, which contains the usual information about the number of applicants at each college and university but also reports the test-score ranges of successful applicants and the percentages of students who finished in the top tenth, top fifth, or top quarter of their class. Although this information would not be enough to create a specific table of probabilities so that a student who finished with a 3.6 grade-point average and a 1300 SAT score would know that he or she had a 36 percent chance of being admitted, it does provide us with some additional insights into the probabilities of admission.

To return to our Ivy League university, the *Report* tells us that 90 percent of the successful applicants to Harvard were in the top 10 percent of their class and 99 percent were in the top quarter of their class. As far as SAT scores were concerned, 75 percent of the Harvard applicants noted in the *Report* scored at or above 1400 whereas 25 percent scored at or above 1590. Whether this means that the scores tended to cluster around these two indices is unclear but it is probably more likely that the scores tended to approximate a bell curve of some sort. But because these are supersecret statistics that cannot be allowed to fall into unfriendly hands, we cannot say anything further about the prospects for admission to Harvard because these are the only guidelines with which we are able to work.

Suppose, just suppose, that you really are not interested in going to Harvard but that you do like the idea of going to another Ivy League school because you have no interest in seeing your alma mater play in a college national championship football game. If so, you might want to consider Yale or Princeton, which are also very competitive but which do not start with an "H." There are a few other differences between these schools such as one being located in Connecticut and the other in New Jersey but they are really so insignificant so as to not merit any additional discussion. Anyway, the prospective Yalie or Princetonian will still have to surmount significant hurdles to obtain the coveted admission letter.

For someone who wishes to enjoy the exotic tropical splendor of downtown New Haven, Connecticut, Yale University may provide the ideal undergraduate experience. About five thousand fewer applicants applied in 1999 to Yale than to Harvard (13,270), but about 2,135 were accepted—an acceptance rate of about 16 percent as compared to a little more than 11 percent at Harvard. Although Yale has very stringent admission standards, the potential applicant does have an appreciably greater chance of being admitted than he would if he were applying to Harvard, all other things being equal. This somewhat smaller class of applicants also posts a slightly lower range of SAT scores with 75 percent of the applicants described in the *Report* scoring at or above 1380 and 25 percent scoring at or above 1550 on the SAT. These score differentials are not significantly different from those posted by the group admitted to Harvard but they may provide enough breathing room for a partic-ular applicant to squeeze in at Yale even though he might have otherwise missed the cut at Harvard and its lovely vibrant Boston area. One final point is that 90 percent of Yale's entering freshmen graduated in the top 10 percent of their high-school class and 99 percent graduated in the top quarter of their class—an array of class rankings almost identical to those found in Harvard's incoming class. Presumably, the other 1 percent at both Harvard and Yale, who did not make the top quarter cut, were able to demonstrate compelling reasons for being admitted to their respective schools—such as the prospect of the applicant's parents paying for the renovation of the arts and sciences faculty lounge.

The same sort of comments we have made about Yale also apply to Princeton, which lies to the west in Princeton, New Jersey. Princeton, too, provides another Ivy League alternative to Harvard—with the ski slopes of Aspen and Vail a mere twenty-five hours away by car. As with Yale, it attracts a slightly smaller pool of applicants than Harvard with some 14,875 applying in 1999 and 1,694 being accepted—an acceptance rate of 11 percent. But because of its smaller number of acceptances, Princeton actually has a lower acceptance rate than Harvard (11 percent versus 11.3 percent) and, in that sense, is actually more exclusive than Harvard. But Princeton's successful applicants posted a slightly lower range of SAT scores, with the *Report* stating that 75 percent of the applicants scored at or above 1360 and 25 percent scored at or above 1540. Moreover, 92 percent of Princeton's prospective students graduated in the top 10 percent of their high-school class and all 100 percent graduated in the top quarter of their class—a group of class rankings that is a couple of percentage points better than both Harvard and Yale. Even though the test scores garnered by the Princeton and Yale groups are admittedly a little lower than those posted by the Harvard group, the former two groups would probably still find that they would have many career opportunities beyond that of crossing guard and sanitation worker.

But perhaps the prospect of attending a university in the northeast does not appeal to you or perhaps budgetary considerations dictate that you consider a public university. There are a number of so-called public Ivies which offer first-rate educations to students but at a more affordable price than those generally available with the private Ivy League universities. They also offer a little more geographical diversity and perhaps a slightly less onerous burden for potential applicants to overcome in order to gain admission. Two of the most famous public Ivies—the University of Virginia at Charlottesville and the University of California at Berkeley—are located on opposite sides of the country but share an enduring tradition of scholarship and excellence. Moreover, Berkeley, once known as a hotbed of student activism, would be the ideal institution to offer a degree in civil disobedience. As far as their respective class numbers are concerned, Virginia received 16,461 applications in 1999 and accepted 5,588—a rate of almost 34 percent. Berkeley, by contrast a much larger institution, received 31,108 applications in 1999 and accepted 8,044—a rate of about 25.8 percent. Certainly both these acceptance rates are more generous than those stingy private Ivies with their elitist attitudes and, coupled with somewhat lower SAT ranges (the *Report* states that 75 percent of Virginia's [Berkeley's] successful applicants scored at or above 1210 [1200] and 25 percent scored at or above 1410 [1430]), 82 (98) percent of Virginia's (Berkeley's) successful applicants ranked in the top 10 percent of their high-school classes and 96 (100) percent of Virginia's (Berkeley's) successful applicants ranked in the top quarter of their class. Indeed, Berkeley can claim a higher class-rank average than any of the private Ivies—an honor that will bring a special feeling of pride to the students there when they storm the administration building.

In summary, the fate of any single applicant cannot be precisely predicted because the gods of the admissions offices are human and are not going to admit every person whom we would otherwise think would be a surefire winner. There are simply not enough seats for all of those students who are truly deserving of admission. The sparse percentages that we were able to cull here merely underscore the point that statistics offers us guidance as to the general probabilities that a candidate can expect to be admitted but they cannot be used to predict with certainty the admission of any single applicant. Perhaps the best strategy any student can utilize is to apply to a number of schools that seem to be within range as well as at least one "reach" school that might otherwise be too competitive for the student. At any rate, as we have seen elsewhere in this book, a bachelor's degree from any no-name school arms the graduate with a competitive edge in the job-salary sweepstakes.

13

BECOMING A
FILM STAR,
ROCK STAR, OR
BEST-SELLING AUTHOR

Everyone wants to be a star. Many people will have an opportunity to enjoy their "fifteen minutes of fame"—a phrase coined by pop artist Andy Warhol, who had a marvelous talent for drawing oversized soup cans and silk-screened celebrity portraits. Many people seek celebrity and a certain chosen few have it thrust upon them. But as we live in an age in which people as well as the national media are obsessed with fame and fortune, it is not surprising that more people want to grab that brass ring of glamour and riches that is usually available to only a chosen few. But the demand for those few places in the pantheon of celebrity is intense and many persons would probably not hesitate to run over their grandmother with their car if it would ensure their being enshrined on the Hollywood Walk of Fame or even winning a recurring role on *The Young and the Restless* or *All My Children*.

THE SILVER SCREEN

The most famous people in the country are not politicians or doctors or lawyers but instead a tiny group of individuals who would call themselves "actors" but who are dubbed "movie stars" by the popular press. Now we are not talking about those people who star in such enduring nature films as *Flight of the Bumblebee* and *Cacti of the Desert Southwest* in which we get to see the host stick his hand into a beehive for the tasty honeycomb or probe the lower intestine of a water buffalo for samples of the local flora and fauna. These films, though certainly deserving of notice and immortality, do not generally get distributed to most movie theaters but instead find themselves passed from elementary school teacher to elementary school teacher much like the proverbial single fruitcake that makes it rounds from household to household each holiday season. Nor are we talking about cinema classics such as *Hot Babes in the Locker Room* or *Vixens Take Driver's Ed*, which showcase the acting talents of many attractive women who have unfortunately been unable to make a living in mainstream movies due to the prejudice in Hollywood against actresses who have twenty pounds of silicon implants in their breasts and a proclivity for running through meadows and along beaches without a stitch of clothing. No, the movies we are talking about are those films which may feature fifteen car crashes or a tearful love affair or even a murder mystery and, at the very least, must cost $20 million. This cost threshold naturally excludes all the fine nature films and cinema classics ever made even though some feature films rely more on special effects and big-name stars than plot or quality scripts or character development for their effectiveness.

But the media is drawn to that small group of actors and actresses who headline these major motion pictures. These are the elite few who can command $10-million, $15-million, or even $20-million salaries for a single film which, in a few cases, is sort of justified. There is no mystery why these few people are paid so well for a few months' work because they are so well known and so beloved by the movie-going audience that their presence will virtually guarantee a profitable movie. Artistic considerations are generally not considered to be vitally important to the commercial success of a film even though all actors and directors want to be known as "serious artists." Of course it is difficult to be taken seriously by the critics when your movie is dependent upon the simulated destruction of the state of California by a gigantic falling antelope or the tragic story of three female bullfighters who battle tradition and prejudice for the right to play professional nude volleyball with a bull's head. But the star power brought to any mainstream film by these select few is undeniable and can make the difference between a runaway hit or a huge flop.

But the pathway to movie stardom is a difficult one in which success does not invariably arise from talent, hard work, and the frequency with which one spends his or her time auditioning on the casting couch. Perhaps the single biggest obstacle is the vast discrepancy between the number of actors and the number of available acting jobs. For example, the Screen Actors Guild reports on its Web site that in 1993 it had 46,745 members who earned a total of $280,379,856 in television movies and series work, a total of $188,217,009 in movies, a total of $183,436,066 in commercials, and $2,778,852 in industrial films. This translates to an average salary of $5,998.07 per actor for television movies and series work, an average salary of $4,026.46 per actor for movie work, an average salary of $3,924.18 per actor for commercials, and $59.44 per actor for industrial film work. Now there are some actors who work only in one of these areas and other actors who work in two, three, or even four of these areas. As such, it is difficult to get a clear idea as to the range of distribution of salaries among actors. But when we take into account that the average salary for actors doing television movies and series work is less than $6,000 per year, it suggests that there is a very large pyramid in terms of the salary structure in the television film and series in which there are a few very highly paid actors and actresses at the top who are starring in hit shows and able to demand seven-figure salaries. Then there is a second tier of "second banana" actors and actresses who may, at best, make several hundred thousand dollars a year. Then you get to the third tier of "character" actors and actresses, most of whom earn far less than $50,000 per year. Finally, there is the group of occasional part-time actors who earn so little each year from acting as to make their incomes earned as waiters and as sales clerks appear as a small fortune. Like the dumb kids in the public schools who helped the rest of us do well when graded on a curve, the vast majority of the working actors and actresses earn very little money from their profession and, indeed, would be happy to be earning the industry average. Indeed, even those earning the industry average would find themselves able to qualify for government assistance because they would be characterized as living below the poverty line which, in 1999, was $8,667.00—about $2,668.93 above the average actor's television movie and film earnings.

If you are an actor who has decided to concentrate on a career in films because you consider the world of television to be too vulgar, then you will not be pleased to find that the average earnings per actor are a comparatively paltry $4,026.46. The good news is that an actor who earns the average amount from movie work will not have to fear losing any benefits such as welfare, public housing, or any other form of government assistance. The bad news, of course, is that this is not very much money and will not be enough for you to purchase both the thirty-room mansion in the hills overlooking Hollywood *and* the 400-horsepower turbocharged two-seat roadster. Perhaps the outlook will change, however, if you lower yourself to take on some extra television series and film work in industrial films. Unfortunately, the roles that you are probably playing to earn the industry average are not necessarily those that will catch the attention of a casting director. In other words, you may be an extra in a biblical epic in which you are carrying out one of the finest acting performances ever recorded on film amidst the twelve thousand other persons who are crossing the seabed of the Dead Sea's parted waters, but your fine thespian efforts may never be seen by anyone who can do your career any good.

As with the actors who worked exclusively in television movie and series roles, the average income for movie actors is not enough to support a family of gerbils comfortably and underscores the huge gap between the few haves who earn millions of dollars per year and the many have-nots who earn no more than a few thousand dollars a year and dream of being named a beneficiary in the will of one of the aforementioned haves or, even better, marrying one of the really old haves and staying married until their new decrepit spouse drops dead of a heart attack.

There are a variety of intangible factors which also figure into the ultimate likelihood of success in Hollywood, including simple twists of fate which may cause a virtual unknown to be thrust into the spotlight as sometimes occurs when a famous actor or actress marries a person who is unknown to the wider audience. Or a person may become famous for performing some heroic deed such as pulling someone from a burning building or capturing an enemy tank on the battlefield. Such fleeting moments of fame can serve as a platform from which to launch a career in the movies or television. More recently, the comedy club circuit has proved to be a fertile source of talent for television and, in some cases, movies. Many situation comedies have been created around the routines of comedians who have managed to parlay their nightclub successes into national television fame. Here again, classical training as an actor and "serious" stage performances may have less to do with one's ultimate success in the movies than whether you have a "gimmick" or a certain look that is suddenly all the rage in Hollywood.

The pyramid of actor salaries in Hollywood is also, not surprisingly, reflected in the success of its movies. Just as there are a few "blockbuster" actors who command vast salaries for appearing in a single film, there are comparatively few "blockbuster" feature films which generate the lion's share of audience revenue and help to offset the losses incurred by most of the other films. Indeed, the Hollywood dream factory churns out about seven hundred films per year according to the *New York Times Almanac 2001*, about half of which are submitted to the Motion Pictures Association of America for ratings. The other half of these films presumably provides the fodder for drive-in grope palaces and late-night cable programming with such titles as *Fraternity House Party* and *Hot Tub Hotties.* The average cost of making a major motion picture now exceeds $50 million even though it is a fair bet that you could make thirty or forty *Fraternity House Party* sequels and perhaps a dozen extra *Hot Tub Hotties* for $50 million. When we talk about $50-million films, we are talking about first-run movies that appear in the theater chains and command multimillion-dollar marketing budgets and boast platoons of well-known actors and, sometimes, a plausible plot and intelligent dialogue. Very few such films will feature herds of carnivorous giraffes that attack unsuspecting townspeople or even offer a star or two from the *Hot Tub Hotties* series. Notwithstanding that drawback, the blockbuster films are the ones that command the attention of the financial markets who trade the stocks of the motion picture companies; the critics who review these films; the investors who help finance these films; and the movie-going public that ponies up seven, eight, nine, and, in some cases, even ten dollars per ticket for a first-run performance. But even though the motion picture industry generates more than $7 billion per year, the top twenty films of 1999 collectively generated more than $3.3 billion or almost half of the total revenues. As the other 680 or so films brought in the remaining $3.7 billion—earning an average revenue of around $5.4 million—one can easily see why Hollywood studios are so consumed with finding the next blockbuster. Of course many of these 680 films earned ten, twenty, thirty, forty, or even fifty million dollars, but the number of films in each of these categories declines precipitously as one moves up the earnings ladder. The long and the short of the story is that a very small number of films props up the movie economy. Due to the huge financial risks inherent in most big-budget movies, risk and creativity are not always highly valued by industry insiders even though such elements have clearly figured in many of the leading films of our time. But because so much money must be invested in a major motion picture, there are often irresistible tendencies to churn out formulaic films and sequels that are acceptable to the movie-going audience. Sometimes this mind-set yields a happy result such as *Hot Tub Hotties VIII*, which earned numerous underwater cinematography awards for its group bubble bath scene. But we are not always so fortunate to find such bold originality in the production of quality movies. In summary, the business of movies is like the business of movie actors in that a very small number of films and people are responsible for the commercial success of the Hollywood community. More importantly for our discussion is the fact that the odds against becoming a star or even starring in a major motion picture that grosses over, say, $100 million are so slight as to be discouraging to all but the most tenacious and career-driven of thespians.

MUSIC

Many people who would not be very interested in being a movie star would bite the heads off chickens and bats in exchange for the opportunity to work as the front man or play lead guitar for a famous rock band. There are very few jobs for front men and the requirements are fairly stringent: You must be able to stand on stage, hands on hips, in leather or spandex pants, wiggle your hips and tousle your unnaturally curly golden locks, and emit a wide range of screams and moans in sync with the bombastic chords of your bandmates. Formal music training—let alone voice lessons—is far less important than pretty-boy looks and the ability to move across the stage amidst the screams of thousands of fans without tripping over star-spangled bootlaces or the unplugged guitar which is picked up on occasion to mimic a frenzied guitar riff. Similarly, lead guitarists must learn to master the art of making simple guitar riffs look complicated and also creating strange sounds by biting the strings of their instruments so that they can bask in the oohs and ahs of the stadium crowd. But as the rock-god image is one that has been widely imitated ever since the phenomenal success of Led Zeppelin in the 1960s and 1970s, slavish adherence to this basic rock front-man model will not necessarily guarantee multiplatinum albums or screaming hordes of groupies (which may suffice, for many artists, in the absence of commercial success). Moreover, the members of such bands find, often to their chagrin, that they are expected to create original, catchy songs and new sounds or else they may find themselves criticized by the music critics and abandoned by their fans.

But even though rock bands seem to rise as quickly as the morning sun, there are really very few overnight success stories. Most rock bands labor in obscurity for years—sometimes decades—before they get their big break or record their breakthrough song. Although there are some who may liken the music of these bands to the sounds garbage cans make when hit by a truck, a few of these musical groups will create sounds and songs that attract a wide, often vehement, audience who will study the lyrics of the songs and buy the sheet music so they can play the clumsy three-chord arrangements on their own guitars in the privacy of their homes and examine the album covers for clues and, in some cases, wear the outfits and makeup that are used by the band members themselves. Sadly for these bands, however, the descent is often far quicker than the ascent as today's fans are fickle and very quick to move onto the next sensation—whether it be choreographed lip-synching quintets clad in neon-lined jumpsuits or overweight opera singers wearing Viking helmets and dusty animal furs and hitting boards over their heads. So given the comparatively brief time that most bands have at the top of the heap (which for many bands may not extend beyond a few months of notoriety brought by a single hit such as *Lick My Fingers, Kiss My Toes*—available both on compact disc and in the extended dance version), one must wonder about the odds of success in the music business.

We first need to understand that the conventional measure of success in the recording industry is the platinum and multiplatinum album, the former of which is given to albums selling at least a million copies and the latter of which is awarded to albums selling at least 2 million copies. According to the Recording Industry Association of America (RIAA), 1999 saw thirty albums certified as being multiplatinum and fifty-one additional albums certified as platinum. Needless to say, there were many thousands of albums that were certified conclusively as being neither platinum or multiplatinum—the so-called nonplatinum group that carries with it no distinction or honor at all. For the enterprising rock band seeking to establish itself as a commercial juggernaut, it might want to find out from the RIAA the total number of albums produced for sale in 1999 to get some idea of the sheer mathematical probability that it would be able to create a best-selling album. But there is quite a difference between the haves and the have-nots.

According to the RIAA, 1999 saw about 38,900 releases of full-length audio products or rereleases of audio products previously released by another label. This figure reflected an increase of more than 200 percent over 1992's 18,400 releases. No doubt much of this increase was due to the trend on the part of recording companies to issue recordings previously available only as records or cassettes in the compact disk (CD) form. With a total of eighty-one platinum and multiplatinum albums being sold in 1999, the average artist who does release an audio recording has a 1-in-480 chance of enjoying an album with sales in excess of 1 million units. But these numbers do not tell the whole story because this is a probability calculation based upon both new releases as well as rereleases of previously recorded material. As most rereleased products do not usually generate huge sales, we are probably overstating the probability that the typical recording artist will not sell at least 1 million albums.

The RIAA further informs us that each year sees approximately 27,000 new releases hit the market, of which only about 7,000 are released by the major labels. These figures tell us that there are a lot of independent labels that are manufacturing audio products for market and that—as with most forms of media entertainment—only about one quarter of these new releases are produced by major labels. This profusion of independent releases should make us feel good that we live in America because it makes possible such titles as *Learning Swiss Clog Dancing* and *Teaching Your Dog Not to Bite the Children*. But these sorts of albums—though contributing to our democratic way of life—are not the typical fodder for the major labels that are searching for the new "sound" that will sweep the country and line their pockets with gold. This ongoing attempt to hit a home run (or at least a ground-rule double) is understandable when we learn from RIAA (http://www.riaa.com) that even though the major labels, as we said before, release thousands of new titles (predominantly in the CD format) each year, "after production, recording, promotion and distribution costs, most never sell enough to recover these costs, let alone to make a profit." Indeed, the search for a hit becomes all the more understandable when we learn from the RIAA that less than 10 percent of all CD releases are profitable and that it is these comparatively few releases that finance the plethora of other releases that are never able to find a significant audience. Of course a cursory search along the dial of any radio will reveal many works of audio art which deserve to remain obscure but which have at least some type of promotional backing from their respective labels and therefore a fighting chance to generate the sales needed to turn a profit and possibly make the artists very wealthy.

The low rate of profitability in the music industry would certainly convince most artists that their only realistic possibility of having a successful recording career is to get a recording contract with a major label. This is not to say that there have not been a number of independently produced albums that have enjoyed great popularity. But the production of a commercially successful album not only requires that the artist actually create material that is appealing to the listening audience but also that the label invest in that album by fronting studio production costs as well as marketing and promotion costs. Recording companies must also underwrite the tours of recording artists because only a very

few of the most successful acts are able to attract the corporate spon-
sors and sell the tickets needed to make a national tour (or at least a tour
through three or four really big states) a commercially viable enterprise.
For the rest of a label's acts, substantial out-of-pocket costs must be
fronted, ranging from touring crews (roadies) to venue rentals. As far as
we know, groupies are not typically provided by labels because there are
simply some things which people must learn to get for themselves.

This need to have a corporate "sugar daddy" that can front the production and marketing costs needed to create a successful album suggest that those few artists who are fortunate enough to land a major
recording contract are at least a step ahead in the race to create a platinum album. Even though only a few hundred releases are profitable
each year, the vast majority of these releases are produced by the major
labels. As a result, it is imperative for any recording artist to get a contract with a major label. Once an artist signs with a major label, then
his or her odds of attaining the status of a platinum recording star are
much greater than 1 in 480 because we are no longer dealing with rereleased recordings or independent label recordings. If we assume for
purposes of our discussion that all of the platinum and multiplatinum
albums are released by major labels (which is not necessarily true), then
our odds for attaining wealth and power and being able to afford platoons of fawning yes-men and yes-women (once we sign a contract
with one of these recording giants) will be greatly improved. Indeed,
we would then have about a 1-in-86 chance of realizing the sale of a
million or more copies of our album. If we were interested only in the
probability that we would obtain multiplatinum status, we would find
that our odds would drop to about 1 in 233. But these numbers do not
seem quite so depressing as the well-meaning advice of our parents and
friends to give up the idea of attaining recording success with an electric kazoo band. Yet we do need to recall that only those artists who
appear to have the greatest commercial promise—not necessarily the
most talented or artistic—are signed by the major labels in the first

place. All of the tens of thousands of other acts will have been winnowed out long before that point simply because they did not appear to have the necessary star power to merit an investment in their future that might run to hundreds of thousands or even millions of dollars. So even though these odds do not appear very formidable, they disguise the fact that it is a brutal process getting to the point where an artist or recording group is able to obtain a recording contract with a major label. Only the very best ("best" being a word relating more to commercial promise than artistic integrity) of the nation's bands and singers will ever ink a deal with a major label. But it is this association with a major label that is the ultimate key to the success and long-term career prospects of any recording act.

This discouraging probability should give some cause for concern to the hundreds of thousands of bands laboring away in garages across America and playing at the neighborhood bars and nightclubs. But the very poor odds of securing a recording contract—let alone making a platinum or multiplatinum album—do not seem to dampen the enthusiasm of these would-be rockers. Perhaps it is the desire to leave one's imprint on the landscape of popular music that drives these young persons to continue banging away on their musical instruments. Or perhaps it is the lure of mansions, cars, drugs, and sex—but that is just a crazy theory.

These figures illustrate the feast or famine state of popular music because it, like movie making, depends on a few dozen acts to generate the profits necessary to support hundreds and hundreds of musical acts whose album sales may range from the tens of thousands to a few hundred albums per year. So even though most musicians may deride the commercialism of modern entertainment—particularly the extent to which artistic considerations are secondary to marketing objectives—they want to sell as many albums as possible to the widest possible audience in order to make as much money as possible. In fact, the success of the more popular groups makes it possible for them to subsidize many unprofitable acts that would not otherwise see the light of day. The most successful groups have embraced the concept of merchandising, lending their names and likenesses to a wide variety of products including plastic action dolls, puzzles, lunchboxes, notebooks, and paperback novels.

But is this statistic truly valid or is it something akin to a ghostly fiction? After all, there are certain types of albums such as those featuring rock bands with pouty-lipped lead singers and country singers who have an unnatural affinity for their dogs and horses that claim large audiences toward which albums can be targeted. As such, their albums are designed to appeal to an existing audience. On the other hand, there are certainly hundreds of albums released each year that are more limited in their sales appeal, such as *Lumberjack Songs of the Pacific Northwest* and *Serial-Killer Lullabies*. Indeed, the serious record-buyer can find albums advising listeners how to imitate various birds, albums that showcase the ancestral music of Mesopotamia, and albums with catchy tunes from American labor union rallies of the early 1930s. There are certain categories that are simply too esoteric or too unique to attract a wide audience, and so glockenspiel quartets and kneepant-clad yodelers and Gregorian chanters will doubtless continue to find that few of their "greatest hits" will get much airplay on the leading radio stations—even those catering to "hip" or "groovin'" listeners.

But the odds that a singer will create an album able to reach that magical one million units in sales will depend in great part on the kind of music performed by the musician, the extent to which there are competing titles that could siphon away sales, as well as a host of other factors such as the quality of the music and the production of the album, the intensity of the promotional advertising, its video, and the stage appeal of the group itself. Because some areas of popular music are "hot" at certain times, it becomes progressively more difficult for any single act to remain atop the music world and continue selling millions of albums with each new release. Longevity is not the friend of the popular music group.

BOOKS

Americans may be uniquely obsessed with becoming stars of the silver screen or the television screen or the stage. Some Americans, however, are not as interested in appearing in front of a camera but instead writing the next best-seller that will be made into a major motion picture and confer a sort of indirect stardom upon the wordsmith. After all, authors are not very visible to the general public, especially when compared to television or movie stars. Very few authors make regular appearances on television talk shows and even fewer are asked to play themselves as special guests in sitcoms or made-for-TV movies. In short, even best-selling authors do not command the attention of the public in the same way that persons who appear in more visually oriented media have been able to master. You could walk past some of the biggest-selling authors on the city street and not pay the slightest bit of attention because, after all, they are merely authors who never have their faces splashed across the front pages of the tabloid newspapers. Even though some authors may live outrageous lives and keep a stable of lovers and wear flamboyant clothing, they seem unable to attract the attention of the nation's paparazzi—who will doggedly pursue even the most washed-up movie stars to the ends of the earth. These very same celebrity-crazed journalists and photographers are not often seen searching through the garbage cans of the nation's best-selling murder mystery writers or the most popular syndicated cartoonists. Perhaps the most plausible reason for this lack of attention is that our society has become so visually oriented with the resulting shorter attention spans that those persons who work in areas of the electronic arts are the stars whereas those who labor in the fields of literary endeavor are mere stepchildren. Our true national pastime is being seated in front of a television set for hours watching the news or popular sitcoms or game shows or soap operas or weekly dramas or any of a variety of other programs. Americans are truly fortunate in that we can flip a switch and, through the magic of a satellite hookup, receive several hundred channels of fine broadcasting that will ensure continued immersion in a spoon-fed popular culture that is as satisfying as a lite beer.

The point of this masterful digression is that the written word does not carry the sway of the video image in our mass culture and there is very little that we can do about it. It should also underscore the odds that plague the would-be author who seeks to publish a best-selling book. But before we go any further we need to point out the mushiness of the concept of "best-seller" because it seems that the label is tossed around as freely as undergarments at a fraternity party. What, in fact, is a best-seller? There does not appear to be any uniform definition to the term in a quantitative sense. In part, this is due to the fact that books are characterized as best-sellers based upon their commercial sale success in the markets in which they are sold. In other words, a book does not have to be a roaring commercial success to be dubbed a "best-seller" so long as it is one of the better-selling books in its category. A book on raising pot-bellied pigs called *Dig the Pig*, for example, would probably never make the *New York Times* best-seller list because there are not very many people who are interested in reading about pot-bellied pigs. But *Oink* magazine, the bible of pot-bellied pig farmers, might have a best-seller list on which *Dig the Pig* had been listed. The magazine would believe itself to be justified in calling *Dig the Pig* a best-seller whereas the other 99.999994 percent of the reading population would not believe themselves to have been disadvantaged by a collective failure to reach for *Dig the Pig*. As the sales for most of the titles appearing on this particular best-seller list number in the hundreds and, occasionally, in the few thousands, any book that happens to sell more than a few thousand copies may properly be called a "best-seller" even though such sales figures would not enable the author to purchase a new home in Vail, Colorado.

Herein lies a basic problem about which all authors are in agreement: their books would be best-sellers but for (1) the shortcomings of

the publisher's publicity department; (2) the inadequacies of the advertising budget; (3) the poor quality of the book cover art; (4) the lack of
planning for the book tour; or (5) the stupidity of the reading public.
Surprisingly, very few authors will point to the actual subject matter of
the book, the author's style of writing, or the title itself (e.g., *Dig the
Pig*) as reasons for the cold reception given to the book by the book-
buying public. Of course some authors (yours truly included) feel
themselves to be rather dense when it comes to providing a snappy title
and will often leave it to the publisher to offer a title so that a new
reason number 6 can be added to our list of factors contributing to the
book's commercial demise.

But these problems do not disguise the fact that we do not have a
single standard for determining a best-seller because we have many different types of books competing in their own markets, be they mass
market or more limited specialty market books. The nature of the book
itself is of crucial importance in determining the number of copies that
must be sold in order to plaster the "best-seller" label on the cover. A
trade book or popular book, for example, such as a presidential biography or a self-help book, may have to sell several hundred thousand
copies in paperback in order for it to be deemed a best-seller. However,
the very same books need sell only a fraction of the same number of
copies in hardcover in order to carry the same mantle because hardcover copies are typically three to four times as expensive. From a publisher's standpoint, they are primarily concerned with the amount of
net revenue generated by book sales and so they will be happy to settle
for fifty thousand hardcover sales as opposed to 150,000 softcover sales
if they can make more money on the sale of the smaller number of
hardcover books.

Assuming that none of these factors figure into the commercial
sales of the book, all authors have to contend with certain basic elements of the publishing world that seem to conspire against best-seller
status for any given book. First, the nation's publishers spew out tens of

thousands of new books each year, meaning that the bookshelves of both traditional bookstores as well as their virtual counterparts must make room for tens of thousands of new titles, all seeking to appeal to that discriminating book buyer. These books may be trade books, works of fiction, textbooks, or any other of a variety of other categories of published work. But they must all compete against other books that have already been published. The important point here is that the publishing of tens of thousands of new books each year further saturates an already glutted market and makes it even more difficult for any one book to get the attention to sell the hundreds of thousands of copies needed to provide a more luxurious lifestyle for its author, including a palatial mansion, Porsche, Lear jet, and plentiful friends for hire.

But the author seeking the glory of a best-seller might do well to consider writing a specialty market book in which much smaller sales are needed to get to the top of a best-seller list. However, one must also keep in mind that different best-seller lists use different benchmarks— some are based more on sales in the major bookstore chains whereas others are based upon sales by independent bookstores. One could take a stab at a cooking book, for example, and hope, by virtue of selling several tens of thousands of copies, to write a best-seller. Given the plethora of such books on the market, however, it would be very difficult to come up with a novel cookbook. Indeed, it may be that the author's primary challenge would be to come up with a new slant on a tried-and-true topic. An enterprising author might therefore take a traditional French cookbook and devise recipes showing how soufflés, crepes, and other delicacies could be barbequed or cooked Cajun-style. Regardless of the merit of the book itself, however, the fate of the book on the relevant best-seller list would depend on its sales in the particular stores which are included in the tabulations used by that list.

But specialty books are books with limited sales and little fame. Many authors find it galling to think that their ten-year effort to create a seventeen-hundred-page opus on the migration patterns of geese

Number of Books Selling More Than 100,000 Copies (Hardcover)

Type	Number of Books Published	100,000+ Sales	1,000,000+ Sales
Fiction	11,570	92	8
Nonfiction	88,835	121	5

Source of Statistics: *Publishers Weekly* 1999

would have little chance of becoming a national best-seller. But such are the vagaries of public taste. But someone has to be at the top of the real best-seller lists—the mainstream, top of the top, *New York Times* and *Publishers Weekly* best-seller lists. Nothing short of a *New York Times* or *Publishers Weekly* best-seller will land you a coveted table at Elaine's. One must be a best-selling author if one wishes to attract any attention at all and enjoy any of the perks of the literary life—most of which involve lunches with editors and spending nights in second-rate hotels when doing the talk-show circuit to promote your latest literary work and, occasionally, being spotted in the frozen-food aisle at the grocery store.

So if you are one of the tens of thousands of authors who publishes a book in a given year, what are the odds that you will have a best-seller? According to *Publishers Weekly*, the competition to be a best-selling author is becoming more difficult because authors must sell increasingly greater numbers of books in order to secure even a position on the best-seller list. Whereas a hardcover book might have only needed to sell 300,000 copies to secure the number fifteen spot for sales for the entire year a decade ago, it might have to sell two or three times that number in order to secure that coveted rung on the best-seller ladder in 1998, as was the case with Danielle Steele's *Granny Dan* which sold 775,000 copies. Though this suggests that more people are reading the books that rise to the top of the best-seller lists, we would be mistaken to conclude that each of the top best-selling books for each year had outsold each of the top best-selling books for all the previous years. But it must be heartening to publishers to find that the market for the top-selling books has continued to expand over time. Does this mean that the population as a whole is reading more? This is more difficult to answer because we would expect that an expanding population would consume more books along with more of everything else. But today's population has so many entertainment options ranging from video games to Internet gambling to movie rentals as well as a host of live forms of entertainment from on-line chat rooms to professional sports to all-nude male revues that it seems unlikely that people are reading more on a per capita basis. Furthermore, books must compete with the beast called television that has dominated the entertainment landscape of America so completely for the past half century that the days when the literary intelligentsia flourished in America are almost all but a distant memory.

The degree to which television soaks up the leisure time of the American population has been documented by the A. C. Nielsen Company, which reported that at least one television in each of the households it monitored was on for about 7 hours and 37 minutes per day during the 1998–99 television season, a jump of about 20 percent from the 6 hours and 19 minutes of average daily viewing of television in 1971. Of course such measurements are not perfect but merely an approximation of American viewing habits. But the nation's advertisers who are constantly in search of the widest possible audiences for their advertising budget apparently are satisfied with the existing measures of television viewership even though we could imagine that some monitored households might take special glee in leaving the monitored set on the Chess Channel eighteen hours a day in order to confuse the Nielsen company statisticians who might wonder why viewership of championship chess matches had doubled. But the important point of this discussion is that Americans claim to be busier than ever with their jobs and their lives but they are still spending more time with their eyes glued to the tube.

But what about the actual numbers involved in the book publishing business? First, we need to begin with the total number of books published each year. The *Bowker Annual: Library and Book Trade Almanac* reports that there were 100,405 new books and editions published in 1999. The two largest categories were 11,895 in sociology or economics and 11,895 in fiction. Aspiring novelists will note that only about one out of every ten books published that year was fiction; these are odds that do not bode well for any would-be first-time novelist to find a publisher—unless he or she is unusually gifted in describing scenes of violence, gore, and sexual debauchery or is a relative of a famous celebrity and can offer a gossipy biography. But the fact of the matter is that only 2,835 books of fiction were published in 1980. So it is fair to say that there was a virtual explosion amounting to nearly a fourfold increase in the number of novels published in those two decades but it still represented only about one new novel published for every 23,539 people living in the United States in 1999.

Those seeking to quantify the gross probability that their book would be a best-seller would have to consider the sobering figures provided by *Publishers Weekly*. Leaving aside the term "best-seller," which is not really quantifiable, we should focus more on sales figures. By most standards, the sale of 100,000 copies will qualify any book for best-seller status. According to *Publishers Weekly*, 92 hardcover novels and 121 books of nonfiction sold more than 100,000 copies in 1999. Although there are obviously many paperback versions that sell in excess of 100,000 copies, let us focus on the available hardcover sales. We can then get some idea of the odds that every author must consider when trying to write a book that will appeal to a substantial segment of the book-buying public.

The writer seeking to pen the great American novel must bear in mind that the book market is very fragmented but can always absorb another timeless tale of senseless violence and lurid sex that aims to satisfy the most base instincts of its readers. Anyway, the novel is an enterprise that is rarely destined for best-seller status because only 92 out of 11,570 of all novels published will actually attain the coveted 100,000 sales level. This of course means that the other 11,478 will generally be consigned to commercial oblivion and mundane uses ranging from props in furniture store displays to doorstops for use in the home to unwanted holiday gifts to be given to friends and family members alike. (Remember that copies of the typical author's novel can usually fit into the goodie bags given to the children attending that author's daughter's fifth birthday party.) But the obvious point is that the novelist will have only about a 1-in-125 chance of realizing sales in excess of 100,000 or more. Now this might not seem so tragic but for the fact that many novelists would like to purchase their first mansion and Mercedes with their first royalty check. One cannot maintain such a lifestyle unless one is able to sell a lot of books—indeed, considerably more than 100,000 copies. The reason for this is purely economic in that a hardcover novel which is sold at a 50 percent discount of its list price of $30 with a royalty payment, say, on the net sales price of 15 percent to be paid to its author ($15 net price multiplied by 15 percent) will earn about $2.25 in pretax profits off the sale of each book. If the author is fortunate enough to sell 100,000 copies of his latest book, *Passion in the Laundry Room* (the heartrending story of a beautiful young couple's search for the meaning of life, the truth in religion, and a dryer that would not steal their quarters or burn their clothes), then the author will realize pretax royalties of about $225,000.00. This is nothing to sneeze at but it will probably not be enough to buy the garage of a first-rate mansion—much less the rest of the house—or the shallow but voluptuous trophy wife (or muscular trophy husband). Indeed, a first-rate exotic sports car will require most of that $225,000.00, leaving very little money to allow for a move from the author's current third-story walk-up studio apartment.

Yet what would be the likelihood that the author might be able to write a million-copy best-seller, a book that would take America by storm and make it possible to at least move to a nicer apartment building with an elevator and a concierge who does not rob the tenants' mailboxes? Well, *Publishers Weekly* informs us that only eight novels in 1999 sold more than 1 million copies. Eight. Using our previous example of *Passion in the Laundry Room*, we can quickly determine that sales of one million copies would yield pretax royalties of $2.25 million. This still may not be enough to swing one of the premier residences in the hills above the city but it should be enough for the novelist to actually purchase a home with electrical and plumbing systems that meet all applicable government regulations. But it is even more striking to consider that only about six-tenths of 1 percent of all novels published attain that million-copy mark. Such a remote chance of attaining such commercial success does not seem to deter the tens of thousands of writers who labor away on their keyboards and typewriters day in and day out because, quite frankly, they have a story to tell and they love to write and they are completely delusional about their possibility of making barrels of money.

Okay, so novels are a long shot. What about the wonderful world of nonfiction which, as we have already seen, makes up nearly 90 percent of all books published each year? Surely the fact that there are so many more nonfiction books published each year must reflect a booming market for nonfiction books and a correspondingly greater number of best-selling titles. Well, that is the assumption and it would appear to be a logical one. But there is not a huge amount of logic in the publishing world these days and the figures offered by *Publishers Weekly* would appear to contradict this conclusion. Indeed, as we have seen, only 121 works of nonfiction sold more than 100,000 copies in 1999. Even though these 121 literary masterpieces could very well include titles such as *How to Caulk Your Tub* and *Getting Your Kids Out of the House Without Paying for College*, their comparatively small numbers would offer little comfort to the aspiring nonfiction writer. Given the fact that 88,835 nonfiction titles were published in 1999, only about one-tenth of 1 percent or 1 in 734 reached the coveted 100,000-copy status. These are not particularly encouraging numbers and they certainly would not convince one to drop a promising career as a door-to-door magazine salesperson to pursue a writing career on a full-time basis. This conclusion is further borne out by the fact that only five (yes, five) nonfiction titles sold more than one million copies. So even though ten times as many nonfiction books are published each year compared to fictional books, fewer nonfiction books attained the status of a million-copy best-seller. Of course we need to remind ourselves that these numbers are reflective only of hardcover sales, but they still do nevertheless illustrate the imposing odds that will likely prevent most authors from being able to purchase their dream mansion with their first royalty check.

So even though the odds are not impossibly long, they are not so favorable as to suggest anyone could sit down at a typewriter (or keyboard) and create a literary work that would be in all the bookstores by the end of the year. Of course if your ambitions are not so grandiose and you would be willing to settle for the top spot on a more localized best-seller list such as the Stud Poker Book Best-seller List or more geographically limited compilations such as the Upper Hudson Valley Arts and Crafts Best-seller List, then your possibility of success may not be so far-fetched. But you will still have to create a work that will appeal to an audience that, while far smaller in number than the readers who buy the books that top the mainstream best-seller lists, may in fact be more demanding and unforgiving of errors in the books they do choose to purchase.

But writers have always been discouraged by well-meaning friends, relatives, and annoying busybodies from spending their time putting pen to paper because the odds of commercial success are so slight. However, it may be this very same lack of encouragement that has caused many writers to develop a steely determination to succeed that will compel them to continue butting their heads against the doors of the nation's publishers until they get the break that they so richly deserve. It is only through this perverse form of social evolution whereby the most determined and, occasionally, talented writers can climb to the top of the heap and thus make it possible for classics such as *I'm Okay, You're in Pretty Bad Shape* and *One Thousand Ways to Snub Your Friends* to find their widest-reading audiences.

FINAL WORDS

Whether your dream is to star in a major motion picture or play lead guitar for the world's biggest rock band or write a novel that will move the world to tears, the likelihood of becoming a star is, at best, remote. The entertainment industry is a gigantic pyramid and there are only a few persons—whether they are actors, musicians, or writers—who are able to realize extraordinary income that is generated by those few who have "star power." Unfortunately, there is no surefire way to become a star because fame and fortune may be more dependent on luck, connections, and timing than on actual talent. Some people with extraordinary talents may simply be ahead of their time and, hence, may not attract the attention that their works might have otherwise warranted. As a result, aspiring movie stars, musicians, and writers are advised to reach for their dreams but to keep their day jobs just in case their dreams come crashing down.

EPILOGUE

At this point I hope it has become clear that the purpose of this book was to explore the probabilities that certain events will occur in our lives—events that are sometimes humorous, sometimes tragic, and sometimes bizarre. There is no single underlying narrative structure to this book because the types of probabilities that were featured were those that appeared to me to be interesting or amusing or silly.

Statisticians may wonder why this book has not included discussions about or examples of standard deviations or other basic concepts of statistics; these subjects I have dealt with elsewhere in previous publications such as *Conquering Statistics*. Here, I was more concerned with finding interesting types of probabilities—such as the probability that a meteorite will land on your house or that you will find the perfect mate. Needless to say, one cannot claim complete accuracy on some of the probabilities calculated in this book because we do not always know whether our basic mathematical assumptions are correct. However, most of the topics lend themselves to accurate statistical analysis. Moreover, I decided to write this book to entertain the reader in an informative matter and to provide some examples as to how probabilities can affect us in the real world.

I have also tried to point out the limitations of statistics—indeed, our ability to draw conclusions from all types of data—throughout this book. In other words, the quality of the statistics we have is totally dependent on the care and competence of the person selecting, collecting, and analyzing the data. Whenever we conclude that there is a certain probability that an event will occur, we do not mean to say that it is inevitable that it will take place because the very essence of probability theory is to deal with the likelihood of an event taking place— not the certainty that such an event will take place. Unlike the television psychics who promise to predict your future but somehow cannot figure out a winning combination of Lotto numbers and thus afford a more elaborate stage or even a more desirable time slot, we are only concerned with the statistical likelihood that an event will take place. Whether it actually does take place or not is of no concern to the statistician; he is merely interested in defining the general parameters of its likelihood of occurrence.

This book is therefore very much of a book in that it is intended to inform the reader about the featured events themselves and provide some numerical illustrations for those events. It is rudimentary in its use of statistics—there is no mention of any statistical concepts beyond that of probabilities themselves and a note or two about standard deviations. It is a narrative and I have tried to avoid equations throughout the book because it was my desire that the book would be accessible to the lay audience. Another reason for trying to avoid the use of various statistical formulas and laborious explanations of their use and applications is that most readers do not have a great deal of interest in learning about the mathematical foundations of statistics. I do believe, however, that most readers can find very general discussions of probability theory palatable when they are interwoven through an ongoing series of vignettes.

What I have instead tried to do is to discuss in various parts of the chapters the limitations that must be taken into account when drawing a conclusion about a certain event. Indeed, my desire is to discourage any slavish devotion to the notion that statistics is immutable or infallible. Certainly the fact that the use of statistics is a product of human ingenuity as much as any social or behavioral science ensures that they will not always be pristine, perfect edifices but instead will be marred and even occasionally led astray by incorrect theories or conclusions. Probability theory, then, should be recognized as a tool that helps us to analyze data and bring some degree of understanding to the world around us. If this book shows how we may draw some conclusions about the seemingly chaotic events that take place each day in the world around us, then it will have served its purpose.

INDEX